TSQ Transgender Studies Quarterly

Volume 8 * Number 4 * November 2021

The Transsexual/Transvestite Issue

Edited by Emmett Harsin Drager and Lucas Platero

413 **General Editor's Introduction**
Jules Gill-Peterson

417 **At the Margins of Time and Place: Transsexuals and the Transvestites in Trans Studies**
Emmett Harsin Drager and Lucas Platero

426 **Transgender: A Useful Category? Or, How the Historical Study of "Transsexual" and "Transvestite" Can Help Us Rethink "Transgender" as a Category**
Marta V. Vicente

443 **(Trans) Sex Sells: Star Distributors Ltd. and Trans Sleaze**
RL Goldberg

462 **Standards of Care: Uncertainty and Risk in Harry Benjamin's Transsexual Classifications**
Beans Velocci

481 **The Others of the Ravine**
Daniasa Curbelo

498 **The Collective Scene: Transvestite Cabaret during the End of Francoist Spain**
Iñaki Estella

516 **Mariela Muñoz: Citizenship, Motherhood, and Transsexual Politics in Argentina (1943–2017)**
Patricio Simonetto and Johana Kunin

T0339293

TRANSLATION

532 **Trans-, Translation, Transnational**
Cole Rizki

SPECIAL SECTION: TRANSSEXUAL/TRANSVESTITE SCRAPBOOK

537 **Dedicated to the Last Pearl: Jojo "Josefina Larina Queen of the Congolina" Gilbert, of the Pearl Box Revue**
Harrison Apple

539 **Button Rhetorics**
K.J. Rawson

542 **Rebels, Criminals, Pioneers: Jack Starr and Friends in the QPA Queer Photo Archive**
Jenni Olson

545 **A Most Unusual Volume**
Ms. Bob Davis

548 **Drag Attack: The Celebration of the Posthuman Transvestite in the Spanish Party Underground**
Andrés Senra

550 **Transformers**
Diego Marchante

553 **Catalan Scenes**
Frau Diamanda

555 **Femme4Femme: Remembering Cousin Robert**
Lindsey Shively

557 **Samantha Hudson**
Ira Terán

ARTS & CULTURE

559 **"Can We Be Visible in This Culture without Becoming a Commodity?": An Interview with *Disclosure* Director Sam Feder**
Laura Horak

BOOK REVIEWS

572 **"Naming Their History"**
Review of *Female Husbands: A Trans History*, by Jen Manion
Emily Skidmore

575 **Breaking All the Rules**
Review of *Unbound: Transgender Men and the Remaking of Identity*,
by Arlene Stein
Billy Huff

579 **Parenting Trans Kids in a Cisgender World**
Review of *Trans Kids: Being Gendered in the Twenty-First Century*,
by Tey Meadow
Alithia Zamantakis

582 **A Gender Journey: Without Gender Studies**
Review of *Passing to América: Antonio (Née Maria) Yta's Transgressive,
Transatlantic Life in the Twilight of the Spanish Empire*,
by Thomas A. Abercrombie
Lazarus Nance Letcher

585 **Transgressing Criminology and Victimology**
Review of *Transgressed: Intimate Partner Violence in Transgender Lives*,
by Xavier L. Guadalupe-Diaz
Sergio Domínguez Jr.

General Editor's Introduction

JULES GILL-PETERSON

I have long been confounded, as a brown transsexual as much as a scholar and
historian of trans of color life, with the realism ascribed to the 2015 film *Tangerine*, a Sundance hit that chronicles the Christmas Eve of Sindee and Alexandra,
two trans women of color and best friends hustling the streets of Los Angeles.
Certainly the film's director, Sean Baker, who describes *Tangerine* as "an entertaining film and socialist-realist film," lent the term to critics and reviewers. Much
was likewise made of the fact that *Tangerine* was shot entirely on iPhones with two
lead actresses who actually lived in the life, serving as Baker's supposed "conduit to
the world of transgender prostitution around the Hollywood intersection of Santa
Monica Boulevard and Highland Avenue," as one review put it (Thompson 2015).
Yet the claim of realism, of the specific location and authenticity of Sindee's and
Alexandra's performances, has always struck me as infelicitous. Much like the cis
men who buy sex from the protagonists, the celebration of *Tangerine*'s ostensible
realism has always seemed, to me, to say much more about the desires and pro-
jective expectations of its audience than what the film depicts—a work of fiction,
need it be repeated, no matter how much it might be said to be verité.

Why would Sindee and Alexandra reflect realism as opposed to, say, *realness*, a term actually invented by Black and brown trans femmes? Perhaps the
answer has something to do with how trans women of color and Black trans
women, especially when saturated with sensational narratives of sex work, poverty, and transsexual desire, have long been a punching bag for not only mass
culture but also high theory. Think only of Judith Butler's (1997) egregious (but
quite typical for queer theory at the time) reading of Venus Xtravaganza's death
in *Paris Is Burning* as some kind of inevitable comeuppance for her literal failure
and ideological failure to be queer enough to righteously subvert the desire for a
happy, safe life. Even in the 1990s, when the word *transgender* was still in its Anglo-
American infancy, both as a term used by social service organizations working
with poor trans women of color sex workers and as an umbrella category for

nonmedical identities that differed from transsexuality (Valentine 2007), queer theory was willing to indict realness with a failure to be realist because Black and brown femmes dared to desire to be beautiful, legendary, safe, loved, and secure.

In other words, perhaps *Tangerine*'s reception as realism instead of realness is as much a matter of wishful nostalgia as anything else. In seeing Sindee and Alexandra as tragic, however sincere and sympathetic trans women of color trapped by their circumstances, the audience is both able to imagine they are peeping at a prurient subculture while also reassuring themselves that things are changing and that Sindee and Alexandra do not represent the transgender future. Rather, they would incarnate an atavistic transsexual and transvestite past from which they will be recuperated, one day, by the inexorable rise in liberal trans inclusion that is supposed to typify the twenty-first century despite the overwhelming evidence that nothing of the sort is occurring but for the whitest, most propertied.

This issue of *TSQ*, "The Transsexual/Transvestite Issue," marks a powerful objection to the dominant figuration of "trans" in the field. Skeptical of what has been forgotten, erased, suppressed, and racialized in the passage from a "post-transexual theory" (Stone 1992) to "trans studies" (Stryker 2020), editors Emmett Harsin Drager and Lucas Platero ask temporal and geographical questions that seem long overdue. What ever happened to the transsexual and the transvestite, the two primary signifiers of trans life for the majority of the twentieth century? How is it that the ascendancy of *transgender* and then *trans* has periodized trans identity, life, and appearance, so that the transsexual and the transvestite are seen as relics of the past, when in fact there are many transsexuals and transvestites living in the trans metropoles of the global North? Similarly, how has an implicit geopolitics of trans as a colonial marker of modernity—or postmodernity, depending on whom you ask—relegated the transsexual and the transvestite to the global South? This thoroughly colonial temporality and geography, by which the transsexual and transvestite are backward, literal, or failed trans social forms displaced in the metropole by contemporary trans and nonbinary identities, or remain only in racialized global South contexts where they are implicitly parochial, provincial, and too particular to signify as the subjects of the field of trans studies, deserves a thorough critique.

As *TSQ* continues to reckon with the English-language domination and American centrism of trans studies, issues like these, helmed by Harsin Drager, a historian working on the unacknowledged racial history of trans patients in American gender clinics, and Platero, a trans studies scholar based in Spain, offer an important transnational model that builds on previous special issues. So it is that this issue's dozen plus articles cover not just subterranean or overlooked American case studies in the erasure of transvestites and transsexuals but are joined with extensive work on Spain and Latin America, where differences of language, racial schemas, colonialism, political structures, and categories provincialize any simple recuperation effort. This issue does not rescue the transsexual and transvestite from their relegation to the past or global South; on the contrary, it dissolves the very temporal and geographical imaginary through which that relegation would function. This issue brings forth instead rich and incommensurable analyses of *travestis*, transsexuals, gays and lesbians, Black transvestites, sex workers, and many other heterogenous social forms that do not submit to a north/south, past/present, American/non-American rubric. Likewise, the issue's contributors are nearly half non-American or scholars working primarily in Spanish. Significant thanks are due to Josh Marzano and Lucas Platero for assisting me with translations.

While interrupting the temporal and geographical current of trans studies to treat the transvestite and transsexual as meaningful and irreducibly different social forms in different times and places, each of the articles in the issue also offers substantial interventions at once historiographical, theoretical, conceptual, methodological, and political. Marta Vicente's opening essay illustrates how transgender, "a category created to include all trans* experiences," has expressly failed to do so. RL Goldberg's history of trans erotic pulp novels offers an essential reading of how narratives of forced feminization, sissification, and the erotic field of gender transitivity relied on a narrative environment of whiteness contrasted with Black gender, which was fantasized by contrast as stolid and unchangeable. Beans Velocci turns the history of transsexual medicine on its head by showing the degree to which transsexuality was not a matter of clinical ontology (that is, being a woman or man) but rather a functional matter of whether patients passing would protect surgeons from lawsuits. Turning to the Canary Islands, Daniasa Curbelo's poetic oral histories with transsexuals and travestis from the island's *barrancos* (ravines) curates an impressive vernacular archive of indigenous and antifascist resistance to Spanish dictatorial rule. Writing about the metropole of Barcelona, Iñaki Estella's essay on the travesti cabarets of the waning years of the Franco regime show how trans political resistance can germinate in the private or intimate sphere, behind closed doors, before it moves into the streets. And finally, Patricio Simonetto and Johana Kunin's reading of Argentinian travesti and transsexual public figure Mariela Muñoz's remarkable nationalist, maternal politics upsets easy relegations of transsexuals and travestis to the outside of the political, or as always already radical subjects in relation to the state.

These six articles are followed by a special section, "Transsexual/Transvestite Scrapbook," which pays homage to one of the most important handmade and do-it-yourself mediums employed by transsexuals and transvestites—and, not coincidentally, one of the most abundant, albeit privately generated and owned, of archives. The scrapbook is a multimedia collection of short images, objects, or other archival fragments from a range of locations around the world mirroring the locations of the issue's research articles. Each scrapbook item is accompanied by a short reflection written by the person who submitted it, both placing it in context and, in some cases, reflecting on their personal and intimate relationship with it. This loving tribute to the incommensurability and heterogeneity of the lives that travel under the signs *transsexual* and *transvestite* is a humble and mundane reminder that trans life cannot be contained by any taxonomy or heuristic, nor need it be.

The cover image for this issue, likewise, is drawn from the personal archive of Lindsey Shively's cousin Robert, whose photobooks of femme4femme life in the San Francisco Bay Area work much like the closing scene of *Tangerine*, in which all the cisgender characters in the film are alone and in grief on Christmas Eve, while Sindee and Alexandra find themselves in a laundromat, together. The final shot of the film shows them making up after the climactic fight of the film's diegesis, reaching their hands for one another in sisterhood. What strikes me about this moment is how these two femmes of color show, but don't tell, all it is that they know, that they live, and that makes them happy together, unlike the cis cast of the film. When we look at a cover image of two femmes like the one for this issue, it is worth practicing humility. There is far more that we do *not* know about transsexuals and transvestites than we ever will, but this is nothing like a deficit or lack to which trans studies is the appointed heir and savior. In their colorful and resplendent ephemerality, these trans femmes remind us that it is at best our radical humility as interested and thoughtful scholars that grants us access to the rich worlds of those who have truly *lived* at the margins of not just the social but also the field of trans studies.

Jules Gill-Peterson is an associate professor of history at Johns Hopkins University. She is the author of *Histories of the Transgender Child* (2018) and a general coeditor of *TSQ*.

References

Baker, Sean, dir. 2015. *Tangerine*. New York: Magnolia Home Entertainment. DVD.

Butler, Judith. 1997. "Gender Is Burning: Questions of Appropriation and Subversion." In *Bodies That Matter: On the Discursive Limits of Sex*, 81–98. New York: Routledge.

Stone, Sandy. 1992. "The *Empire* Strikes Back: A Posttranssexual Manifesto." *Camera Obscura*, no. 29: 150–76.

Stryker, Susan. 2020. "Introduction: Trans* Studies Now." *TSQ* 7, no. 3: 299–305.

Thompson, Patricia. 2015. "*Tangerine*." *American Cinematographer*, February. theasc.com/ac_magazine/February2015/Sundance2015/page5.html.

Valentine, David. 2007. *Imagining Transgender: An Ethnography of a Category*. Durham, NC: Duke University Press.

At the Margins of Time and Place

Transsexuals and the Transvestites in Trans Studies

EMMETT HARSIN DRAGER and LUCAS PLATERO

This special issue began with a simple provocation: "Where do we find the transvestite and the transsexual?" The ascendance and mainstreaming of *transgender* and its offshoots in its Anglo-American idiom represent more than a shift in nomenclature. While *transsexual* and *transvestite* were central categories that organized trans experience across a wide array of geographies, genders, and racial and class coordinates during the twentieth century, these categories have receded into the background of anglophone activism and academia. Trans studies, which has been dominated by US and English-based scholarship, has largely moved on from transsexuals in favor of ostensibly more open-ended and proliferating models of gender variance. Transvestites, for their part, have never occupied the center of the field of trans studies. Rendered anachronistic, both groups are more vulnerable than ever to long-standing stigmas with a new temporal twist. They are viewed as either tragic figures who could never be their "true" selves, in the case of transvestites, or hyper gender-conforming figures limited by the time in which they lived, in the case of transsexuals; the forward march of transgender has buried the fact that there are many living people who still identify with and live under those signs.

Defining transsexuality is a thorny business. In creating this special issue, we imagined *transsexual* to signify a particular subject position in relation to the body and the process of changing one's body. As trans studies has moved toward *trans* as a kind of prefix, able to attach itself to a variety of suffixes (Stryker, Currah, and Moore 2008), to use the term *transsexual* is to refer to a particular relationship between bodies and medicine. In naming this connection, we run the risk of collapsing transsexuality as only medical. For us, transsexual is both a medical category and more than a medical category. It describes a relationship to bodily transformation, via hormones and surgery; however, transsexuality is not the literal

TSQ: Transgender Studies Quarterly ∗ Volume 8, Number 4 ∗ November 2021 **417**
DOI 10.1215/23289252-9311018   © 2021 Duke University Press

by-product of medicine. Transsexuality emerged dialectically, in conversation with medicine over the second half of the twentieth century, a global medical accumulation of diagnoses, treatment protocols, public and private clinics, and flows of trans people and trans-derived knowledge in and out of clinics (Aizura 2018). Transsexuality describes the experience of having one's body poked, cut open, sutured back together, and made anew. In this regard, transsexuality is as much about the material as it is the discursive. It is about the phenomenological as much as it is about the medical. *Transsexual* is then a historical category that emerges in certain geographies, thanks to certain technologies, in the twentieth century (Preciado 2008). And as this issue attempts to demonstrate, *transsexual* is also a category of/for the present.

The terms *transvestite, travesti, cross-dresser*, and their various idiomatic iterations are too often understood (especially in mainstream and cisgender contexts) as not fully actualized transgender. They are imagined to be stalled, trapped in the wrong time or the wrong place, oppressed by cultural conventions, or otherwise unable to achieve "transgender" owing to the limitations of their life circumstances. This progress-oriented notion of transness, from sad transvestite pasts or liminal travesti geographies to open-ended trans presents and futures, renders these identities and embodiments backward or anachronistic.[1] Transvestites have historically represented the most visible sign of rupture with the binary norms in many national and local contexts (Berkins 2007) and consequently have suffered intense repression, mockery, and punishment. Transvestites, particularly in the case of travestis in the Americas, are a plural reality, defined by economic precariousness, body maladjustment, transgression of the gender binary, and dense theoretical reflection (Rivas San Martin 2012: 247). As Cole Rizki (2019: 149) writes in the introduction to *TSQ*'s special issue "Trans Studies en las Américas,"

> As a politics of refusal, travesti disavows coherence and is an always already racialized and classed geopolitical identification that gestures toward the inseparability of indigeneity, blackness, material precarity, sex work, HIV status, and uneven relationships to diverse state formations. To claim travesti identity is to embrace a form of opacity and fugitivity that resists necropolitical systems that pointedly rely on capture.

Transvestite and travesti positionalities are often unintelligible in the register of coherent "identity," which is to say one that follows the Western sexological narrative of separating an internal gender identity from sexual orientation. The lack of bourgeois coherence on this axis is often registered in how the ostensible enmeshment of gay and trans styles of being stand in for a range of negative valuations based on the many axes that Rizki enumerates.

Lacking coherence, however, is not an epistemological deficit that trans studies needs to repair. The current search for a term that is "good enough" (Wayar 2019) to describe the global experience of those moving away from the sex assigned at birth comes up against a certain political correctness that imposes a proper way to talk about transgender and nonbinary.[2] This search has the effect of erasing the particularities of the vernacular, the historical, or the chosen names for one's experience. We adapt the concept of the "good enough" from Donald Winnicott's (1953) "good enough" mother, which challenged the notion of the possibility of a perfect mother to recognize the psychic value of their failure, allowing children to live in an imperfect world. *Transvestite* and the *transsexual* may likewise not be politically or taxonomically perfect terms for some dominant trans scholar and activist communities nowadays, but they simply make sense for some of us within the myriad of experiences of gender disidentification (Muñoz 1999). *Transvestite* and *transsexual* are imperfect, sometimes even uncomfortable terms, especially when they "embody a parody of the fragmented corporeal rhetoric that brings irony to the female and male essentialism as well as questions the center/periphery colonial legacy" (Richard 2018: 31). Historically, transsexuals and transvestites have contributed to make explicit the failure in the binary ideology. For example, *la loca* as a militant gender and desiring subject (Perlongher 1997) has functioned as a figure "desencaje" (out of joint) in the Catholic lineages of Latin America and Spain, proving that ours is an imperfectly gendered world, despite centuries of colonial violence meant to cement a binary ideology as natural and immutable. The imposition of the new internationalized gay identity as well as the medical technologies that make possible the modification of the body profoundly transform the meaning and the space inhabited by travestis, cross-dressers, *transformistas*, *femminiellis*, and other trans social forms.

As transsexual editors from two different continents, with two different primary languages, we wanted to ensure that this special issue concerns not only the historical but also the geographical. A colonial spatial logic has also exported transsexuality and tranvestism out of the global North, embedding them as racial markers of gender in the global South. This process is taking place despite vocal counterclaims from communities that reject a Euro-American telos of trans identity and politics. We refer to multiple places in which *travesti* is used nowadays to defend communities from transfeminicide (Bento 2014) and travesticide (Berkins 2015), building on an activism that is rooted in experiences of sex work, and anticolonial and class resistance (Radi and Sardá-Chandiramani 2016). These are often heterodox spaces in their broader regional or national context, where inhabiting the transsexual enables an intelligible transition, a diagnosis that becomes a sort of refuge for some (Pérez 1993). While investigating local epistemologies of trans life and the social forms it takes that exceed or simply do not correspond to a colonial presumption about transsexuals and transvestites from the perspective of the metropolitan global North, this issue seeks to loosen the ease with which the dominant assumed geopolitical and temporal relations between "transgender," "transsexual," "transvestite," and "travesti" circulate.

This issue means to challenge the relegation of the transsexual and transvestite to another time and place in a broad sense, not just by or in transgender studies. Aiming to problematize how these categories do and don't easily characterize people across transnational, temporal, and linguistic boundaries, we aim to create a way for opening up the pages of *TSQ* to those outside the Western academy by welcoming submissions of varying lengths, languages, and written registers. This particular goal has resulted in the issue's "Transsexual/Transvestite Scrapbook." The scrapbook as a genre is a gesture to an important source of transsexual/transvestite history. As Sandy Stone (2006: 224) writes in "The *Empire Strikes Back: A Posttranssexual Manifesto*": "Many transsexuals keep something they call by the argot term 'O.T.F.': The Obligatory Transsexual File. This usually contains newspaper articles and bits of forbidden diary entries about 'inappropriate' gender behavior."

Scrapbooks are assemblages of varied meaning that rarely become part of the official institutional archive of law, medicine, and social movements. Scrapbooks allow us to know fragments of private lives. They also trouble the line between public and private, official and unofficial narratives, by indexing those fault lines as organizing constraints on many trans lives. They are objects of memory making, but as scrapbook contributor Lindsey Shively notes, in queer and trans communities they are also ephemeral. Scrapbooks often bear memories made to be forgotten, or were put together without the intention of recording anything like an official history. As many of the contributions to this special issue's scrapbook attest, finding rare visual or textual evidence of the trans past's richness is often haunted by a lack of clear names, locations, dates, or other corroborating information that can be used to look further into the lives they represent. The scrapbook and the personal photo album are meant for the act of telling stories; the author uses these materials for the purpose of making sense of themselves but also sharing narrative of who they are, what happened to them, and how they want to be seen (Rosón, 2016). For that reason, in the absence of the authors acting out their stories, many old scrapbooks cannot easily be a pathway into further historical retrieval. They are not a transparent archive that can be read and interpreted in a straightforward manner, apart from their creators. It is left to the interested amateur or scholar to find a more labile mode of engagement with the scrapbook as evidence. In similar fashion, this special issue's scrapbook is not offered as an encyclopedic, indexical, or in any way comprehensive archive or account of transvestite and transsexual life, let alone the medium of the scrapbook itself. On the contrary, the varied geographies, intimacies, private spaces, objects, and feelings traversed by the scrapbook are offered in their incommensurability, their evocations over their declarations, and in the desire that we hope they ignite in the reader. The contributors to the scrapbook have written short texts to accompany their visual object, reflecting on what it means to each of them to be pulled into the historical and the visual by the archive.

The research articles in this special issue unfold likewise in various geographies and spaces—the clinic, the cabaret, and the ravines of the volcanic Canary Islands, to name only a few—showing where transsexuality and transvestism have been consolidated, resisted, and experimented with in ways that refuse to add up to a grand narrative of the passage toward a transgender present and future. From the pages of smut novels to courtrooms in Argentina, the issue aims to highlight the expansive and capacious qualities of transsexuality and tranvestism. Rather than an obituary of categories now rendered obsolete, or a mission of rescue and recuperation, the issue enlivens the categories, welcoming them into the pages of *TSQ* to imagine what they could make possible in trans studies.

In the opening article, "Transgender: A Useful Category?," Marta Vicente traces a genealogy of the ascension of the term *transgender* as an umbrella for drifting from one's assigned gender at birth. Analyzing the continuous search for a term that "encompass[es] the multiple and sometimes contradictory relationships between one's body and its social recognition," the category *transgender* then becomes a "rubric for understanding the variability and contingency of gender across time, space, and cultures," always intertwined with other identities, as a sort of social assemblage. This genealogy poses several questions, such as how to think about dissident experiences when terms like *transgender*, *trans*, or *transsexual* did not exist (Halberstam 1998), highlighting the need to focus on the language people used in regard to their lives. Vicente proposes a focus on first-person narratives to build this genealogy and comprehend the "multiple terms used to express the diverse and sometimes contradictory identities an individual can embody."

In "(Trans) Sex Sells: Star Distributors Ltd. and Trans Sleaze," RL Goldberg examines trans erotic fiction from the 1970s–1990s, focusing on the pedagogical nature of trans sleaze, that is, the ways in which these pulp novels explored the negotiation of gender in a Cold War moment. Troubling sleaze scholarship, Goldberg explores how trans erotic fiction was not about enforcing a rigid category of masculinity but, rather, about the possibility of willfully (or forcefully) allowing oneself to be feminized. Yet this process of gendered equivocation and femininization was also fundamentally conditioned by an anti-Black imaginary that Goldberg teases out of the titles sold by Star Distributors. As they explain, this pulp literature shows how "Black gender—depicted exclusively as stable masculinity—is the context from which white trans exploration emerges. Quite simply, the white psyche cannot admit the possibility of Black femininity." "(Trans) Sex Sells" offers a story about the circulation of transsexuality and the genres in which it was constructed/constituted that challenge the supposed dependence of transsexuality on the medical sphere, expanding our understanding of the anti-Black foundations of gender transitivity in the United States.

Beans Velocci's "Standards of Care: Uncertainty and Risk in Harry Benjamin's Transsexual Classification," argues that in the mid-twentieth-century medical milieu of endocrinologist Harry Benjamin, regret and danger were the unofficial criteria in determining whether someone was eligible for gender-affirming surgery. Through the correspondence of Benjamin with Los Angeles urologist Elmer Belt, Velocci tracks how fears of retribution and legal exposure, rather than ontological claims about gender and womanhood, had the final say in the clinical decision-making process. As Velocci writes, "The transsexual emerged as someone to be feared, not for their potential to unsettle gender norms and hierarchies but for the hypothetical harm they might cause to medical practitioners who treated them." Velocci's article allows us to imagine transsexuality not as a neatly contained medical category, let alone an ontological one, but as an unruly terrain, often perceived to be dangerous.

Daniasa Curbelo undertakes a rereading of the concept of *barranco* (ravine), which they identify with the history of indigenous Canary Islander resistance to the colonial order and with political dissidence to the Francoist order in Spain during the mid-twentieth century. These ravines were also where a transvestite/transsexual community lived along with other dissident and marginalized people during the dictatorship. Thinking of the barrancos, volcanic scars on the landscape, as a possible place from which to resist order leads Curbelo to create an oral history with its protagonists and to uncover the strategies of resistance in a context of prostitution and delinquency. This methodology allows them to show the complexity of sexual and gender nonbinary identities in which transvestites and transsexuals endure. Curbelo thereby signals the current exile of the concept of transvestite in Spain, which is produced not only through its pejorative connotation but also through the medicalization of gender transitions from the 1980s onward. The transit of water through the barrancos and of the people who do not fit within binary norms and assigned sex, as well as the transit between the urban and the rural, are appropriate descriptions for these experiences of Canary Islander transvestites and transsexuals, which are often not well known.

The transvestite resistance in the Barcelona cabarets of the 1960s and 1970s, which was possible even under absolutist regimes such as the Franco dictatorship, is the focus of Iñaki Estella's analysis in "The Collective Scene." Habitually, academic literature has focused on the Francoist repression as an overall fact, making invisible the specific practices of resistance to fascism that did exist (Rosón 2016; Platero 2015). These practices of resistance, especially in their transvestite iterations, often occurred in private, which, in Estella's analysis, was the overlooked prerequisite to their public expression. Estella explores the existence of a counterpublic (Warner 2002) that frequented cabarets in Barcelona and showed its admiration for transvestites who in turn were navigating, not without risk, censure from the Franco regime. Although some readings of countercultural practices place the spotlight on individuals such as the artists Ocaña or Copi, it is important to not divest them of their social and activist context. Cabaret has been an ambivalent site for transvestite and gay life, but also a site of refuge (Mérida-Jiménez 2016), where humor has been a fundamental strategy for navigating mockery and shame and for making desire for transvestites possible.

Finally, in "Mariela Muñoz: Citizenship, Motherhood, and Transsexual Politics in Argentina (1943–2017)," Patricio Simonetto and Johana Kunin retell the story of Mariela Muñoz, an Argentine travesti mother who, thrust into the national spotlight after her adopted children were taken away from her, deployed the strategic role of mother to further transsexual and travesti rights in Argentina. A complex figure, often at odds with feminist and LGBTQ movements in Argentina, Muñoz does not easily fall into the role of beloved trancestor, styling herself as something more like a nationalist transsexual mother to the nation in the wake of years of dictatorship. As the authors write, "Her trajectory defied the limits of cis-gendered and antimaternal feminisms and showed how demands that could be initially considered conservative can lead to unexpected public support and legitimation of a marginalized community."

With this issue, and the accounts of transsexuality and transvestism that it showcases, we hope to inspire the desire to toss aside the "umbrella" of trans and transgender, instead encouraging trans studies to pivot toward more specific (historically, geographically, linguistically) identities and categories. In doing so, we want to contest the imposition of a proper and correct way to enunciate ourselves, encouraging the act of listening and learning from those that often are not at the center of trans studies. Being able to talk about what is materially and symbolically different about being transsexual or transvestite versus transgender or nonbinary allows us to more fully account for a heterogeneity of gender experiences. There is a lot to be gained from having an abundance of terms to differentiate between specific trans positionalities and embodiments. Lastly, we acknowledge that the linguistic nuances of a much larger semantic trans field can help to spotlight the entanglements of these experiences with the imposition of colonial, racial, and ableist logics that are at the root of our lives.

Emmett Harsin Drager is a doctoral candidate in the Department of American Studies and Ethnicity at the University of Southern California. Their dissertation, "To Be Seen: Transsexuals and the Gender Clinics," focuses on the trajectory of trans therapeutics in the United States in the twentieth century. Their research has been supported by UCLA Special Collections and the ONE Archives Foundation. Their writing can be found in *TSQ*.

Lucas Platero is assistant professor of social psychology at the King Juan Carlos University of Madrid and also serves as director of the University Press at Bellaterra Publishing House. His current collaborative research focuses on two projects: the experience of LGBTQA+ people with COVID 19 in Spain and the experiences of trans* men who give birth in Spain. His work has been published extensively, with eleven books and over fifteen journal articles.

Notes

1.   Our thinking about the retrograde character of transsexual and transvestite identities is highly influenced by the work of Kadji Amin and his book *Disturbing Attachments: Genet, Modern Pederasty, and Queer History* (2017).

2.   In her book *Travesti: Una teoría suficientemente Buena* (*Transvestite: A Good Enough Theory*; 2019), Marlene Wayar uses this very same term when discussing the violence against transvestites and the long list of lost and dead transvestites in Latin America. Also, building on her own childhood travesti memories, she poses the question of how to raise our children with the hope that they can have a travesty future.

References

Aizura, Aren. 2018. *Mobile Subjects: Transnational Imaginaries of Gender Reassignment*. Durham, NC: Duke University Press.

Amin, Kadji. 2017. *Disturbing Attachments: Genet, Modern Pederasty, and Queer History*. Durham, NC: Duke University Press.

Bento, Berenice. 2014. *Brasil: O país do transfeminicídio*. Rio de Janeiro: CLAM. www.clam.org.br /uploads/arquivo/Transfeminicidio_Berenice_Bento.pdf.

Berkins, Lohana. 2007. "Cómo nos decimos: Las travestis en Latinoamérica." *E-misférica* 4, no. 2. www.pagina12.com.ar/diario/suplementos/las12/13-9791-2015-06-12.html.

Berkins, Lohana. 2015. "El travesticidio también es femicidio." *Página/12*, June 12. www.pagina12 .com.ar/diario/suplementos/las12/13-9791-2015-06-12.htm.

Halberstam, Jack. 1998. *Female Masculinity*. Durham, NC: Duke University Press.

Mérida-Jiménez, Rafael. 2016. *Transbarcelonas: Cultura, género y sexualidad en la España del siglo XX*. Barcelona: Bellaterra.

Muñoz, José Esteban. 1999. *Disidentifications: Queer of Color and the Performance of Politics*. Minneapolis: University of Minnesota Press.

Pérez, Kim. 1993. "La transexualidad." Presentation at Jornadas Feministas Estatales: Juntas y a por Todas, Universidad Complutense de Madrid, December 4–6.

Perlongher, Néstor. 1997. *Prosa plebeya: Ensayos 1980–1992*. Buenos Aires: Colihue.

Platero, R. Lucas. 2015. *Por un chato de vino: Historias de travestismo y masculinidad femenina*. Barcelona: Bellaterra.

Preciado, Paul B. 2008. *Testo yonki*. Madrid: Espasa Calpe.

Radi, Blas, and Alejandra Sardá-Chandiramani. 2016. "Travesticidio/Transfemicidio: Coordenadas para pensar los crímenes de travestis y mujeres trans en Argentina." *Publicación en el Boletín del Observatorio de Género.* www.aacademica.org/blas.radi/14.pdf.

Richard, Nelly. 2018. *Abismos temporales: Feminismo, estéticas travestis y teoría queer.* Santiago de Chile: Ediciones Metales Pesados.

Rivas San Martín, Felipe. 2012. "Travestismos." In *Perder la forma humana: Una imagen sísmica de los años ochenta en América Latina*, edited by Roberto Amigo et al., 247–53. Madrid: Museo Centro de Arte Contemporáneo Reina Sofía.

Rizki, Cole. 2019. "Latin/X American Trans Studies." *TSQ* 6, no. 2: 145–55.

Rosón, María. 2016. *Género, memoria y cultura visual en el primer franquismo.* Madrid: Cátedra.

Stone, Sandy. 2006. "The *Empire* Strikes Back: A Posttranssexual Manifesto." In *The Transgender Studies Reader*, edited by Susan Stryker and Stephen Whittle, 221–35. New York: Routledge.

Stryker, Susan. 2008. *Transgender History.* Berkeley, CA: Seal.

Stryker, Susan, Paisley Currah, and Lisa Jean Moore. 2008. "Introduction: Trans-, Trans, or Transgender?" *WSQ* 36, nos. 3–4: 11–22.

Warner, Michael. 2002. "Publics and Counterpublics." *Public Culture* 14, no. 1: 49–90.

Wayar, Marlene. 2019. *Travesti: Una teoría suficientemente buena.* Buenos Aires: Muchas Nueces.

Winnicott, Donald. 1953. "Transitional Objects and Transitional Phenomena—A Study of the First Not-Me Possession." *International Journal of Psycho-Analysis* 34: 88–97.

Transgender: A Useful Category?

Or, How the Historical Study of "Transsexual" and "Transvestite" Can Help Us Rethink "Transgender" as a Category

MARTA V. VICENTE

Abstract This article seeks to start a discussion that may help us understand why the category "transgender," created to include all trans* experiences, has excluded some. If "transgender" cannot fully include all trans* people, can it still be a useful category to adequately capture and analyze the lived experience of historical actors? It is in tracing back the genealogy of *transgender,* in the search for a name that could encompass the multiple and sometimes contradictory relationships between one's body and its social recognition, that we may attempt to discover why *transgender* has eclipsed terms such as *transsexual* and *transvestite.* The article first examines the parallels between recent debates in the historiographies of gender and transgender as terms that can express the complex social representation of bodies negotiated by language. Second, it studies how much a genealogy of transgender in the past reveals in fact a multiplicity of terms to express a realignment between body and a self that can be read by society. Ultimately, the author proposes the study of first-person narratives as the best way to comprehend the multiple terms used to express the diverse and sometimes contradictory identities an individual can embody.
Keywords history of gender, transsexual, transvestite, narratives, identities

I would like to start by addressing some of the fundamental questions posed by the editors of this special issue: "Where do we find the transvestite and the transsexual? How have these categories been rendered untimely, retrograde, or counterrevolutionary?" Categories such as transvestite and transsexual have been overshadowed by the increasing acceptance of *transgender* as an umbrella term that includes all trans* experiences.[1] Has *transgender* instead become a category that, created to embrace all, has excluded some? If, as the general editors of *TSQ* (n.d.) propose, "'transgender' comes into play as a category, a process, a social assemblage, an increasingly intelligible gender identity, an identifiable threat to gender normativity, and a rubric for understanding the variability and contingency of

TSQ: Transgender Studies Quarterly * Volume 8, Number 4 * November 2021 **426**
DOI 10.1215/23289252-9311032 © 2021 Duke University Press

gender across time, space, and cultures," then we must also rethink *transgender* as a historical term open to variations and multiple crossroads with other identities that is not only "a category, a process, a social assemblage" but also offers "intelligible gender identity" to those who dare to trespass gender boundaries. Transgender identities are the result of shifting productions of knowledge throughout history, grounded in a language that operates as a form of bridge between genders and bodies by translating the visual and physical body into a legible and social entity.

In this article I seek to start a discussion that may help us understand why a category created to include all trans* experiences has faced difficulties in doing so. If "transgender" cannot fully include all trans* people, can it still be a useful category to adequately capture and analyze the lived experience of historical actors? I believe that in tracing back the genealogy of *transgender*, in the search for a name that could encompass the multiple and sometimes contradictory relationships between one's body and its social recognition, we may discover why *transgender* has eclipsed terms such as *transsexual* and *transvestite* and what to do about it.

Words are a microcosm of larger social debates in which they are born. In a similar way to Paul B. Preciado's (2020: 78) "amnesic feminism that suffers from a chronic lack of knowledge of its own genealogy," the word *transgender* also needs to reclaim its linguistic past and trace back the complexity of its genealogy. As Michel Foucault saw it, a genealogical analysis points at an intellectual system that is at the mercy of historical incidents and power relations. To Foucault, the genealogical method is "the undermining of all forms of historically grounded truth claims, all those that are based on a retrieval of lost origins and simple lines of development" (Sax 1989: 769). Thus the genealogy of *transgender* also aims to avoid a simple line of development to reveal the complexity of a term and its transformation to serve the needs of individuals in their different historical and geopolitical contexts. The genealogical search of *transgender* takes us to unearthing how the search for a term came about at the same time as the production of knowledge about the body. Such knowledge production reveals the ability of different forms of knowledge to coexist and the multiplicity of languages to describe them. To analyze this genealogical process of the making of *transgender*, I will first examine the parallels between the recent debates in the historiographies of *gender* and *transgender* as terms that can express the complex social representation of bodies negotiated by language. Second, I will study how much a genealogy of *transgender* in the past reveals in fact a multiplicity of terms to express a realignment between body and a self that can be read by society. I will propose the study of first-person narratives as the best way to comprehend the multiple terms used to express the diverse and sometimes contradictory identities an individual can embody.

An issue to consider is whether using terms such as *trans** and *transgender* in a context in which these categories did not exist is valid for historical analysis. The same question has been raised regarding the use of terms such as *homosexual* (Reay 2009), *lesbian* (Velasco 2011), or *pornography* (Vicente 2016) before the nineteenth century. One cannot use categories that may impose modern values onto historical subjects. For this reason, we need to pair them with the language people used at the time to describe their historically situated trans* experiences, meanings, and lives. Albeit the possible errors that using a term that people did not recognize as such involves, *trans** and *transgender* are terms of convenience that allow us to encompass the diversity of experiences of people in the past whose gender did not coincide with the gender assigned at birth. Moreover, avoiding the modern terms may also result in being part of the silencing that brought us to study this very same subject (Velasco 2011). Likewise, it is risky to generalize *transgender* and its meaning and application in different cultural contexts. The same can be said with *nationalism*, which in some contexts has excluded feminism while in others it has empowered feminists (Rodó-Zárate 2020). Equally, categories such as "transgender" become useful in embracing all trans* experiences, depending on how much they can intersect with different groups and the alliances they create.

(Trans) Gender

The title of this article refers to Joan Scott's groundbreaking text "Gender: A Useful Category of Historical Analysis," originally published in 1986 in *The American Historical Review*, in which the author examines the possibilities and limitations of the category "gender" to refer to the body's social constructions.[2] To Scott, the meaning of gender goes beyond the social construction of bodies and instead addresses relations of power and the creation of knowledge that embrace symbolic relations of subordination and hierarchy. Thus, gender provides the basis for giving meaning to "the organization and perception of historical knowledge" (31). More than two decades later, in 2011, Judith Butler and Elizabeth Weed reexamined Scott's proposal, questioning how much "gender" as a category is in fact useful to the study of human relations. Butler and Weed restored the question mark in "Gender: A Useful Category of Historical Analysis?"—the same question mark that the editors of the *AHR* had removed from Scott's article in 1986, perhaps looking for a certainty in the usefulness of gender that the author had never intended.[3]

By bringing back the question mark in Scott's article, one can explore the instability of the category "gender" and the difficulties it offers in classifying human behavior. Butler and Weed (2011: 3) warn us, "It is not possible to know whether gender is a useful category of analysis unless we can first understand the purposes for which it is deployed, the broader politics it supports and helps to produce, and the geopolitical repercussions of its circulation." The circulation of "gender," the way it arises within the dialectics of power in each time, may make "gender" a useful category, but it underplays the relations that brought it in the first place. In many cases, a gender identity presupposes the supremacy of gender over other identities. Instead, one needs to acknowledge that gender is part of the multiple embodied identities a person has and that are a response to the production of knowledge of the body: how a body is perceived and accepted by others. As Lucas Platero (2014: 83) has argued, the production of knowledge always responds to certain expectations and forms of recognizing and validating. It does not work in a void; knowledge production is the result of "how relations of power are negotiated."

The parallels between the categories "gender" and "transgender" cannot be missed. Like "gender," "transgender" is also a category that presupposes a social construction of one's body. Like "gender" as well, "transgender" ultimately runs the risk of giving primacy to the social in shaping the meaning of the body. Both "gender" and "transgender" are "linguistic tools which extract certain informa-tion, experiences, and feelings about ourselves and others" (Valentine 2007: 31).[4] These linguistic tools need to make the body intelligible to society. But, first, those "experiences and feelings about ourselves" must be dug out, extracted, unearthed from what is hidden inside us, out into the world for others to see and recognize. All this is taking us to the primordial place of the body in the creation of the self, as the threshold between the inside, and truthful self, and the outside, the social and cultural recognition of the self. Any word that seeks to categorize the human experience—and its social existence—needs to acknowledge this. Both "gender" and "transgender" do so. If "gender" wants to include "sex," "transgender" also seeks to include body-focused terms like *transsexual* or *transvestite*. However, despite their aims of inclusion, both terms have in many ways failed to embrace the bodily experience of the self.

By pointing at the need to bring back the body in "gender" and "trans-gender," I do not intend to suggest that the body is an entity separate from the social and being obscured by these categories. Instead, I support the argument of those who have posited that the body can be only experienced from the inside and projected onto the outside. It is what José Ortega y Gasset (1929: 123) defined as the *intracuerpo* (intrabody): "Our psychic life, our external world, are both based on this internal image of our body that we always carry with us and becomes the measure for all." Or it is a bodily experience difficult to explain but that may reveal the genuine truth of the self, something Katie Rain Hill (2014: 44) felt "in the core of myself: that my external body did not match with how I felt inside." Any category must be able to express this multidimensional aspect of the body that goes beyond the social to embrace the intimate, personal, and almost spiritual aspect of the self. It is a difficult task, since a linguistic expression of this complete self may risk the prospect of failure. Yet the genealogy of *transgender* can provide the roots to this multidimensional component of the embodied self and the attempts throughout history to find the name to define it.

Transgender first appeared as *transgenderism* in John Oliven's 1965 *Sexual Hygiene and Pathology* (Williams 2014: 233). Used in the 1970s by those who sought to distinguish themselves from transsexuals, *transgender* became in the 1990s a category celebrated for reflecting the flexibility and fluidity of gender (Hill 2013). It soon became an alternative term to *transsexual*, in vogue from the 1960s until the 1980s. "Transsexual" emphasized the medical and pharmacolog ical aspect of changing one's sex, while "transgender" was meant to embrace any gender realignment of an individual's body. "Transgender" also offered hope for creating bridges that would make "possible a broad alliance among different gender-variant people, including cross-dressers and transsexuals" (Papoulias 2006: 231). Although "transgender" never completely replaced "transsexual," the term "transsexual" was progressively judged as reflecting a flawed transgender iden-tity. From this perspective, "transsexual" was a term too closely connected to the body and the medicalization of the trans* body. Such focus on "transgender" as connected to a specific gender identity, even if fluid, made it a term less wel-coming to other terminologies such as not only *transsexual* but also *transvestite*. Transvestites in their temporary assumption of a different appearance suggested a transitional and mutating practice rather than a solid identity, and this excluded them in practice from the transgender umbrella.

Scott saw the rise of the category "gender" as a phenomenon taking shape in the American academy. The category of "transgender" as well bears an Anglo-Saxon component. Yet, while American scholars generally shy away from using *transsexual* and *transvestite*, Vek Lewis and Manuel Roberto Escobar have shown how such categories have symbolic currency in many countries in Latin America. Rather than hiding trans* identities, by reclaiming the word *travestis* and *trans-sexual*, the person is in fact turning the queer body into a site of protest and subversive potential (Lewis 2010: 38). The body as "a site through which sub-jectivity is constructed and difference is articulated" keeps reclaiming its place in this story (Lewis 2013: 466). The trans* body is the result of a specific and histor-ically based crossing of "regimes of knowledge-power" (Escobar 2016: 105). It is "a baroque construction," displaying multiple sides, socially translated by a diversity of languages. Defining oneself with words such as *marica* (fag), *puta* (whore), and *gai* (gay) and still thinking themselves as trans*, Escobar's subjects express a definition of the self that tries to maneuver through these "regimes of knowledge-power" to establish their own space of resistance.

Lewis's and Escobar's studies show the ways in which the body's space of resistance is constructed through the politics of recognition and the visibility of a body, which allows us to connect the variations of the meaning of *transgender* to visual marks of identity. If "all of our identifying traits are forms of appearance, and the first content of our nature (and its first place of realization) is our appearance," then the key is to know how much one can find the language to identify those traits and translate them into marks of identity (Coccia 2016: 80). This identity may translate deeper characteristics of the human self, which is what, as we saw before, appears at the root of the trans* self. Zoologist Adolf Portmann (1967: 17) saw no difference between humans and other animals: all display a zest for trying to connect "what is visible and tangible to what is more and more deeply hidden." The outside is an expression of the inward individuality of each animal. It is what makes an animal sociable and therefore able to survive. From the zoologist's perspective, animal life and behavior teach that in the practice of living the outside and the inside become blurred, as there is a constant "desire" to be recognized by others. In the human world as well, there is this desire to be recognized, to blur the lines that separate the outside from the inside. Appearance is meant to guarantee survival and mating, but only humans can bridge the gap between the outside and the inside through cognitive language. Words translate the individual's different lived experiences into multiple identities. Identities become the individual's perception of the self as well as how it appears to others, the legibility of the representation.

A Genealogy of *Transgender*: In Search of Identities

In the twentieth and twenty-first century the terms *gender* and *transgender* have been closely intertwined with issues of identity. Gender has become such a fundamental part of people's self-definition as human beings that it is difficult not to think of it as one of the main marks of identity. However, the reality of a sovereign and all-reigning gender identity is difficult to sustain when looking at the many other identifications that are connected to gender, mainly, sexual identity. Moreover, in the current discussion on gender in Europe and America there has been a need to break down the term *gender* itself, with a multiplicity of subterms: *genderqueer, nonbinary, gender nonconforming, bigender, demigender, pangender,* and *agender,* just to name a few. The world of possibilities is wide open to what Rogers Brubaker (2016) has referred to as the "unsettled identities" that have characterized contemporary societies. To Brubaker, in the past few decades the "landscape of identities has become much more complex, fluid, and fragmented. As new categories have proliferated and old categories have come to seem ill fitting, we increasingly face uncertainties and ambiguities in identifying ourselves and categorizing others" (41). However, such unsettled identities have been constantly present in the past, at least of the last five hundred years.

But what is identity? Is it, as Susan Faludi (2016: 49) has asked, "what you choose, or what you can't escape?" Faludi's memoir about her transgender father explores the maze that her father's transition to womanhood represented. Identity, or the sense of belonging to a group and what identifies it, is inexorably connected to the politics of recognition, and national and religious recognition adds layers to gender identity. To me it appears as a seesaw because, as much as one wants it to remain steady, it never does. The pivot point of the seesaw represented by the body is never wide enough to allow for trans* individuals and society to maintain a stable identity. From Faludi's perspective her father sees her acceptance and recognition as a woman as part of the identity recovery of her nation, Hungary, and her conflictive Jewishness. In Faludi's case the politics of recognition were at play. One may feel belonging to a group, but it becomes a social reality only when the group recognizes us as one of them. In fact, the bases for existence and "the desire to persist in one's own being is fulfilled only through the desire to be recognized," or to match the outside with the inside (Butler 2005: 43). This desire seems to drive the need to proclaim one's identity to the world. Faludi's question, however, remains unanswered: Does one choose one's identity or is it something ingrained in ourselves, something we cannot escape? Does one's identity need to match society's expectations of the limited number of identities available to each individual? When we examine the narratives that trans* individuals produced throughout history, we can say at the very least that transgender is one of multiple identities that can define an individual. Moreover, "transgender" itself is the result of multiple identities that in twentieth-century Western societies may well include "transvestite" and "transsexual." Choosing one over the other would be as anachronistic as the term *identity* itself.

In the recent study of three gender stories from nineteenth-century France, Rachel Mesch (2020) points at the difficulties of talking about identity in history. Quoting Lisa Duggan's (1993: 793) definition of identity as the "story or narrative structure that gives meaning to experience," Mesch (2020: 11) refers to gender identity as "stories" rather than labels, a "necessary and vital tale to tell" for trans* people. This is also Jen Manion's (2020) proposal in Manion's analysis of "female husbands," people assigned female at birth who lived as men and married other women in the eighteenth and nineteenth centuries in England and the United States. To Manion, it is in the first-person account, in the intimate projection of the self to seek social recognition, that one can grasp at the multiple marks of identities of an individual and which are favored and why. The body of trans* stories may in fact create a "transgender time" that "challenges traditional chronology and highlights the temporal dislocations necessary for self-narrative" (Devun and Tortorici 2018: 521). It is in this storytelling where the visual recognition of someone, and the language to express this recognition, come together to bridge the gap between the body and the social. The external appearance and behavior of someone can establish the forms of knowledge that help identify that person. As the title of the 2014 edited collection *Otras formas de (re)conocer (Other*

Ways of (Re)cognizing) (Mendia Azkue et al. 2014) references, the act of (re)cognizing allows one to recall something already (visually) experienced. In the process of recalling that image, allowing the memory of something that has always been there to resurface, the brain generates new knowledge. This process lies at the core of the politics of recognition in an ongoing process of first recognizing and then offering entitlement to what is recognized. From this perspective it is the first-person account that may reveal "the dialectics of power" Butler and Weed referred to. Autobiographical narratives had the potential of revealing the trespassing of identities—gender, race, religion, and nationality—and the power relations behind the construction of the self.

Many writers have pointed out how much identities are the result of stories we construct and tell to ourselves and others, from Jay Prosser's (1998) concept of "narrative work" to Joan Didion's "we tell ourselves stories in order to live," Adriana Cavarero's (2000) "narratives of the self," or Julia Kristeva's (2001) "life is a story." Certain narratives have a prearranged script, and it is difficult to (re)cognize them without that symbolic guidance. As if it we were trying to put into words a dream that we had just woken up from, the narrative line offers us the possibility of making sense of a life made up of "disparate images" (Didion 1979: 1). This narrative line can be as eclectic and dissonant as one may wish, and only the individual has the potential to destabilize gender with their first-person narratives, sometimes mixing narratives and voices. In their autobiography *Heaven*, Emerson Whitney (2020) brings several voices in the asymmetrical construction of the self, but it is Maggie Nelson's (2015) *The Argonauts*, promoted as "a genre-bending memoir, a work of 'auto theory' offering fresh, fierce, and timely thinking about desire, identity, and the limitations and possibilities of love and language," that offers multiple and conflictive layers of relations. Nelson's view of trans* experiences and the language to describe them may better express the core of trans* narratives throughout history—the use of terms that change in relation to power relations and creation of knowledge. The naming of the self occurs in accumulative form, and earlier concepts are never forgotten but in fact are kept as alternatives (Daston and Galison 2007). Equally new words to describe trans* ways of living are produced across time, not to replace old ones but to coexist with them. At the same time, the search for genealogy and historical precedents relates to the attempt to "stabilize" the conflict between the individual and society. While the individual tends to express in their personal narratives a multitude of identities and tries to find the language that defines them, the receptor of these narratives will tend to choose a single denominator that reduces all those identities into a single category.

A historical analysis of narratives of the self offers a window into the multiple constructions of identities and how they can produce knowledge toward the politics of recognition. In my work I found that the confessional genre is, among the first-person narratives, the one that offers the best possible window into this difficult-to-grasp relation between the inside and the outside of trans* experiences. Because of the direct association between confession and truth production when confessing, individuals reveal their "most secret nature" through the penitent's examination of the sins of the body or through the corporal violence or coercion authorities applied to the accused (Foucault 1980: 60). Departing from Saint Augustine of Hippo's *Confessions* (2008), confessants not only reveal a truth they had been hiding inside themselves, but the process happens only through a painful revelation that involves a transformation, the root of conversion to the new self that was the original and truthful self. This spiritual component inherited in the confession allows the trans* confessant to access the intrabody that Ortega y Gasset was referring to. Confession can extract this deep and hard-to-explain knowledge of the self that only the person themselves knows but only through confession can be made public. This was the Inquisition's intent in making Elena/Eleno de Céspedes, the Spanish "mulatto" surgeon accused of sodomy, confess before its tribunal. Céspedes appeared before the inquisitors on July 17, 1587, ready to provide a "genealogy" to the tribunal. Confession before the tribunal of the Inquisition, expected from each convict, was part of a set of power relations—the dialogue between the accused and the accuser, what the confession produced and what the tribunal expected to hear—that produced knowledge about the body and the self. In their confession, the accused was requested to present the truth about oneself by relating their life story through a genealogy account.

Genealogies revealed fundamental information for the inquisitors: the history of the individual as a good Christian, how and when they derailed from the right path as well as the networks created in their journeys toward possible heresy. In their genealogy, Céspedes extracted multiple identities from their selves as a branded former slave, a soldier, a dissident, and a medical practitioner, all shaped by their condition as a possible "hermaphrodite" in a brown body.[5] While Céspedes's actions reveal a multiplicity of identities, they were all merging into one that the Inquisition could recognize as "truthful." Céspedes presented themselves as a good Christian in the body of a hermaphrodite: "Even though I was a woman I was also a man. Since I had the nature of a man. I was suitable to marry" (Kagan and Dyer 2004: 51). Céspedes's narrative is that of a good Christian, marrying a woman thinking themselves to be a man. Céspedes's garments, jobs, literacy, and attraction to women entitled Céspedes to be a man and to highlight the physical part of themselves that was hidden.[6] The contrast lies in Céspedes's personal account to the Inquisition that combines multiple identities and a fluctuant body with a language that wants to find a way to convey a stable self for the inquisitors to read and recognize as a "livable self" (Butler 2016: 18). At the end of the document of Céspedes's declaration, Elen* has an ink stain where the *a* (the female, Elena) or *o* (the masculine, Eleno) should have been.[7] We do not know whether the drop of ink was accidental. But perhaps, despite themselves, the inquisitors were also projecting Céspedes's ambiguity by combining the two names *Elena/Eleno* to describe the accused.

Confessions express the ambiguities and fluctuant definitions of the self that are a common pattern in the genealogy of *transgender*. They are immersed in relations of power, on "the structures that let us live," finding points in common, establishing a compromise (Butler 2016: 19). This contrasts the multiple identities of the confessant with the need to have one single identity that the confessor needs to hear, making the confessant's main identity readable to the receiver. Relations of power also frame the case of the Spanish lieutenant Erauso's confession to the bishop of Guamanga (Perú) in 1623.[8] Born in 1592 in Donostia-San Sebastián (Spain), and placed at a young age by their parents in a convent, Erauso (1992: 64) later told the bishop that before professing the final vows, "I left the convent for such and such reason, went to such and such place, undressed myself and dressed myself again, cut my hair, traveled here and there." In their confession, Erauso saw no contradiction in presenting themselves as a virgin, baptized as Catalina, who nevertheless was entitled to live and dress as a man and wear the name *Antonio* because of their valiant service to the monarch. Erauso portrayed a body that had the potential to be ambiguous. As contemporary accounts reported, Erauso "looks more like a castrato (*capón*) than a woman," a comment that synthesizes Erauso's efforts to portray themselves as more than a man (as a soldier beyond the constraints of sex) and as a hero ("more a valiant soldier than a courtier") (128). Erauso's ambiguity is also reflected in the use of pronouns in their story, referring to themselves in feminine while framing a gender that was clearly masculine in the expected male preference for women, and the violence and aggressivity portrayed throughout the story. Erauso thus ends their narrative with the cutting answer to a cheeky lady who greeted Erauso with the feminine "Señora Catalina," to which the newly named Antonio de Erauso responded, "Señora *puta* (whore), [I have come] to give you a hundred strokes and a hundred gashes to the one who would dare to defend you" (124). The theatrical ending to what is already a problematic text (Erauso's original manuscript was lost and survives only as a late eighteenth-century transcript) reveals, however, a reaffirmation of a masculine gender identity that wants to shine through any possible female component of Erauso. The male gender ending, however, cannot erase the entire text in which Erauso establishes their authority through a female virginity, heroic deeds, and their status as a noble Basc.

Throughout nineteenth- and twentieth-century Europe and America, categories that identify trans* experience reveal the ambiguities and fluctuant definitions of the self. Céspedes and Erauso, for example, saw themselves immersed in the relations of power that create specific knowledge about the body. If Céspedes presented themselves as a hermaphrodite and Erauso as a military hero, they both did it after sorting out multiple identities of themselves: Céspedes as a soldier and surgeon, Erauso as a noble Basc and former novice. Equally, three centuries later Ralph Werther/Jennie June, the Connecticut-born author of *Autobiography of an Androgyne* ([1919] 2008) constructed a soul-searching confessional narrative that offered a multidimensional view of the self. The author did not find any conclusive adjective that could identify them as a transvestite or homosexual, but instead searched for the right terminology to label the trans* experience: *fairie, invert, androgyne, hermaphroditos*. To June and others terms such as *homosexual, androgynous, intersex, transsexual,* and *transvestite* were exchangeable and fluctuant; someone could identify with one in a given moment and another in a different time of their lives or be several at once.

Despite the complexity of identities portrayed in the confessional account, both confessant and their audiences tended to narrow the scope of identities to one, perhaps searching for an umbrella term that helped encompass the complexity of human nature and identities. In fact, this was the aim of Alfred Herzog, the Austrian-born physician established in New York who agreed to publish Werther/June's manuscript. To Herzog *Autobiography of an Androgyne* was the product of a homosexual in search of redemption. The same single identity was behind the arrest in 1968 of M.E. in the Catalan town of Hospitalet. Because M.E. was arrested "in suspicious attitude and dressed as a man," their actions easily fell under the "homosexual" umbrella used by medical and policing authorities during the dictatorship in Spain, an umbrella that gathered "different sexualities and gender expressions" (Platero 2015: 16, 26). The labeling of M.E. as "transvestite" and "homosexual" probably contrasted and clashed with the multiple words available at the time for those accused of homosexuality. Much like the "transgender" umbrella, the "homosexual" umbrella of the 1960s failed to acknowledge the complicated and rich diversity of gender and sexual identities, revealed in recent interviews of Silvia Reyes Plata, a Spanish entertainer arrested in Barcelona in 1974 for "making ostentation of his homosexuality" (se hallaba haciendo ostentación de su homosexualidad) (Terrasa Mateu 2016: 463). In both the documentary *Bones of Contention* (dir. Andrea Weiss, 2017) about the memory of the repression of LGBTQ rights in Spain as well as in an interview by the doctoral candidate Jordi Terrasa Mateu in 2016, Reyes refers to herself as "homosexual," "gay," "transvestite," and "transsexual" alternatively. According to Terrasa Mateu (2016: 168), Reyes explained she felt "absolutely comfortable with the word gay" and that she "lacked prejudgments in choosing a word that defined her sexual orientation and gender." Reyes is probably not unique in embracing a multiple terminology that helps her define what to her is a way of living and feeling.

The sense of the self as multifaced, body- and soul-searching contrasts, then, with a desire from the other to find a single word that would embrace this complex denomination. When in 1966 the German American endocrinologist Harry Benjamin popularized the term *transsexual*, he did it by obscuring other terms such as *transvestite, androgynous,* or *homosexual* that *transsexual* was meant to encompass. Yet the body has always had the potential to be a site of resistance refusing to be circumscribed. Trans* experiences kept projecting this hesitance (and resistance) to being labeled. Louis Graydon Sullivan, a native of Milwaukee, and the first well-known gay trans* man in the United States, wrote in his diary in September 1979, "I don't know if I am a deluded transvestite or an overly cautious transsexual" (Reay 2019: 140, 148). At the end of his life, Sullivan settled for a gay male identity, but one cannot erase the journey that took him there, full of ambiguities that, as Sullivan himself saw, were "far more revolutionary & futuristic than trying to resolve it along some obscure conventional lines" (148). Fixed terminologies never fully satisfied Sullivan, but perhaps he ended up acknowledging that he also had to aim at securing a "livable life" to be able to survive as a trans* man.

Conclusion

"Transgender," initially meant to offer visibility and acceptance to the bearer, has now become a sort of cloak that renders invisible all the nuances and multiple identities of trans* people. To be able to grant visibility to all trans* experiences, the need to destabilize language seems key. If, as David Valentine already expressed in his 2007 *Imagining Transgender: An Ethnography of a Category*, the category "transgender" was in the 1990s a useful construction mostly for activists and meant to include all "gender-variant individuals," then the category may have already worn out its own use as new power relations are being established in the evolving genealogy of *transgender*. As Valentine (n.d.) pointed out, "This vision carries with it assumptions about gender and sexuality that reinforce racial and class hierarchies." Many others within the queer community have echoed Valentine's concerns and questioned the fixed language that constrains the multiplicity of identities. Perhaps unwillingly and unintentionally, "transgender" has become linked to an identity that presupposes a legible body. Even if "transgender" wants to include all trans* possibilities, at the end of the day it grants visibility to those who display a stable identity, even if it entails an ambiguous gender. It is important to make identities concrete—real—or we risk the invisibility that mutable identities threaten to bring. In seeking to stabilize, we may leave out—render invisible, hide—what does not fit. This is at the core of the relations of power at work in the rise of "transgender" and its evolving place in our linguistic map. Perhaps it would be useful here to refer to J. L. Austin's (1962: 4–7) contrast between "constative" and "performative" utterances: the former is a speech that states or reports, while the latter implies an action added to the description of what one is doing. The various terms that refer to the trans* experiences are meant to be "constative" or descriptive, while in the practice of their daily use they appear as "performative," constructing realities and with the potential of transforming the very same utterance they had originated from. The performative use of a term such as "transgender," initially intended as descriptive, ultimately creates tensions expressed in the debate over the use of "transgender" as a common denominator for the diversity of trans* experiences.[9]

The need for a creation of a stable identity that the genealogy of the word *transgender* reveals is a process, the historical journey to progressively demand a single identity from individuals. This gender purity has historically developed in tandem with racial purity, even before the abolition of slavery in the colonial world and the inclusion of former slaves into the community of free citizens of a nation (Martínez 2013). Multiple gender denominations as much as mixed races grew progressively unwelcomed and, worse yet, unreadable (Snorton 2017). The fear has always been to remain invisible. As Viviane Namaste (2000: 2) argued, "Transsexuals are continually and perpetually erased in the cultural and institutional world."[10] Wrongly read, the body that is asymmetric appears as monstrous, this being a recurrent fear in trans* narratives (Mercier 2019). Worse than risking invisibility throughout history, individuals who were not recognized as either male or female were at risk of becoming targets of violence (Butler 2005: 31). Transphobia emanates mostly from seeing the trans* body as a monstrosity that does not fulfill the human patterns and thus invites aggression and violence (Stryker 1994). Identifying oneself as either transsexual or transvestite may open this wound by presenting the trans* body as incomplete, a medical project or a mutable self, a body that defies normality and therefore acceptance.

Yet the potential subversive element of any transgender lies in its lack of stability. Can we then recover the categories "transsexual" and "transvestite" to continue making *transgender* a subversive word? But how? Perhaps by recognizing the instability of terms that language must express and that the term *category* itself denies. The reality would be a "blending of categories" that David Valentine foresees in "transgender, gay, transsexual, transvestite, and others" (Reay 2020: 207). Yet "category" itself may be a word that lacks the porosity of other concepts such as experience. Kimberlé Crenshaw (1989: 139), in the now classic work "Demarginalizing the Intersection of Race and Sex," emphasized the benefits of approaching the study of "categories" from the perspective of "experiences." Like category, identity is also a concept that may lack flexibility, and perhaps we should be, as Preciado (2019a: 37) suggests, "thinking in terms of relation and potential of transformation, instead of terms of identity." It is interesting to note that in the Spanish version of *An Apartment on Uranus* Preciado (2019a: 25) uses the word *nociones* (*notions*) to refer to "a system of visibility, of representation, and of granting of sovereignty and political recognition."[11] Preciado seems to propose the need to stay away from categories, by connecting notions with a "system of visibility, representation." Categories, "a division within a system of classification," are an effort to create "legible individuals" so that the reading cannot be confusing. Yet the English translation of Preciado's work uses the word *categories* instead of *notions*, explained by the fact that the translator uses the French version of *An Apartment on Uranus*. Preciado wrote both the French and the Spanish versions, which came out simultaneously in spring of 2019. The two, *Un appartement sur Uranus: Chroniques de la traversée* (2019b) and *Un apartamento en Urano: Crónicas del cruce* (2019a), are almost identical texts but bear differences in the use of the language to address what Preciado calls his place as "un disidente del régimen binario sexo-género" (a dissident of the sex-gender binary regime) or "un dissident du système genre-genre" (a dissident of the gender-genre system) (Preciado 2019a, 2019b). The multiple versions of Preciado's work make us question: What are categories? Are categories differently constructed in distinct languages portraying different notions of the body evolving from specific power relations? Is *transgender* or anything that has as its root *gender* a useful notion to get at the origin of the notions of human divisions? I need to leave the reader with these open questions so we can all continue discussing the difficulties of inclusion in an age of division and dissent.

Marta V. Vicente is professor of history and women, gender, and sexuality studies at the University of Kansas. Her most recent publications are *Debating Sex and Gender in Eighteenth-Century Spain* (2017), "Queering the Early Modern Iberian Archive" (2018), and "The Medicalization of the Transsexual: Patient-Physician Narratives in the First Half of the Twentieth Century" (forthcoming). She is presently working on a book manuscript titled *Trans Confessions from the Inquisition to the Internet*.

Notes

1. I use the term *trans** to refer to the wide spectrum of transgender identities and experiences. Although I risk the possibility of falling into the same limitations that *transgender* has, by removing *gender* from *trans*, it may result in a term that reaches further out from the constraints of *gender* and, as Susan Stryker, Paisley Currah, and Lisa Jean Moore (2008: 11) suggested, make it more open ended and relational.
2. Scott's article was revisited in 2008 in an *AHR Forum* (Scott 2008).
3. In a reissue of the article, Scott expressed her desire to maintain the question mark.
4. Valentine's quote refers to *gender* and *sexuality*, but it can also apply to *transgender*.
5. Several scholars have studied the case of Céspedes: Israel Burshatin, Richard Kagan and Abigail Dyed, Emilio Maganto Pavón, Francois Soyer, Sherry Velasco, and Lisa Vollendorf, just to name a few.

6.   Céspedes seemed to lack facial hair and had pierced ears, traditional among Castilian women, but this was also the practice of men in some African countries.

7.   The scribe also changed pronouns, depending on the context in which Céspedes was described (when listing Céspedes's jobs, the scribe noted Céspedes with the masculine pronouns).

8.   Erauso confessed before the bishop after having sought ecclesiastical protection to avoid arrest for murder. Secondary literature on "the Lieutenant Nun" is extensive. Among the long list of authors who have analyzed the manuscript of Erauso's confession are Nerea Aresti, Christopher Kark, Carolyn McCarthy, Eva Mendieta, Pedro Rubio Merino, Cathy Rex, Michele and Gabriel Stepto, Rima de Vallbona, and Sherry Velasco.

9.   I would like to thank the anonymous reader of this article who suggested this idea.

10.   Namaste uses both the term *transsexual* and *transgender*.

11.   Both quotes are my own translation from the Spanish.

References

Augustine of Hippo, Saint. 2008. *Confessions*. Translated by Henry Chadwick. Oxford: Oxford University Press.

Austin, J. L. 1962. *How to Do Things with Words: The William James Lectures Delivered in 1955*. Oxford: Clarendon.

Benjamin, Harry. 1966. *The Transsexual Phenomenon*. New York: Julian.

Brubacker, Rogers. 2016. *Trans: Gender and Race in an Age of Unsettled Identities*. Princeton, NJ: Princeton University Press.

Butler, Judith. 2005. *Giving an Account of Oneself*. New York: Fordham University Press.

Butler, Judith. 2016. "Rethinking Vulnerability in Resistance." In *Vulnerability in Resistance*, edited by Judith Butler, Zeynep Gambetti, and Leticia Sabsay, 12–27. Durham, NC: Duke University Press.

Butler, Judith, and Elizabeth Weed. 2011. *The Question of Gender: Joan W. Scott's Critical Feminism*. Bloomington: Indiana University Press.

Cavarero, Adriana. 2000. *Relating Narratives: Story Telling and Selfhood*. Translated and with an introduction by Paul A. Kottman. London: Routledge.

Coccia, Emanuele. 2016. *Sensible Life: A Micro-ontology of the Image*. Translated by Scott Alan Stuart. New York: Fordham University Press.

Crenshaw, Kimberlé. 1989. "Demarginalizing the Intersection of Race and Sex: A Black Feminist Critique of Antidiscrimination Doctrine, Feminist Theory, and Antiracist Politics." *University of Chicago Legal Forum* 140, no. 1: 139–67.

Daston, Lorraine, and Peter Galison. 2007. *Objectivity*. New York: Zone.

Devun, Leah, and Zeb Tortorici. 2018. "Trans, Time, and History." *TSQ* 5, no. 4: 518–39.

Didion, Joan. 1979. *The White Album*. New York: Simon and Schuster.

Duggan, Lisa. 1993. "The Trials of Alice Mitchell: Sensationalism, Sexology, and the Lesbian Subject in Turn-of-the-Century America." *Signs* 18, no. 4: 791–814.

Erauso, Catalina [Antonio] de. 1992. *Vida i sucesos de la Monja Alférez: Autobiografía atribuida a Doña Catalina de Erauso*. Edited by Rima de Vallbona. Tempe: Center for Latin American Studies, Arizona State University.

Escobar, Manuel Roberto. 2016. *Cuerpos en resistencia: Experiencias trans en Ciudad de México y Bogotá*. Bogotá: Ediciones Universidad Central.

Faludi, Susan. 2016. *In the Dark Room*. New York: Metropolitan.

Foucault, Michel. 1980. *An Introduction*. Vol. 1 of *History of Sexuality*. Translated by Robert Hurley. New York: Vintage.

Hill, Katie Rain, with Ariel Schrag. 2014. *Rethinking Normal: A Memoir in Transition*. New York: Simon and Schuster.

Hill, Robert. 2013. "Before Transgender: *Transvestias'* Spectrum of Gender Variance, 1960–1980." In *The Transgender Studies Reader 2*, edited by Susan Stryker and Aren Z. Aizura, 364–79. New York: Routledge.

June, Jennie [Ralph Werther]. (1919) 2008. *Autobiography of an Androgyne*. Edited and with an introduction by Scott Herring. New Brunswick, NJ: Rutgers University Press.

Kagan, Richard L., and Abigail Dyer. 2004. *Inquisitorial Inquiries: Brief Lives of Secret Jews and Other Heretics*. Baltimore: Johns Hopkins University Press.

Kristeva, Julia. 2001. *Hannah Arendt: Life Is a Narrative*. Translated by Frank Collins. Toronto: University of Toronto Press.

Lewis, Vek. 2010. *Crossing Sex and Gender in Latin America*. New York: Palgrave MacMillan.

Lewis, Vek. 2013. "Thinking Figurations Otherwise: Reframing Dominant Knowledges of Sex and Gender Variance in Latin America." In *The Transgender Studies Reader 2*, edited by Susan Stryker and Aren Z. Aizura, 457–70. New York: Routledge.

Manion, Jen. 2020. *Female Husbands: A Trans History*. Cambridge: Cambridge University Press.

Martínez, María Elena. 2013. "Sex, Race, and Nature: Juana Aguilar's Body and Creole Enlightened Thought in Late Colonial New Spain." Paper presented at the "Race and Sex in the Eighteenth-Century Spanish Atlantic World" symposium, University of Southern California, Los Angeles, April 12–13.

Mendia Azkue, Irantzu, Marta Luxán, Matxalen Legarreta, Gloria Guzmán, Iker Zirion, and Jokin Azpiazu Carballo, eds. 2014. *Otras formas de (re)conocer: Reflexiones, herramientas y aplicaciones desde la investigación feminista*. Donostia-San Sebastián, Spain: SIMReF.

Mercier, Thomas Clement. 2019. "Resisting the Present: Biopower in the Face of the Event (Some Notes on Monstrous Lives)." *New Centennial Review* 19, no. 3: 99–128.

Mesch, Rachel. 2020. *Before Trans: Three Gender Stories from Nineteenth-Century France*. Stanford, CA: Stanford University Press.

Namaste, Vivian. 2000. *Invisible Lives: The Erasure of Transsexual and Transgendered People*. Chicago: University of Chicago Press.

Nelson, Maggie. 2015. *The Argonauts*. Minneapolis: Graywolf.

Ortega y Gasset, José. 1929. *El espectador*. Vol. 5. Madrid: Revista de Occidente.

Papoulias, Stan [Constantina]. 2006. "Transgender." *Theory, Culture and Society* 23, nos. 2–3: 231–33.

Platero, R. Lucas. 2014. "¿Es el análisis interseccional una metodología feminista y queer?" In Mendia Azkue et al. 2014: 79–96.

Platero, R. Lucas. 2015. *Por un chato de vino: Historias de travestismo y masculinidad femenina*. Barcelona: Ediciones Bellaterra.

Portmann, Adolf. 1967. *Animal Forms and Patterns: A Study of the Appearance of Animals*. New York: Schocken.

Preciado, Paul B. 2019a. *Un apartamento en Urano: Crónicas del cruce*. Barcelona: Anagrama.

Preciado, Paul B. 2019b. *Un appartement sur Uranus: Croniques de la traversée*. Paris: Bernard Grasset.

Preciado, Paul B. 2020. *An Apartment on Uranus: Chronicles of the Crossing*. South Pasadena, CA: Semiotext(e).

Prosser. Jay. 1998. *Second Skins: The Body Narratives of Transsexuality*. New York: Columbia University Press.

Reay, Barry. 2009. "Writing the Modern Histories of Homosexual England." *Historical Journal* 52, no. 1: 213–33.

Reay, Barry. 2019. *Sex in the Archives: Writing American Sexual Histories*. Manchester: Manchester University Press.

Reay, Barry. 2020. *Trans America: A Counter-History*. Cambridge: Polity.

Rodó-Zárate, Maria. 2020. "Gender, Nation, and Situated Intersectionality: The Case of Catalan Pro-independence Feminism." *Politics and Gender* 16, no. 2: 608–36.

Sax, Benjamin C. 1989. "Foucault, Nietzsche, History: Two Modes of the Genealogical Method." *History of European Ideas* 11: 769–81.

Scott, Joan W. 1986. "Gender: A Useful Category of Historical Analysis." *American Historical Review* 91, no. 5: 1053–75.

Scott, Joan W. 2008. "Unanswered Questions." *American Historical Review* 113, no. 5: 1422–30.

Snorton, C. Riley. 2017. *Black on Both Sides: A Racial History of Trans Identity*. Minneapolis: University of Minnesota.

Stryker, Susan. 1994. "My Words to Victor Frankenstein above the Village of Chamounix: Performing Transgender Race." *GLQ* 1, no. 3: 237–54.

Stryker, Susan, Paisley Currah, and Lisa Jean Moore. 2008. "Introduction: Trans-, Trans, or Transgender?" *WSQ* 36, nos. 3–4: 11–22.

Terrasa Mateu, Jordi. 2016. *Control, represión y reeducación de los homosexuales durante el franquismo y el inicio de la transición*. Barcelona: Universitat de Barcelona.

TSQ. n.d. "About the Journal." read.dukepress.edu/tsq/pages/About.

Valentine, David. 2007. *Imagining Transgender: An Ethnography of a Category*. Durham, NC: Duke University Press.

Valentine, David. n.d. "David Valentine." cla.umn.edu/about/directory/profile/valen076 (accessed July 7, 2021).

Velasco, Sherry. 2011. *Lesbians in Early Modern Spain*. Nashville: Vanderbilt University Press.

Vicente, Marta V. 2016. "Pornography and the Spanish Inquisition: The Reading of *Le Portier des Chartreux* in Eighteenth-Century Madrid." *Comparative Literature* 68, no. 2: 181–98.

Whitney, Emerson. 2020. *Heaven*. New York: McSweeney's.

Williams, Cristan. 2014. "Transgender." *TSQ* 1, nos. 1–2: 232–34.

(Trans) Sex Sells

Star Distributors Ltd. and Trans Sleaze

RL GOLDBERG

Abstract In this article the author considers the vexed relationship that Star Distributors' trans sleaze had with taxonomy. The author argues that linguistic slippage and the inability to define a precise trans identity as object speaks not only, or exclusively, to a sloppiness on the part of sleaze writers but is also a deliberate illumination of the degree to which white trans is not reducible to something known or necessarily stable. Because it is irreducible to knowledge and finality, these texts delight in the possibilities of plurality, in teaching, and in learning to work one's gender in excess of cis practice. Finally, this article explores the bifurcated way these novels depict pedagogy for white and Black trans characters.

Keywords pedagogy, transvestites, sleaze, genre

"A 'Pornucopia' of Crime"

S tar Distributors Ltd. was once one of the largest porn wholesalers in the United States, dominating the market from the early 1960s to the early 1990s. Though Star Distributors had an outsize role in shaping the pornography industry, it is remarkably difficult, today, to learn very much about the company. It's not terribly hard to find a post office box (362 Canal St. Station, New York, New York, 10013), or the address of their former office in Manhattan, 150 Lafayette Street, in Little Italy. And what they distributed isn't itself a mystery: for three decades, Star Distributors distributed sleaze, erotic fiction, and pornography through their multiple mail-order book series. Running the gamut of erotic interests, proclivities, fetishes, and fantasies, their wares were advertised as "erotic novels for virtually every taste! Sexy tales that thrill! . . . Stimulate! . . . Excite! Full of explicit erotic action . . . Bold! . . . Daring!" (*Cross-Dressing Daddy* 1981). The Private Journals series published, for example, *The Diary of a Debauched Debutante*, *The Diary of a Ship's Slut*, and *The Diary of a Minister's Mistress*. Among the titles in the All-American Series were *Jane's Insatiable Aunt*, *She Took on the Team*, and *Co-Eds in Heat*. Strange Tales was a sexual bestiary of bestiality—*The Ape Girl*,

TSQ: Transgender Studies Quarterly * Volume 8, Number 4 * November 2021 **443**
DOI 10.1215/23289252-9311046 © 2021 Duke University Press

Snake Charmer, Stud Horse—and Lesbian Erotica included titles such as *Chained Lesbians, Black Lesbian Teacher, Lesbian Mother*, and *Her Strange Aunt*. There were numerous series on domination and submission, rape, and assault. The War Horrors series was one of the more historically sourced series, with a catalog that included *Gestapo Lesbian, Kremlin Horrors*, and *Swastika She-Devil*. Star Distributors also had multiple long-running series on gender-nonnormativity—Trisexual Books, Transvestia, She Males, Transvestite Tales, Satin Slaves, Gender Bender, Chicks with Dicks, Crossdressed, Men in Lace, and Cross Dresser's Club—which addressed topics primarily concerned with transvestism and transsexuality [1]

Star Distributors had not always trafficked in sleaze. Incorporated in 1948, Star Distributors began as a magazine distribution company that specialized in nonsexual niche trade publications. When Theodore Rothstein took over a financially insecure Star in the 1960s, he looked to new markets and initially began selling softcore pinups. But he never managed to make a profit; the pornography industry—such as it was, then—was controlled by New York and New Jersey mob families, and Star simply did not have the resources to compete. How, precisely, Robert DiBernardo, a capo of the DeCavalcante[2] family, became involved with Star Distributors is unclear. But at some point in the decade he and Rothstein formed a working partnership.[3] Though Rothstein remained Star's president, DiBernardo became the vice president, financial backer, and de facto head of the company. Under DiBernardo's leadership, Star shifted its interest from niche trade publication to hardcore pornography dealing in any and all aspects of gender and sexuality, especially those considered to be salacious or exploitative. DiBernardo diversified Star's distribution to include sleaze—mass-produced paperbacks, published anonymously, often written by precarious writers. These texts were genre snarls of pulp, "educational" material, case study, and fiction, and they catered primarily, though not exclusively, to heterosexual men.[3] In short, these texts were, as Susan Stryker (2001: 89) notes, "throwaway books designed for one-handed reading" (fig. 1).

Scholarship on pulp and sleaze has tended to focus on representations of sexuality, and rightfully so. Pulp is known, above all else, for comprising little more than erotic scenes loosely connected by narrative, like pearls on a slack string. Brilliant character development was not the point of these narratives; sexual gratification was. Still, mid-century pulp served other functions. Yvonne Keller (2005: 387) argues that one of the effects of pulp, and their ready accessibility, was putting "the word *lesbian* in mass circulation as never before," especially from 1950 to 1965. Not only did this allow heterosexual people to encounter the "shadowy" homosexual underworld, but pulp's "truly impressive quantities helped create the largest generation of self-defined lesbians up to that point" (Keller 2005). Beyond affording readers insight into new identities—or identities new to them—

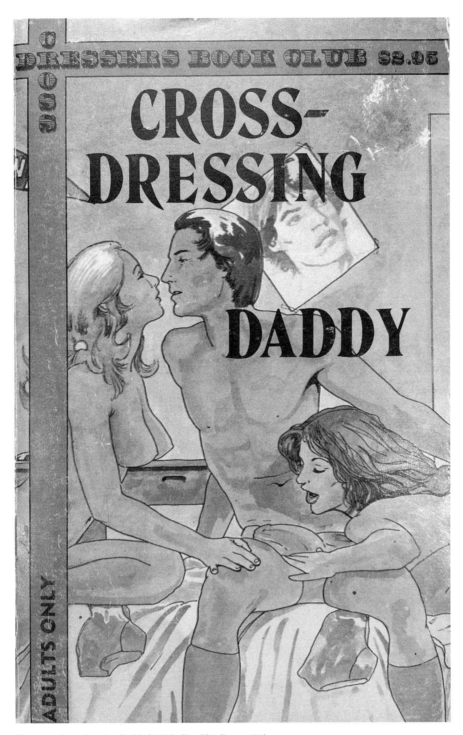

Figure 1. *Cross-Dressing Daddy* (1981), Star Distributors Ltd.

mid-century gay pulp both validated gay male desires and revealed more than just gay sexuality, as Michael Bronski (2003: 8) notes: "Hidden within their plots and their characters' lives were maps, hints, and clues that told gay men how they might live their lives." This meant anything, from depicting what gay sociality looked like, to describing the interior of a gay man's home, to simply committing to paper the steaminess of an erotic encounter. Though a great deal has been written about queer pulp, there is significantly less analysis of trans in queer pulp studies. In part, this is a question of periodization. Lesbian and gay pulp peaked from the 1950s to the 1970s. Trans erotic fiction, on the other hand, was not ubiquitous until the late seventies. Another crucial difference, however, is that texts that centered trans people were not only sexual or about sexual identification. Accessible, cheap, and easily portable, these novels captured fantasies that were primarily about gender, particularly as gender was renegotiated in the public sphere during the Cold War.

In his 2018 *Street Players: Black Pulp Fiction and the Making of a Literary Underground*, Kinohi Nishikawa (2018: 6) defines *sleaze* as "mid-twentieth-century print commodities (pulps and pinup magazines) whose aim was to circulate fantasies of putting women in their place." To put women in their place highlights how gendered and racialized political anxiety was interjected into the content of sleaze, providing the underpinning for both textual narrative and character development (such as it was). As Nishikawa (2018: 6) writes, "Readers of sleaze felt that they were victims in a world given over to feminization, or the idea that masculine self-possession was being squelched by the demands of social conformity and domestic life. Sleaze rebuffed that trend, assuring readers that men were still on top, and that, despite many challenges to it, the male ego remained intact."

Trans sleaze from the 1970s–90s, however, poses a unique problematic in studies of sleaze and smut: if the aim of these texts was, as Nishikawa argues, to circulate fantasies of putting women in their place, this dynamic changes in trans feminine sleaze, in which men's place is inherently unstable and seems to be one in which they accede—willingly, happily, and sensually—to their own feminization. Might we read anxiety over feminization and gendered stability that manifests, concurrently, as a pedagogy for enthusiastically losing, or ecstatically clinging to, one's gender? Which is to say, trans sleaze literalizes Nishikawa's definition of sleaze: it made discursive those fantasies of masculine readers by literally putting women in their place, offering a kind of generative, gendered equivocality, often framed as scenes of staged pedagogy. To put women in their place was for these men to fantasmatically, narratively, learn to become women. Such equivocality was a privilege, not only of having a good teacher, as I will argue, but also of whiteness not directly identified as such. Instead, in these texts, whiteness masquerades as theoretically nonracialized, but essentially coded-white spaces—"college" or the kind of "professionalization" of finance work (as in, for instance, the novels *Stockbroker's*

Secret Life [1983] or *Banker's Secret Lust* [1986]). These spaces are defined in relief to Blackness, framed as a noninstitutional, "natural," "essential," "inborn" sexuality. In these texts, Blackness is always a teacher instrumentalized in the service of white sissification. If white men are put in women's place through forced feminization, they are doubly so through gender's racialization, specifically through the hyper-masculinization of Blackness, both male and female. In relief, whiteness is feminized (and obtains a particularly dated femininity at that). When Black characters are admitted into the world of the text, it is only as masculine, self-assured feminizer or as a trans character with no sense of gendered ambiguity. Hortense J. Spillers describes a similar trend to conflate Blackness and masculinity in her 1987 article "Mama's Baby, Papa's Maybe: An American Grammar Book." Responding, in part, to the Moynihan Report (1965), which pathologized Black American families for emasculating men and being headed by "masculine women," Spillers traces a genealogy of Black gendering—or, more specifically, what she calls ungendering—to slavery and how, for one to be made property, one becomes not a body with gender, desire, and subjectivity but flesh with a productive or reproductive function.

This feels like a tough claim to make—that Black characters are afforded no gendered subjectivity—in books that are premised on a fundamental lack of subjectivity. But if the plotline in these narratives is that someone learns to become trans, a sissy, or a woman, these are plotlines that Black characters are never afforded. Indeed, across these novels, Black characters are needed for a kind of gendered stability against which whiteness can explore gender. Said differently: in these texts Black people are capable of teaching, by juxtaposition, but not of learning.

Across these novels, whiteness is, unsurprisingly, the unnamed background that affords gender's lability or the possibility of expressing incoherent gender in relative safety. This allows readers access to trans fantasy, but also permits the reassertion of the privilege of whiteness in, to borrow from Nishikawa, a world given over to Blackness and Black masculinization. These novels, written between the 1970s and 1990s, don't so much as directly respond to contemporaneous Black organizing—and here I'm thinking of masculinist and nationalist organizations like MOVE, the Black Panther Party, the New Black Panther Party—as pivot away from it, allowing Blackness to enter the world of the text to shore up white femininity. The clearest, and most consistent way these novels do this is through their nearly identical, monolithic representations of Black gender as—in addition to the ugly racialized and animalized categories we often see in sleaze—natural, organic, stable, strong, consistent, certain, and unquestioned. Even when Black characters are trans, their identities are afforded a certain kind of stability and coherence that doesn't permit—and certainly isn't interested in—

any narratological exploration, as we see with white characters. Black gender—depicted exclusively as stable masculinity—is the context from which white trans exploration emerges. Quite simply, the white psyche cannot admit the possibility of Black femininity. We see this exemplified, for instance, in a passage in *Stockbroker's Secret Life* (1983) in which the white Anton—feminized as Annie—is engaged in a scene with Nokoma, a Nigerian dom. "There was contrast between Nokoma's all-male organic excellence and Anton's silky feminized she-maledom. A case of opposites attracting. Anton felt the power of Nokoma's body especially below the waist, where the master's erection nuzzled Anton's own" (110). Though this is not simply a case of "opposites attracting," Anton's feminized "she-maledom" is defined in relief, juxtaposed with Nokoma's racialized "organic excellence."[4]

Little critical attention has been afforded Star and its overwhelming influence not only on trans sleaze and pulp but also on the overall pornography industry in the mid- and late twentieth century. In what follows, I closely attend to two books from Star Distributors' catalog: *Dressing Up Bobby* (1982) and *Black Transvestite* (Hunter 1982). I pair these texts because they are representative of the genre's depiction of race and pedagogy. *Dressing Up Bobby*, a "campus novel," suggests pedagogy—whether learning in college or learning to be trans—is an expansive, slapstick, and jubilant process reserved for white queer and trans people. *Black Transvestite*, on the other hand, draws out the ways in which pedagogy is disciplinary and corrective, and the ways in which Black trans gender is not worth narratological exploration. When white characters appear in this novel, it is only to prove, again and again, the limits to Black education. Much of the distinction between how Black and white characters are depicted is around identity formation: in white campus novels, the books tend to be far more ponderous and slippery in describing identity; indeed, this is much of the fun of education as characters claim many queer and trans identities and are rarely disciplined into one (thus white characters are inconsistently named sissy, transvestite, cross-dresser, transsexual, and so forth). *Black Transvestite*, however, models the opposite: identity exploration is not a form of valuable, or valued, education. Language offers far fewer opportunities for Black characters to learn about themselves; rather, it is used narratively to show the limits to Black trans. In reading these texts, I argue that the linguistic slippage, the inability to define a precise trans identity as object speaks not (or not only) to a sloppiness on the part of sleaze writers but is also a deliberate illumination of the degree to which white trans is figured as irreducible to something known or necessarily stable. Because it is irreducible to knowledge and finality, these texts delight in the possibilities of plurality, in teaching, and in learning to work one's white femininity differently.

What these novels share is a combined fantasy of forced feminization and white supremacy.[5] If the consensual nonconsent of forced feminization is, reductively, "about gender," I think these books leave open the question about the knotty relationship between whiteness and force, whiteness and nonconsent, and a repudiation of whiteness's claim to supremacy for a fantasy of helplessness. To be sure, this is not at all a claim that these books show a way in which white guilt, or something like it, might be productively sublimated into a kind of gender exploration. Instead, these books reveal how the racialization of gendered pedagogy does something else to Hortense Spillers's theorization of Black ungendering. If the conditions of slavery meant that, as Spillers writes in her 1987 essay "Mama's Baby, Papa's Maybe," "we lose at least gender difference in the outcome," then these books don't so much ungender Black people as misgender them: Blackness and gender are not inconsonant but are, quite simply, not interesting enough to warrant specificity, exploration, and the possibility of difference. Yet this is not the gendered integrity Spillers urges us toward: integrity functions not unlike ungendering—body and flesh become captive. Spillers writes that "the captivating party does not only 'earn' the right to dispose of the captive body as it sees fit, but gains, consequently, the right to name and 'name' it" (69). In transfeminine sleaze these names are various—sissy, TV, cross-dresser, trans— but they are all white.

For all of their rote, surgical blandness—I find sleaze is not often a genre that lends itself to especially compelling textual analysis or hermeneutic engagement,[6] and the plots within each genre are impressively, committedly unvarying—these texts do, I think, offer a compelling provocation in their representation of pedagogical subjectification. Pedagogy is represented, in trans feminine sleaze, as something rendered explicit and accountable in a language of gendered teaching. Over the course of the narrative, a man comes to learn—is taught—that he is, in fact, trans feminine (in the most capacious sense: terminology varies across the same page from *transsexual* to *transvestite* to *sissy*, and so on). Or, alternatively, a transvestite comes to recognize that transition to living full-time is possible. One question we might thus ask about this pedagogical bent involves attending to its intended audience: Star Distributors was not producing trans feminine erotic fiction—at least not intentionally—for trans readers. If trans readers found themselves, or found something validating and sustaining in the text, all the better. But the primary audience for these texts were not trans people; they were mainstream consumers, largely comprising nontrans men.[7] What, then, might we glean from Star Distributors' relatively loose taxonomies?

Dressing Up Bobby

In a 1974 *New York Magazine* article, Ron Sproat describes his experience writing sleaze—or, as he titled the piece, "the working day in a porno factory." Sproat briefly worked for the unassumingly named Typographics Systems, Inc. (TSI). There he was expected to produce no fewer than 40 pages of text each day, or 180–

200 pages each week—a demand he asymptotically approached but never quite accomplished. The work, as he describes it, was unforgiving and tedious: each day he was entirely given over to his typewriter, writing canned erotic narratives with limited direction from management save for a few quantitative requirements (page count, number of sex acts, and frequency of sex scenes); workplace camaraderie was nonexistent: writers had no time to do anything but write if they wanted to meet their exacting quotas. Turnover was exceptionally high. Sproat never learned, he claims, the names of the other writers who worked at TSI during his brief tenure there. But this doesn't seem terribly extraordinary; alienation was an essential feature of TSI's business model. Sproat enumerates a rather typical Marxian account of alienation, but with a twist: the books TSI's writers produced were published anonymously—and remained a mystery even to those writing them: "Every night, the pages we had written that day disappeared from our desks," Sproat writes. He continues,

> Only the last page was left so we could remember where we'd left off. We were never allowed to see the galleys. When a book was completed, we were instructed to write a preface, a blurb for the back jacket, and three alternate titles. We were not allowed to know what the final choice of title was. The books were published under pseudonyms, as books of this kind usually are, but we were not allowed to know what our pseudonyms were. When asked where the books were distributed, Bob said, "All over the country," but would not be more specific. Of course we were not allowed to see the final product. It was clear the company wanted to keep us as far from our work as possible, presumably in case the question of rights came up. (40)

If narrative continuity and quality control were at all of concern for Star Distributors, refusing to let writers refer back to the earlier pages of their manuscripts can only be described as an audacious workplace hazard. It also might explain, at least partially, the way in which many trans sleaze books fail to track characters in the brief distance of a few paragraphs. Though attention to proper pronoun use was likely not a priority of writers, there's something comically egregious about the way in which a character's pronouns change over the course of an uncomplicated, nonacrobatic sex act. This switch seems less to do with abrupt changes in gender identification and more to do with material working conditions that required writing at breakneck speed, often without the luxury of a complete manuscript to refer back to. So, too, do we see a comedic lack of object permanence: characters present in one scene are suddenly disappeared with no explanation or recourse; less ominously, and more frequently, characters' names abruptly change in the space of a page break. In *Black Transvestite*, for instance, a character introduced as Oliver Strong is, two pages later, and for no discernible reason, rechristened Ollie Brown.[8]

I've found no indication that Sproat's work was ever published in any of Star's trans sleaze series. In fact, I've been unable to locate any account, other than Sproat's, of a writer whose work was distributed by Star. Perhaps, like Sproat, these writers worked for other unassumingly named companies that worked production side and told their writers about as much as Sproat learned about distribution. If writers did discover their sleaze out in the world, it was mere chance.

Nevertheless, Sproat's account is useful, I think, in explaining why keeping writers alienated from their work was the case: doing otherwise could be bad for business. Many of the writers of trans sleaze were precariously employed, aspiring writers and journalists making ends meet by temporarily doing hackwork. Though it's unlikely they would have had the means to sue for rights to their books—after all, if they did, in all likelihood they wouldn't have been doing hackwork—double blinding the writing was an effective strategy to preempt any additional legal complications. No doubt the management of Star had their hands full dealing with the various obscenity cases always already thrown at them.

Trans sleaze of the 1980s is also a marked departure from sex publications and digests produced in the earlier decades of the twentieth century—like *Sexology Magazine*, for instance—that at least creatively, reachingly hinted that the publication was not of, or not primarily of, prurient interest. Often masquerading as case studies, as science, or as sex education, these other texts were polyvocal in a way that sleaze was certainly not. Nor did it aspire to be (fig. 2).

From the cover image, trans sleaze unambiguously telecasts its contents. Transvestia Books depict photographs of trans women, alone, reposed, frontally nude, irrepressibly genital, and exposed to the viewer. Crossdresser's Club and Men in Lace tended toward something coy, suggestive, and pink: the emphasis was on the physical and psychic subordination of the trans figures, not their anatomy. Trisexual Books' house style was cartoonish, graphic, extrusive, and phallic. Characters are depicted as mushrooming out of the hemmed limits of their skimpy lingerie; they have disproportionately large breasts and large hair, held up by the severe taper of their legs. The cis-women depicted have sharp features, sharp chins, sharply angled eyebrows, and tremendous breasts. The trans women all appear shocked, terrified, humiliated, and terrifically aroused. Their penises—an unmissable feature in each illustration—are comically large, enormously tumescent.

Dressing Up Bobby (1982, fig. 3) begins as Jenny Doerr, a college English teacher, instructs one of her students, Bobby, to put on a pair of panties and "let the feminine part of [his] nature come out." With Miss Doerr's support, Bobby recognizes what Miss Doerr has already seen latent in him—a "girlishness" that must be expressed. Though Bobby seems to have had a hazy sense of his own femininity, it is only after Miss Doerr's instruction that Bobby is able to adequately articulate these feelings:

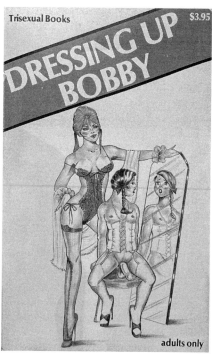

Figure 2. *Mother's Strange Lover* (1984), Star Distributors Ltd.

Figure 3. *Dressing Up Bobby* (1982), Star Distributors Ltd.

> Bobby often wondered what a real man did feel like. In truth, he did not feel like a real man, not even when he fucked Jenny. There was always that girlish part of him, begging for release, and it seemed to Bobby that that girlish part had always been begging. It had taken Jenny's firm but sexy hand, her guidance in things that Bobby had never even suspected, to make him find that good girlishness in his own soul. (8–9)

To say that this novel has a plot would be generous—essentially, we follow from viewpoint character to viewpoint character, as each explores their own trans gender or transsexual attraction in reductive shorthand. Affectively, the world of the novel is somewhere between a Todd Solondz film and one of John Waters's more grotesque sequences.[9] Though, ostensibly, the context for Bobby's (and Jenny's and Jeff's and Kris's and Bonnie's) awakening is a college campus, the writer makes but a few halfhearted attempts to remind us of this, or to maintain anything but a petty fidelity to setting: when Jenny goes to an academic conference in Chicago, she is stood up by a former flame. This incident takes up the whole of our learning of the conference, save for the moment in which she dismissively reflects: "She certainly could not go to meetings of English teachers and hear speeches on grammar and the teaching of technical writing and shit like that" (83). Earlier, Jenny proleptically mourns the upcoming graduation of another student, Linda. We're made to understand that this interaction is one between a professor and student by their witty academic repartee: "After graduation, Linda would leave the campus and go to another, larger university for graduate school. . . . 'Don't think about graduation,' [Linda] said softly. 'Don't think about parting, Jenny. You know what Shakespeare said. Journeys end in lover's meeting.' 'Every wise man's son doth know,' the teacher said sweetly completing their favorite quotation from the Bard" (29–30). Elsewhere, the writer's use of simile betrays the fact that, perhaps, Miss Doerr falls somewhere in the break between teacher and playactor: "'Do you feel your feminine soul, Bobby?' she asked, her voice firm as a teacher's again" (104).

But the climax of the book—or one of a great many climaxes—occurs when Bobby earnestly reflects on Miss Doerr's most important pedagogical intervention: teaching Bobby to be—and become—a woman. In Bobby's narration, Miss Doerr assigned, for her freshman composition class, a paper in which students had to articulate "something about themselves that they were having trouble figuring out" (93). Because "it was not really clear in his mind," Bobby wrote about feeling feminine. Office hours having ended, Miss Doerr invites Bobby over to her apartment to continue their conversation. This is an offer Bobby refuses to refuse because "she was an excellent teacher. Bobby had already learned a lot about writing from her" (95). Praising his courage in writing such a vulnerable essay, Miss Doerr explains that the only way that Bobby will become a good writer is if he continues to have courage, to open himself up to new experiences. Melodramatically, she promises: "I will teach you to wear high heels and hose. I will teach you to put on makeup. I will teach you to be the prettiest girl in the world. But first I have to fuck you. You have to fuck me, Bobby. I need it. You need it. The whole world needs it, Bobby" (105–6). In her promise, Bobby hears this: "She would fill him up again with masculine and feminine feelings. She would guide him back to the Garden, back to Paradise, and he would be happy and sexy there. He would not be confused, and he would write so fucking well" (110). Intrinsic to Bobby's sense of pedagogy is that, beyond being "filled" with feminine and masculine feelings, he would no longer be confused about his femininity and, more crucially, he would be able to write "so fucking well." As gendered pedagogy is presented to him by Miss Doerr—not without bias, of course, since her intentions are hardly chaste—to learn to do one's gender is to simultaneously develop the capacity for written self-expression that exceeds gender performance. Gender, like writing, is an epistemology that offers Bobby the experience of new genre, as Sandy Stone might say. Crucially, it is not language, per se, that Bobby needs: throughout the text, his sense of self, and how he names his identity, undergoes endless revision. What Miss Doerr is able to provide for Bobby is sexual possibility and options as yet undetermined; she doesn't offer the language of transvestitism or transsexuality, but she offers transvestitism as an epistemology he can work through to become more feminine and a better student and writer.

Just before putting on panties for the first time, Bobby conveniently, suddenly remembers a recurring dream: in a de-eroticized retelling of Salome, he imagines a beautiful woman dancing the dance of the seven veils, only to realize that it is he who dances. "He shivered. He had never understood that dream at all, had never wanted to remember it before. But now he remembered it and he wondered what it all meant. And, still wondering, he reached out and took the panties from Miss Doerr" (102–3). The temporal convenience of this remembering suggests, I think, that pedagogy—for all the ways Miss Doerr forces feminization on Bobby—merely draws out something already dormant. All Bobby needed was the (in)appropriate teaching and the safety of the college campus for him to end up where he started: back to the Garden, back to Paradise. At the same time, Bobby's remembering conditions the scene of pedagogy. Not only does Miss Doerr want to teach him, but he also wants to learn; he requires an analytic framework—or, in this case, embodied praxis—to understand what, exactly, his dream means. (Though, to be sure, it doesn't seem all that impenetrable.)

At the book's conclusion, Kris, one of Bobby's sexual partners, now newly initiated into erotic enjoyment thanks to Bobby's second-order teaching, realizes how much she's learned, and how much she has yet to learn. After crediting her discovery of bisexuality—both the concept and her own—to attending college (27), she reflects on her many sexual options as a Kuhnian paradigm shift: "That would be a wild world, too and she loved both worlds and would never be able to live in just one world again" (174). Indeed this seems to be the pedagogical promise that Bobby holds out hope for: the opening up of new possibilities, a glimpse of a new world and decampment from the old. While, on one reading, gendered flexibility seems like a fairly unsurprising fantasy for a text produced at the height of neoliberal flexibilization, on another, Bobby and the others seem hopeful for a kind of ontological unfamiliarity that has less to do with gender and more to do with equivocality writ large. Perhaps one overly generous reading: if gender might be changed with such facility and voluptuousness, perhaps greater structural change—the things in the world that seem most impervious to change—might follow. Or, more likely, and probably more in keeping with sleaze's aspirations: there's something very very sexy about learning, and the kind of learning that can be done in all-white spaces. Bobby, spent after an evening with Jenny and Jeff, certainly feels as much: "It seemed to Bobby that he had liked everything since he had come to college" (9).

Black Transvestite

For all of its libidinousness and vacuity, there is a moment in the text when Jenny Doerr does contemplate a rather serious lesson to teach "her boys." She wakes up one morning at the conference hotel to learn that "a transvestite had been murdered by a crazy salesman, right here in this hotel, it seemed. Too bad, Jenny thought. She hoped that none of her boys were ever murdered. She had to tell Jeff and Bobby about this case when she got back to the college. She had to warn them to be careful" (*Dressing Up Bobby* 1982: 84). Jenny doesn't know that the person killed is Tom Laramie, the selfsame Tom Laramie she believes has stood her up. Regardless, Jenny does not make it back to the college to warn Bobby about safety and self-protection, derailed, as she gets, when she finds herself reluctant to leave a brothel of transvestites in Chicago. So much for the academic conference, so much for tenure.

This moment in the book is significant: in an otherwise ludicrous staging of pedagogy as the conceit for transsexuality, the author points to a desperately serious concern: how trans people—trans feminine people—might stay alive. It seems that part of the conceit of *Dressing Up Bobby* is that nothing bad really happens to these college students, inured, as they are, by their whiteness. There are Shakespearean reversals and moments of buffoonish levity in which the characters suddenly realize that, surprise, no one's really as straight or cis, or as gay, as they seem: "'Jeff!' Bobby yelped. 'Kris!' Bonnie squealed. 'Bobby!' Jeff croaked. 'Bonnie!' Kris squealed" (156–57)—but all's well that ends well. Even in moments that may look like (*Write* it!) disaster—when, for instance, Bobby and Jeff, in drag, pick up two truckers, go back to their motel room, and do not disclose that they are cross-dressing—the situation pans out all right. Better than all right, in fact: the truckers are also cross-dressers. They're butch dykes passing for men, and, even more convenient for Bobby and Jeff, they're very keen to sleep with "the two fake females" (69). The scene ends, a just-so fairytale: "And the seedy motel room was filled with the sounds of cock-sucking, sounds that had been heard in that room before, but the variations that these four had known probably had never before been seen by these dirty walls" (82). Indeed, the "sexual confusion" that all four experience around their genders and sexualities makes the experience that much more enlivening (81).

Those characters not safeguarded by their whiteness are less fortunate. Such is the case for Georgina, the titular *Black Transvestite* (fig. 4). Where *Dressing Up Bobby* relies on shorthand tropes of white collegiate life to communicate the safety of the pedagogical space and the safety of equivocality, even as it extends to the truck stop at the edge of town, *Black Transvestite* leisurely, and with a pornographic relish (what Hortense Spillers [1988: 67] names "pornotroping"), piles abuse onto Georgina as a horrifying caricature of Black urban impoverishment.

Transvestia $3.95

BLACK
TRANSVESTITE

Adults Only

by Raquel Hunter

Figure 4. *Black Transvestite* (1982), Star
Distributors Ltd.

When Georgina ends up, like Bobby had, in a motel room with several men unaware of her trans status, she is brutally gang raped. If college enables safe and dirty exploration for Bobby and his cohort, the same is not true for Georgina.

Like *Dressing Up Bobby*, *Black Transvestite* (Hunter 1982) begins with a foreword that doubles as narrative foreplay: there is only the faintest breath of exposition. We've hardly met the titular character—the first line is "Georgina lay on the bed"—before she's being jerked off, in the second sentence. In the space of these eleven prefatory sentences we learn very little about Georgina save for the fact that she has a "hot hard cock" (3–4). Indeed, this is a detail restated a staggering seven times in the first eleven sentences of the book.

The plot of the book—such that it has one—is typical sleaze: Georgina, a sex worker from Harlem, is late to meet Bobby, her pimp.[10] In her lateness she reflects on her life:

> All his life, George had known he was not really a man. His penis was a lie, a chance genetic accident, for his mind was that of a female. From the very first he knew it. His mother, a whore herself, had left him to live his lonely daydreams from the inside of the Harlem apartment. The days were spent in front of the mirror, playing his dress up games, dreaming of being a tall black woman, an actress, a model, something fine and proud. (7–8)

From the narrative's beginning, Georgina is certain that she is a woman. Yet unlike *Dressing Up Bobby*, this book is entirely involute, offering Georgina no escape, no relief, no outside. Indeed, the only pleasure in the book seems to be that which Raquel Hunter takes when, at any opportunity, she might demean and undercut Georgina. Consider the lines of the book's first chapter: "George Duncan stood in front of the mirror. But to say that he was thinking of himself as George at all, was to be greatly mistaken. He had not thought of himself as a man in years. Not since he was a little boy" (3). With a kind of stunning rhetorical cruelty, Hunter quietly moves from an omniscient narrator to free indirect discourse. What's lost in the movement: the unequivocal sense that the narrator sees George, not Georgina. Yet the narrator's "mistake" is not one to be corrected. Such is the tenor of the book—foreclosure. On the following page the narrator predicts that Bobby, Georgina's brutal pimp, "was the only person that George had ever loved, or ever would love" (8). Signaling narrative foreclosure from the start of the book, there's little hope for Georgina. It seems, for a young Black girl in Harlem, the daughter of a sex worker, there never had been. Little surprise that the book ends this way: "All of Georgina's dreams were once more dashed to the ground. It would seem that she was never to get the thing she wanted most in the world" (177). Throughout the text, Georgina's sole desire is to have genital surgery; when she is, as a teenager, immediately pimped out, she finds solace in the fact that she will be trained to "be a proper paramour" (41), and, with time, will save enough money for surgery. What she is taught is brutal and final: for her, there is no out, no way of meeting her desire. Pedagogy happens not in the classroom, as it does for Bobby and his classmates, but through the merciless teachings of pimps Carlos, the Countess, and Bobby. Only at the novel's close does Georgina finally internalize the lessons she has been relentlessly trained in: unmitigated hopelessness. As Carlos puts it, "There ain't gonna be no operation, you mean too much green the way you are" (161). For Georgina it is never about learning to become a woman: it is learning that she'll never be able to accomplish womanhood in a way that is meaningful to her and consonant with her desires.

No big surprise, then, that the novel doesn't end with the same gesture toward openness that concludes *Dressing Up Bobby*. Rather, we recognize Georgina, lying on the bed, not having moved from where we encountered her in the preface. Resigned to her situation, receiving, in a rare act of narrative forbearance, a "less brutal john" (which is to say, it is still a brutal scene), "her own hot cock was throbbing as a feeling of real hopelessness washed over her" (180). As readers, we know from the beginning of the book that Georgina's life is not going to turn out as she hopes. Hunter's rhetorical play with prolepsis always and only indicates impossibility, closure, unattainability. Yet the temporal equivocation—a kind of anterior posterior—holds out space, if not for readers, for Georgina's education. But unlike Bobby, Georgina already knows that she is trans; the novel's pedagogical fantasy is not one of gender expression. The novel's fantasy is far bleaker than the impossibility of desire, much less Georgina's desire for surgery. Titled *Black Transvestite*, the novel is a pedagogical lesson in effacement, desubjectification, and denial until Georgina comes to identify only with type—as a Black transvestite.

> If she had known that she was jumping from the frying pan into the fire, then she never would have asked [Bobby] to help her. But who else could she have turned

to. It's not like a TV from Harlem has the chance to meet many rich and generous people. He used her as they all had. . . . She would never get her pussy, this she knew. . . . It would be so fine to wake up, as from a dream, and find she was a woman. All woman and nothing but woman. But she knew that it would never be. (178–79)

Hunter poses a question that is not a question—but who else could she have turned to. It is a question that needn't be asked, since, through and through, Georgina has learned that she is entirely alone and without recourse. Through the narrative's temporal equivocation, its propulsion forward only to return us to the same place the preface begins, she comes to see this, too. Yet where communicability structured *Dressing Up Bobby*—finding the language, then the instruction to convey one's subjective experience—the opposite problem maintains for Georgina. The novel's basic premise is one of miscommunication—Georgina naively thinks that someone might help her. This lesson, no less useful for its difficulty, points up another pedagogical fantasy at the heart of sleaze: if learning can be sexy, it can also be brutal. Indeed, it might be futile to separate the two. But as we see in the difference between Bobby's and Georgina's narratives, brutality without genuine aftercare—what Georgina experiences—offers little respite. To what degree, then, does Georgina learn anything at all in the course of her education?

Undoubtedly, the brutality Georgina experiences is different, not only in magnitude but also in kind, from the mostly slapstick (and sometimes consensually and goofily sadistic) brutality we see in *Dressing Up Bobby*. On one level, we might attribute this to setting: Bobby and his cohort are safeguarded by their whiteness and sheltered by the broader whiteness of the college campus. Georgina, on the other hand—neither white nor a college student—is not. But the differential treatment of trans femininity in these texts crystallizes the distinctive ways in which sleaze can "put women in their place." If, as Nishikawa argues, sleaze "assured readers that men were still on top, and that, despite many challenges to it, the male ego remained intact," we do see in *Black Transvestite* this rather conventional understanding of sleaze. I have argued, however, that trans sleaze complicates this paradigm insofar as trans sleaze literally puts women in the place of men. This does not seem to pertain, however, to *Black Transvestite*. This is, I think, because of the genre's disinterest in Black sexuality as anything other than instrumental or trope. In *Dressing Up Bobby*, Bobby manages to put himself in a woman's place; by the novel's conclusion Bobby has accessed a comfortable trans femininity. But Georgina is, from the outset, unambiguously trans. That Bobby's narrative is pedagogical is clear: he learns, in college and through conversation, to become trans. For Georgina, everything—her future, her opportunities, and even her transness—are framed as foregone.

This has, I think, a significant implication for the genre, and for the way the genre represents trans pedagogy. If we understand pedagogy as opening up a space for equivocation and learning that is not about reifying a kind of traditional gendered stability, Star's corpus suggests this is true only for white characters, for whom there is the possibility of political efficacy, coalition, change, and reconciliation. By embracing the possibility of college learning, and the equivocation such learning allows, the dominant presentation of white trans in these texts—beyond the sensational—is one of fascination. It is interesting, the novel suggests, to explore Bobby's journey into transness, not just the wild sexual acrobatics Bobby performs with Miss Doerr and at her behest. White trans becomes something to think—for Bobby, and for readers. Black trans does not; it is thoughtless and unthought; pedagogy is only ever a study in disciplining.

The lack of investment in Black trans subjectivity is not surprising in sleaze, but it does stand in contrast to concerted efforts to give white trans characters fertile—if single-minded—inner lives. Equivocation, not on offer for Black trans, stunts our obligation to Black trans, in the pedagogical sense of learning from, recognizing, or accompanying Black trans development. Perhaps, in some sense, we don't want to accompany Georgina in her development; certainly, the brutality meted out to her renders *Black Transvestite* a pornographically violent, disturbing encounter. But there is a danger, too, in looking away from the novel's racist exploitation. To do so would be to miss how, in trans sleaze, Black ungendering does not seem to be the primary mode of dehumanization. Presuming Black genders to be transparent, obvious, uncomplicated, and not worth exploration, these texts, instead, blithely misgender Black characters. In the context of trans sleaze, these books teach us to do the same, uninterested as they are in the possibility of Black gender, Black fantasy, and Black futurity.

RL Goldberg is a postdoctoral fellow in the Dartmouth Society of Fellows. Their work has appeared, or is forthcoming from, the *Paris Review, TSQ, ASAP/J*, the *Los Angeles Review of Books*, and elsewhere.

Notes

1. The identities of their writers remain a mystery. Most books were published anonymously or pseudonymously. Further, it remains unclear how many—and which—texts were outsourced, since Star was primarily a distribution company, not a producer of content.

2. As early as 1970, "witnesses at public hearings of the New York State Commission of Investigation . . . had linked Star Distributors, Ltd., and Robert DiBernardo to the New Jersey crime family led by DeCavalcante" (Kaplan 1972). It seems likely that DiBernardo,

one of John Gotti's top lieutenants, controlled Star. The precise nature of his role in Star is unknown; DiBernardo was allegedly shot twice in the back of the head and put through a tree shredder for making jokes about Gotti behind his back. In *Reefer Madness* Eric Schlosser points out that speculation that DiBernardo controlled Star was due to two factors: his relationship to Reuben Sturman (considered to be, as Schlosser writes in a 2003 *New Yorker* essay, the "Walt Disney" of porn, then the largest producer and distributor of hardcore pornography), and the unquestionable involvement of the Cosa Nostra in the porn industry. But, as Schlosser writes, "organized crime families earned most of their income from porn through real estate deals, renting properties to adult bookstores, strip clubs, and massage parlors" (159). Said differently, doing business with the mob did not necessarily mean that that business was under mob control.

3.   Pulp novels were enormously popular. As Yvonne Keller (2005) notes, many pulp novels—like Tereska Torres's *Girls in 3-B* or Vin Packer's *Spring Fire*—sold millions of copies. Yet, as Keller writes, "the genre's undeniably homophobic and voyeuristic appeal to a heterosexual male audience intent on enjoying the 'queer loves' of the 'twilight woman' ties this image of lesbianism to heterosexual pornography" (385). Still, these novels were enjoyed by people of all genders and sexualities and, even if they were largely sold to heterosexual men, the widespread dissemination of lesbian pulp had "nonrepressive effects" (406). David K. Johnson (2019: 18) makes a similar claim about physique magazines, which served men who openly identified as gay but also "catered to fans who merely thought of themselves as fellow 'physique enthusiasts' misunderstood by their families and mainstream society." Physique magazines, like lesbian pulp, thus enabled a gateway into queer culture, networking opportunities, and cohesion around early homophile organizing. Trans sleaze seems to have occupied a similar nonrepressive status culturally. But it is clear that trans sleaze was also marketed to trans people, in magazines like *Transvestite Dating Guide* (1987), for instance, which often included full-page advertisements for Star's erotic novels.

4.   This recalls Frantz Fanon's (1968: 27) description of Blackness as being reduced to being seen as "in total fusion with the world, in sympathetic affinity with the earth, losing [my] id in the heart of the cosmos—and the white man, however intelligent he may be, is incapable of understanding Louis Armstrong or songs from the Congo. I am black, not because of a curse, but because my skin has been able to capture all the cosmic effluvia. I am truly a drop of sun under the earth."

5.   The covers of these two books are also telling: *Dressing Up Bobby*, part of the Trisexual Books series, is an illustration. The cover image of *Black Transvestite* is not an illustration but a photograph, lending the book a kind of reality, a photorealism that the Trisexual Book cover does not share. Though not all women depicted on the covers of Transvestia books were women of color, many were. Similarly, a fairly substantial—though by no means exhaustive—survey of the covers of Trisexual Books showed no nonwhite characters.

6.   *Black Transvestite* (Hunter 1982), part of Star Distributor's Transvestia series, includes lines like: "She bobbed her head up and down and up and down and up and down. She moved her noggin faster and faster and the heat was building up in Georgina" (52) and "She pumped hard and the hot goo made her cunt sound like a sump pump" (50). These lines are not irregular in their tedium, though the second is certainly unique in its creative (?) use of metaphor.

7.   Trans sleaze was, also, of course, read by trans people. But as Michael Bronski (2003) points out, a significant amount of homosexual pulp was consumed by heterosexual people; so, too, with trans sleaze, like all of Star's sleaze.

8.   Beyond such errors, many of these books are riddled with typographical and spelling mistakes, some of which produce fairly absurd results: in *Dressing Up Bobby*, Miss Doerr inspects a nude Bobby as if she were "a buyer at a salve auction" (100). Perhaps this simile is intended, but my guess is the author intended for the more recognizably familiar, and violent, "slave auction."

9.   In the world of the novel everyone seems to be queer or trans of some variety. In a brief scene between two police officers, as they recover the corpse of a trans woman shot by a john, the officers—characters not previously introduced and of no sustained interest in the text—share this conversation: "'But he was drunk when he went out with that faggot, right?' 'Right.' The cop thought of correcting his partner, of saying that the guy who was dead was not necessarily a faggot. He was a transvestite, and some transvestites fucked women all the time. In fact, some of them were known as real studs. But the cop did not want to defend the dead man too much. If he did, his partner might suspect something, might suspect the truth. . . . But Chicago was a rough city, and, if you were a cop, it was not a good idea to let anyone know that you wore women's clothing in your off-duty hours" (*Dressing Up Bobby* 1982: 88–89).

10. Bobby seems to be a popular name among Star's writers; this Bobby is unrelated to the titular Bobby of *Dressing Up Bobby*.

References

Banker's Secret Lust. 1986. New York: Star Distributors.

Bronski, Michael. 2003. *Pulp Friction: Uncovering the Golden Age of Gay Male Pulps*. New York: St. Martin's.

Cross-Dressing Daddy. 1980. New York: Star Distributors.

Dressing Up Bobby. 1982. New York: Star Distributors.

Fanon, Frantz. 1968. *Black Skin, White Masks*. 1st Evergreen ed. New York: Grove Weidenfeld.

Hunter, Raquel. 1982. *Black Transvestite*. New York: Star Distributors.

Johnson, David K. 2019. *Buying Gay: How Physique Entrepreneurs Sparked a Movement*. New York: Columbia University Press.

Kaplan, Morris. 1972. "Pornography and Pirated Stereo Tapes Seized in Raid on Mob-Linked Operation." *New York Times*, December 12.

Keller, Yvonne. 2005. "'Was It Right to Love Her Brother's Wife So Passionately?': Lesbian Pulp Novels and U.S. Lesbian Identity, 1950–1965." *American Quarterly* 57, no. 2: 385–410.

Moynihan, Daniel Patrick. 1965. *The Negro Family: The Case for National Action*. Washington, DC: US Department of Labor. www.dol.gov/general/aboutdol/history/webid-moynihan.

Nishikawa, Kinohi. 2019. *Street Players: Black Pulp Fiction and the Making of a Literary Underground*. Chicago: University of Chicago Press.

Schlosser, Eric. 2003. "Empire of the Obscene." *New Yorker*, March.

Spillers, Hortense J. 1987. "Mama's Baby, Papa's Maybe: An American Grammar Book." *Diacritics* 17, no. 2: 65–81.

Sproat, Ron. 1974. "The Working Day in a Porno Factory." *New York Magazine*, March.

Stockbroker's Secret Life. 1983. New York: Star Distributors.

Stryker, Susan. 2001. *Queer Pulp: Perverted Passions from the Golden Age of the Paperback*. San Francisco: Chronicle.

Standards of Care

Uncertainty and Risk in Harry Benjamin's Transsexual Classifications

BEANS VELOCCI

Abstract In the 1950s and early 1960s, Harry Benjamin and his colleague Elmer Belt corresponded at length about which transsexuals they would and would not approve for genital surgery. Benjamin defined transsexuality primarily through a desire for medical transition, but merely being a transsexual in this definition did not automatically result in surgical eligibility. Benjamin and Belt remained preoccupied with the possibility that transsexuals would regret their surgeries and seek legal or personal revenge, and thus their assessments of who should have surgery focused more on the possibility of a bad outcome than adherence to gender norms or classification as transsexual. The informal clinical practices they worked out to protect themselves in these early years of American trans medicine would ultimately go on to structure more formalized Standards of Care. Benjamin and Belt's fears, and their resulting decision-making processes, thus played a crucial role in the production of the category "transsexual." Throughout their correspondence and clinical practice, the transsexual emerged as a threat to medical providers, and a subject incapable of making their own bodily decisions, needing to be protected from themselves. While assessments of gender identity and gendered behavior factored into these decisions, their decisions about who might regret transition treated gender as primarily practical and functional, and made an unshakable internal gender identity a necessary but insufficient criterion for granting a patient access to surgery.

Keywords surgery, clinical practice, Harry Benjamin, classification, transsexuality

"Each of us will probably die by getting shot by some patient like E. V.," wrote urologist Elmer Belt to Harry Benjamin, endocrinologist and so-called father of transsexuality, in February of 1960.[1] He was joking—kind of. Belt had sent along a citation for a new book on heart disease that struggled to define maleness and femaleness, and the joke was that the two of them were more likely to be murdered by an angry transsexual than to die of heart disease. For nearly two years before Belt sent the letter, he and Benjamin had been debating whether Edie V. Hutchens should be eligible for the removal of her penis and testicles and the construction of a vagina.[2] The longer they delayed, the more desperate

Hutchens became, but they hesitated to allow the surgery for fear that Hutchens would regret her transition and turn on them, whether with gun in hand or by other means.

Since its beginnings, trans scholarship has emphasized the importance of performing normative gender and "proving" that one was "really" a transsexual in the history of medical transition (Stone 2006; Meyerowitz 2002; Gill-Peterson 2018). Belt's sarcastic remark exemplifies another central force in how clinicians made decisions in the early years of American trans medicine: fear of transsexuals' ruining doctors' lives.[3] While adherence to normative gender roles certainly played a part in who doctors allowed to medically transition, fears of being sued or otherwise facing retribution from patients could easily shift the balance in the final decision of who could have surgery. Focusing on this aspect of clinical decision making shows how informal evaluative practices rooted in anticipation of bad outcomes became standards of trans care. It also illuminates how gender operated as a functional, rather than ontological, designation in doctors' understanding of transsexuality. The question for Benjamin and Belt was not whether someone was really a woman but if they could pass as a woman, nor if they were really trans but if they would regret transitioning.[4] The answers to these questions, however, were not remotely self-evident. That uncertainty carried significant perceived risk of getting it wrong, even as it made space for doctors to insist that only their expertise could be trusted to get it right. Throughout the 1950s and early 1960s, as Benjamin and his colleagues, especially Belt, invented new ways of dealing with trans patients, the transsexual emerged as someone to be feared, not for their potential to unsettle gender norms and hierarchies but for the hypothetical harm they might cause to medical practitioners who treated them.[5]

This article takes as its base assumption that the categorical transsexual emerged through a set of practices. As scholars in science and technology studies (STS) have argued, concrete and coherent things do not simply exist out in the world waiting to be described but are, rather, produced through naming and interaction, often in convoluted and contradictory ways (Bowker and Star 1999; Law 2004; Mol 2005; Murphy 2006; Barad 2007). That process played out in the creation of the transsexual (Latham 2019). This article is the result of tracing such productive classification in action, and it builds on the methods of the scholars in STS cited above who have trained their attention toward the on-the-ground work involved in making *things* things. I look primarily to unpublished source materials, especially Benjamin's correspondence with colleagues and patients as well as the subset of his clinical records open to researchers at the Kinsey Institute. Doing so makes visible, in messy and granular detail, how Benjamin and his colleagues negotiated the many ambiguities that emerged as a result of their attempted sortings, which Benjamin largely smoothed over by the time he published texts for wider reading. The approach I take here is part of a broader research agenda that investigates the unnaturalness of cisness and the tremendous amount of effort that went into making it seem as though most people simply fit into their assigned gender category (Velocci 2021). My reading of Benjamin's letters is thus shaped by many years of engagement with scientific and medical experts' anxious grappling with the slippery incoherence of gender and sex writ large.

My approach to the category "transsexual" and its creation opens up a different way to think about how sexual categories function. Historians of transness have engaged in extensive thinking about who should be considered the subject of trans history, particularly before the category "trans" existed, and have largely settled on an idea of someone who "moves away" from the gender they were assigned at birth (Stryker 2008; Skidmore 2017; Manion 2020). The post-mid-twentieth-century trans subject tends to be regarded in contrast as self-evident, with the "transsexual" especially emerging as a particular construct of mid-twentieth-century medical discourse (Meyerowitz 2002; Stryker 2008; Gill-Peterson 2018). Looking solely at the category "transsexual" in Benjamin's published writings would, after all, indicate that the "true transsexual" was merely someone who wanted to change their body, especially their genitals, to "at least resemble those of the sex to which they feel they belong" (Benjamin 1966: 22, 14). Indeed, Benjamin (1966: 21) wrote in his book *The Transsexual Phenomenon*, "The request for a conversion operation is typical only for the transsexual and can actually serve as definition." The way that he actually interacted with transsexuals, though, suggests that the stated classification system did not map onto clinical practice. Not everyone who was diagnosable as a transsexual should, in his measure, have the surgery they wanted. Thus simply being a transsexual wasn't enough to have surgery because the transsexual was constructed as someone whose desire for surgery simultaneously defined them and was likely to produce a bad outcome. Attending to exactly how Benjamin determined who was eligible for surgery demonstrates that even as it was being produced, the category of the transsexual formed less around a set of coherent gendered contents and more in terms of the possible effects of trans surgery. The mid-twentieth-century transsexual was not the self-evident cousin of the less categorically delineated nineteenth-century trans subject. Figures like Benjamin did not define transness by establishing solid criteria and then assessing people by how closely they matched them; rather, they constructed transsexuality as a space of uncertainty through their fear-based practices and used that uncertainty to maintain clinical control.

Wreaking Mayhem

Through a fairly arbitrary series of events—having the right background, knowing the right people, being in the right place at the right time—Benjamin became an obligatory passage point (Callon 1984) in the mid-twentieth-century world of trans medicine. As Benjamin's reputation for being willing to recommend surgery and hormones increased and he became known as *the* doctor who knew what to do with transsexuals, other doctors referred patients they couldn't or wouldn't treat to him, and trans people told each other to write to Benjamin for a sympathetic doctor who believed in the legitimacy of their experience and could help them (Meyerowitz 2002: 133).[6] Throughout the 1950s, anyone seeking what was then called a "conversion operation" essentially had to go through Benjamin's private practice for a surgical referral.

Finding someone to send patients to, however, proved difficult. Many of Benjamin's colleagues thought trans people were mentally ill and needed to be protected from their own desires; the prospect of removing healthy tissue just because a patient wanted it gone seemed absurd, not to mention bad medical practice. Moreover, in the 1950s, trans surgery was decidedly, as Belt described it, "experimental."[7] While doctors affiliated with Magnus Hirschfeld's Institut für Sexualwissenschaft had performed transsexual vaginoplasties in the 1930s, the development of the surgical technique ground to a halt with the rest of the Institut's activities when Nazis destroyed it and burned its records in 1933 (Meyerowitz 2002: 20). Doctors in the 1950s would have to develop new surgical methods, which, as Belt reported on his own experiences, often resulted in complications.[8] Trans medicine, then, offered doctors a chance to be on the cutting edge of a new field, but, with concerns about how individual patients would fare, not to mention how it would be publicly perceived, most surgeons had little interest in it.

Others were more open to the idea and viewed surgery as a positive intervention that could improve transsexuals' lives—but they, too, were reluctant to perform it, primarily on legal grounds. While no law explicitly criminalized genital surgery for trans patients, surgeons and their lawyers interpreted an old statute outlawing "mayhem," intended to prevent the harming of men who might become soldiers, as prohibiting the castration of patients with healthy organs who wanted their testicles removed (Sherwin 1954). In 1948 Benjamin ran into this fear of legal trouble with the first trans patient he attempted to refer for surgery, Val Barry.[9] Barry, whom Alfred Kinsey had stumbled across and sent to Benjamin, had been admitted to the State of Wisconsin General Hospital's psychiatric ward after reportedly attacking her parents when they refused to allow her to leave the house dressed as a woman.[10] According to a note Benjamin attached to the psychiatrist's report, even though the hospital recommended castration and vaginal reconstruction to manage her psychological distress, the attorney general of Wisconsin intervened and refused to allow the surgery to take place because it would be prohibited under the mayhem statute.[11] Undeterred, Benjamin pressed on in his efforts to find a surgeon for Barry, but legal concerns continued to dissuade anyone from operating. Max Thorek, perhaps best known as the founder of the International College of Surgeons, had agreed to perform Barry's surgery but changed his mind after hearing about the legal risks. "As I had expected," Benjamin wrote to Kinsey, "Thorek has been strictly advised by his attorney not to perform the operation on [Val] as he would open himself up to *criminal* charges."[12] Thorek, according to the same letter, eventually agreed to provide Barry with estrogen but recommended that she seek out a surgeon elsewhere in the world, like Mexico, where there was no such mayhem law.[13] For him, it was not worth the legal risk.

A solution to the legal conundrum emerged in further conversations with surgeons: prospective patients could be required to undergo a psychiatric evaluation. Before he declined to operate, Thorek had apparently told Benjamin that he "would perform the operation only on the advice of a psychiatrist, and then only with the permission of the authorities," as Benjamin put it to Barry.[14] To obtain such a recommendation, Benjamin approached Karl Bowman, a psychiatrist at the Langley Porter Clinic in San Francisco. "In attempting to find an urological surgeon interested in [Val]'s case," Benjamin wrote to Bowman, "I was impressed with the fact that probably only an authoritative advice, as it could come from you, could induce a reputable urologist to agree to operate."[15] In another case, a patient named Caren Ecker, who had attempted to remove her own testicles, reported to Benjamin in October of 1953 that Dr. Frank Hinman Jr. was willing to complete her efforts and remove her penis.[16] According to Hinman's lawyer, there was no legal barrier to his performing the surgery, since Ecker had already started the process. "However," Ecker wrote to Benjamin that December, "as it may become an item of controversy, he wants me to obtain a second opinion of both an urologist and a psychiatrist."[17]

The psychiatric evaluation became even more firmly enshrined as a de facto requirement when Benjamin began sending patients to Belt for surgery. Belt, a Los Angeles–based urologist and the protégé of Hinman's father, Dr. Frank Hinman Sr., became Benjamin's go-to referral for penectomies and vaginoplasties as early as 1954, but he remained concerned about the possible consequences of performing trans surgeries for years.[18] The two quickly settled on a psychiatric evaluation as a necessary component of the decision, and their informal practices congealed into a set path toward surgery. First, patients contacted Benjamin, whether self-referred or sent to him by another doctor. If the patients seemed suitable for surgery, Benjamin referred them (although he repeatedly insisted that he was not referring to specific surgeons or recommending surgery, merely offering a name of a sympathetic surgeon and "consenting" to surgery) to Belt. Belt then sent patients to Carroll Carlson, a psychiatrist, for assessment.[19] By May 1958, this process was so engrained that Belt wrote saying that he had sent a patient to Carlson "in accordance with our established routine."[20]

Even with this routine in place, the pair struggled to decide who should be eligible for surgical interventions. Rather than negotiate the ostensible gendered truths of patients' lives, their debate focused on who might cause trouble for them if they regretted their surgery. Belt and Benjamin were both particularly concerned about a patient named Edie Hutchens, the one Belt joked was likely to shoot them. Though Benjamin encouraged Hutchens to make the trip to California for a consult with Belt in May of 1958, by June he had written to Belt to advise that although Hutchens would probably psychologically benefit from surgery, he had concerns about the practicality of Hutchens living as a woman.[21] Belt agreed, writing that he was reluctant to operate on Hutchens because she would likely have to "undergo physical examination in the course of [her] work as a teacher."[22] Because the surgical technique Belt used was still in its infancy, it would be obvious to any examiner and result in Hutchens being fired. Belt was sure that when this happened, "[her] resentment against the man who carried out this work will rise and grow—no matter what [she] thinks of [her] feeling now." A lawsuit, Belt was sure, would follow. "Hardly a jury in the world would condone [the surgery]," he concluded the letter, spelling his professional demise. Over the next six months, Belt continued to obsess over the imagined penalties he would face for operating. Hutchens, he wrote to Benjamin that December, "would most certainly get anyone in trouble who dared to operate on [her]. I still have that feeling about [her] regardless of what the psychiatrists say."[23] To assuage Belt's fears, Benjamin emphasized the role of the psychiatric evaluation in warding off legal consequences. "I understand your hesitation to operate," he wrote, "although the psychiatric evaluation would protect you."[24] The psychiatric evaluation was not, then, for Hutchens's mental well-being or even diagnosis, but for the benefit of Belt, who was afraid of being sued.

Concern about legal censure and public controversy thus produced the requirement of a psychological evaluation, rather than any attachment to diagnostic clarity. Benjamin did not task psychiatrists with making any kind of diagnosis of transsexuality or innate femininity. "All I would expect of a psychiatrist," he wrote to Belt, "is to pass judgment as to whether the respective patient has a sufficiently normal mentality, to allow him to make his own decision."[25] The desire for surgery in and of itself was supposed to be enough for a diagnosis of transsexualism, but it was not enough to convince Benjamin and Belt that the risk of "treating" transsexualism was worth it. Rather, the psychiatric evaluation existed to protect surgeons from legal backlash. Certainly the law didn't require it—again, there was no law specifically outlawing castration or surgical construction of a vagina, and so there were no legal specifications for how to go about obtaining either of those surgeries. But with a psychiatric evaluation, if anyone attempted to sue a surgeon, the surgeon could appeal to the authority of the psychiatrist who had signed off. Another expert's approval would diffuse responsibility for the decision.

Future Regret of Surgery Past

As is clear from the Hutchens case, regret, and ensuing anger toward the surgeon, was a persistent concern for Benjamin and Belt, and managing an imagined future of regret became a key aspect of deciding who would get surgery and who wouldn't. Benjamin did his best to weed out patients who seemed like they might regret their decision because they would not pass as successfully as they hoped, or might change their mind later. The problem with not passing was that people might regret their transition; the problem with regret was that they might blame the people who had facilitated their surgical and hormonal treatments and sue them or, as in Belt's "joke" about Hutchens, show up to their office and shoot them. As Benjamin wrote to Belt about a patient he declined to approve for surgery, "I am afraid if anything is done now it may backfire."[26]

Transsexuals were apparently particularly prone to psychological states that would lead them to both make poor choices and lash out. Whether these states were due to an inherent trait or difficult lives, Benjamin saw trans people as constitutionally unstable and difficult to deal with. "Many of these patients are utterly unreliable," he wrote to surgeon F. Hartsuiker as an explanation for a patient's seemingly erratic behavior. "After all, nature has made them misfits."[27] To Kinsey's associate Wardell Pomeroy, he confided, "Most of these people are narcissistic, completely lack judgment, and some of them easily develop ideas of persecution."[28] In a letter to Kinsey himself, Benjamin said simply, "Those T.V. cases of mine (transvestism, not television) are a damned nuisance most of the time."[29] Trans people thus wound up on a circular path: they were transsexual because they wanted surgery, and they could not be trusted to make their own decisions about surgery because they were transsexual.

Benjamin tended to reject patients he viewed as emotionally volatile, particularly if they seemed likely to question his authority. "Since this young man does not seem to be too cooperative," he said of one patient, "I would not treat [her]."[30] Anyone Benjamin saw as impatient, pushy, or demanding could find themselves ineligible for surgery or at the very least reprimanded. "You will have to learn to be patient," Benjamin told another patient in a veiled threat (see Pitts-Taylor 2020). "Otherwise, you may jeopardize your future chances for the operation."[31] Benjamin sometimes cut off correspondence with patients he felt were challenging him. Early on in their three-year correspondence, Carlotta Dorta shared her experience with doctors who resented patients who tried to assert their own knowledge of transsexuality. "Slowly but surely I reached the conclusion that it doesn't pay to be honest and open-minded about it, specially with medical-doctors, and even more specially, with psychiatrists," Dorta wrote in March 1965.[32] "The minute they have the slightest to suspect or guess that the so-called 'patient' *knows-too much*, or that he knows more than he is supposed to know . . . they cool off and crawl back into their shells, and run away like scared rabbits." Evidently, this experience repeated with Benjamin: he eventually cut off their correspondence owing to the "tone" of a postcard that Dorta had sent to him, as he explained in an October 1968 farewell.[33] He told Margaret Harrison that he could "no longer be your doctor or your friend" because "it was very *inconsiderate* of you to disturb me on a Sunday morning just to request that I should write to your brother."[34] When Stephen Wagner asked Benjamin to write to her physician about her estrogen dosage, and whether Benjamin might send before-and-after pictures of people who had had surgery, Benjamin's research associate and secretary Virginia Allen wrote on top of the received letter, "read—no reply—'TOO DEMANDING.'"[35]

In an attempt to counteract the possibility of regret, Belt and Benjamin both emphasized the irreversibility of surgical interventions as justification for limits on eligibility, as though patients had not considered that. As Benjamin advised Rhonda Wallace, "The operation you are contemplating is a serious and irrevocable step. Safeguards are required."[36] The safeguards Benjamin mentioned, though, were meant to protect him and Belt from transsexual regret, and they used uncertainty about who might regret an irreversible surgery to justify agonizing over their decisions. Belt, too, expressed the importance of scrutinizing and denying surgery to anyone who might have second thoughts. This was not just scrutiny in the present, though, but accurately telling the future. Belt wrote of one patient in 1958, "So far, by carefully evaluating them, we have not had any disappointed patients, but this particular boy seems to be beyond prediction."[37] This unpredictability made Belt want to proceed with extreme caution, and Benjamin concurred: that patient was "one of the most 'dangerous' cases. I say at present, HANDS OFF."[38] In this emotional register, each transsexual was a dangerous, unknown quantity who had to be delicately managed at every step, even as clinical assessors apparently had preternatural powers to see who would cause trouble down the line.

In their selection apparatus, degrees of inherent masculinity and femininity did come up. Occasionally, Benjamin used "wrong body" language that implied a true, stable, internal gender that could be without doubt identified as masculine or feminine. For example, Benjamin told Val Barry that he "would consider [her] definitely a woman that accidently possesses the body of a man."[39] When it came to making the final call of whether surgery was appropriate for a given patient, though, practical considerations came to the fore. In a June 1958 letter written in the midst of the back-and-forth over Hutchens's future, Benjamin outlined three prognostic factors to be considered in approving a patient for surgery to avoid the production of regret: surgical, psychological, and practical outcomes. Benjamin's faith in Belt's surgical technique, he wrote, meant that he was not concerned about the first. The second factor was increased happiness and decreased fear of being arrested for cross-dressing. Benjamin mentioned that all of his patients whom he had approved for surgery had experienced an improvement in psychological well-being as a result of hormonal treatments, and also "due to the realization that they have come as close to the female sex as medicine can provide." But who would benefit psychologically? Those with the best practical outcome. The practical outcome, as Benjamin put it, "refers to the prospect of producing a reasonably successful 'woman.' In this respect, the physical structure and appearance of the patient is of importance. If this appearance is unchangeably masculine, the outcome is, of course, not only problematical but definitely doubtful, if not unfavorable." This practical outcome, he continued, was likely to be problematic in the case of Edie Hutchens, and was why he thought Hutchens should resume living as a man instead of obtaining surgery and continuing with her transition.[40] Hutchens, in this framework, would come to regret her transition because she was, in Benjamin's account, unlikely to successfully pass as a woman.

In other words, what mattered for these outcomes was not who really was a woman, but who would look feminine enough to pass. In a 1957 letter to Wardell Pomeroy, for example, Benjamin mentioned a patient who had managed to have surgery even though he had not agreed to it. "The reason that I did not consent was the strong masculine appearance," he wrote, though he admitted that the patient had had a positive surgical outcome—in part because rhinoplasty had given her a more feminine-looking face.[41] Being a "convincing" woman, meanwhile, could be grounds for surgical approval. A report from Walter H. Peterson, the director of the Chicago Psychological Institute, to surgeon Daniel Lopez Ferrer reported positively that the patient under consideration "gives the impression of a fairly 'handsome' not overly seductive woman," and her appearance "could best be described as an image of a refined, attractive, maiden aunt."[42] Similarly focusing on appearance, Benjamin wrote in a 1958 assessment of a patient for Belt, "I know too little about him to pass an opinion, but agree with you that he may look very well as a girl. He probably ought to be one."[43] By focusing on external characteristics, Benjamin and his colleagues made an unshakable internal gender identity a necessary but insufficient criterion for granting a patient access to surgery.

Passing concerns were not only about appearances. Benjamin also worried about patients' capacity to "do all the things that women do (household duties, etc.)" and particularly to find employment as women.[44] Kinsey told Benjamin that all of the patients he knew of who had had surgery and attempted to socially transition were struggling to find jobs, unless they were willing to earn "their living on the lecture platform or some type of public exhibition."[45] This was also a key point in the Hutchens case. Benjamin and Belt feared that Hutchens would be fired from her job as a result of not passing. This focus on employment echoes a longer history of queerness being attached to a fear of dependency and becoming a public charge, as well as the intense gendering of the labor market at mid-century—not to mention the regret that might stem from being unable to find work posttransition (Canaday 2009; Kessler-Harris 2001, 2003).

A focus on passing—and the consequences of not passing—thus took precedence over gender classification. A prospective patient's failure to adhere to gender norms might lead to regret, but Benjamin and Belt did not categorize people according to intrinsic gender so much as how they might be read by others. While Benjamin believed that transsexuals possessed a degree of what he called "constitutional femininity," he took issue with what he felt was a misreading of this statement that suggested he believed that transsexuals were actually female. Benjamin wrote to the editor of the *Journal of the American Medical Association* to correct an article that had described his perspective as such. The "concept that these subjects (transvestites) are 'constitutionally female' . . . is not and has never been my concept," Benjamin specified. "Naturally an assumption of a certain degree of constitutional femininity is not to say that these subjects *are* constitutionally female."[46] In other words, Benjamin did not assess his patients to determine whether they were women—he assumed that they were not.

True Transsexuals and Real Women

Scholars have discussed the reluctance of medical professionals to grant trans people access to transition care in terms of a defense of binary, stable sex, but neither Benjamin nor his colleagues seemed concerned that the binary, or womanhood, or femininity were under threat (Meyerowitz 2002; Stone 2006; Valentine 2007; Gill-Peterson 2018). On the contrary, they viewed transition as largely functional and cosmetic—while estrogen and vaginoplasty, along with new clothes, a new job, and a new set of familial and social relationships, might enable someone to live in the world as a woman and be more comfortable with herself, none of those things would make her a real woman. In these doctors' framework, their patients were not women but transsexuals. The category "transsexual" served not as a condition of being for which there was an appropriate medical response but, rather, as a state of rejecting reality that required careful handling.

Benjamin stressed that patients had to demonstrate a "realistic assessment" of their future to qualify for surgery. They could not think of themselves as real women, only imitations of such, and if they believed otherwise, they were deluding themselves. Benjamin remained unconvinced that trans women were actually women, even after transitioning, and he was clear with patients on this point. "You must realize, of course," he responded to Edith Williams's inquiry, "that living as a woman and taking female hormones does not make you a woman."[47] To Winnie Dunning he wrote, "Please remember that no operation can ever make a normal

female out of a male. Sex cannot be changed—only the secondary sex characters."[48] So framed, medical transition was a long-term masquerade, an intervention that could treat the symptoms of gender dysphoria but not one that could
produce a fundamental change in someone's sex. Medical transition could certainly help a patient feel better, but only the appearance of the body would be
transformed, and only partially at that. The category that a patient would fit into
would not change, and it was disqualifying to imagine otherwise.

Acceptance of one's "real" sex suggested that a patient would be satisfied
with the outcome of their transition, further enshrining it as a selection criterion.
Belt in particular found it endlessly frustrating that his patients continued to
pester him for more surgical interventions that were beyond his capacity, like
implanting ovaries and a uterus. "No matter what we do for these patients they
will never be satisfied," he wrote to Benjamin in 1956, after he had operated on
several trans women. "As each procedure is performed, they come up with further
desires and requests which makes the job of dealing with them and handling their
problem very difficult."[49] Belt cautioned a patient similarly. "It is in the nature of
things that a transvestite will never be wholly satisfied with her appearance," he
wrote to Barbie Owens. "In the most successful operation we have had, a young
person with so great a tendency toward femininity that her very perineum was
constructed by nature wider than the male, . . . the patient came in after all was done
expressing dissatisfaction because there was not a uterus with tubes and ovaries
projecting into it from above and she could therefore not have a baby. 'You have
performed a miracle so far for me, Doctor, why can't you do just this one more
thing?'"[50] Even with an intrinsic "tendency toward femininity," a "realistic" set of
expectations—here taking the form of an acceptance of material limits—was
apparently lacking.

Beyond casting patients as failing to understand both the limits of modern
science and how sex works, Belt's view on the necessity of realistic expectations
circled back to possible legal problems. In 1969, when journalist Burton Wolfe
asked why Belt had stopped performing trans surgeries, Belt highlighted the
expense of malpractice insurance and legal settlements in light of the perceived
risks of treating trans patients. Belt told Wolfe that he was concerned about lawsuits in which amounts of "money demanded by the dissatisfied transsexual who
had dreams of becoming a mother and other such nonsense were beyond the
wildest imaginings."[51] While turning down Lorna Harding for treatment, Belt
likewise claimed that he had stopped performing peotomies and vaginoplasties
"due to a series of unfortunate experiences with patients who have felt that they
wished this type of work done but who expected more than the surgeon can possibly deliver in the way of alteration even though the limitations of the method were
most carefully set forth preoperatively."[52] Fear about regret, then, was paired with
a frustration with patients wanting more.

Though less personally threatened by the possibility of regret than Belt, Benjamin conflated "unrealistic" hopes with emotional instability. "*Do try hard to give the impression of a well-balanced sensible person* who does not expect miracles," he wrote to Debbie Mayne as she sought a psychiatrist's approval for surgery.[53] His reference to "miracles" firmly placed transsexual hopes in the realm of the fantastic and likely impossible. Benjamin himself had written to Dr. F. Hartsuiker, Mayne's potential surgeon, saying, "It is quite important in my opinion that the patients retain their realistic attitude toward their own status even if they live the life of a woman to which I feel they are entitled."[54] Here, ontological "status" as a transsexual contrasted with merely functioning as, but not being, a woman. Though Benjamin may have coached Mayne on how to convince Hartsuiker that her expectations for her surgical outcome would not be too high, Benjamin expressed doubts about Mayne's grip on reality. "[Debbie] impressed me as so highly emotional as to be almost called psycho-neurotic and certainly very unrealistic," Benjamin wrote in the same letter to Hartsuiker. "I think [Debbie] is a more serious problem than many other transsexualists and it is really often difficult to decide which is the lesser of the two evils: to operate or to refuse operation."

Benjamin would eventually, unlike his patients, come to possess a sense of objective reality in the form of a classification system. Complex diagnostic criteria for transsexuality were developed after Benjamin and Belt had already established their routines for assessing patients for surgical approval. When Benjamin first started recommending trans patients for surgery in the early 1950s, there were no meaningful diagnostic criteria other than his own gut feelings. While an October 1964 letter from Ruth Rae Doorbar to Benjamin suggests an eventual psychiatric approach that put potential surgical candidates through a battery of intelligence, personality, and perception tests, these served more of a research purpose in their early incarnation than a diagnostic one.[55] In the mid-1950s, Benjamin was effectively on his own, making diagnoses of transsexuality according to his own judgment.

To formalize the process, Benjamin developed what he called the Sex Orientation Scale, or the S.O.S. The scale, based on Kinsey's sexual behavior rating system, described seven categories of "sex and gender role disorientation and indecision," from "Type 0," those with "normal sex orientation and identification" who find the idea of cross-dressing and surgery "foreign and unpleasant" and consist of "the vast majority of most people," to "Type VI," the true transsexual of high intensity (Benjamin 1966: 22). However, Benjamin emphasized that the types "are not and never can be sharply separated" and were "approximations, schematized and idealized" (23). Most patients would "fall in between two types and may even have this or that symptom of still another type" (24). Even with this diagnostic tool, then, transsexuality and assessment of who would benefit from surgery was anything but self-evident, and required a clinician's interpretation.

Within the S.O.S., as with Benjamin's earlier interactions with patients, transsexuals were not transsexuals because they were actually a gender other than the one they had been assigned at birth. Rather, they were transsexuals because dressing and living as women was not enough to alleviate their gender dysphoria, because psychotherapy did not work to relieve their symptoms, and most of all because they wanted genital surgery. As is clear, though, clinical action did not directly follow classification. If anything, classification as transsexual itself created barriers to transition, at the same time that those barriers reinforced the need to carefully circumscribe surgical eligibility. After all, barriers would not be needed if transsexuals were not inherently unstable, as evidenced by their resistance to such barriers. The transsexual was constituted as different from the nontranssexual through a separate set of clinical practices that applied only to patients already deemed transsexual (Latham 2017). It was the inability to suppress gender dysphoria that made someone both a good candidate for surgery and a risky candidate for surgery precisely on the basis of their failure to cope with psychic pain.

Diagnostically and practically, little changed with the development of the S.O.S. Benjamin occasionally responded to inquiries with an S.O.S. diagnosis—in November 1961, for example, he sent a copy of the S.O.S. to patient Joan Sewell with the note, "Judging by your description, you most likely belong to Type III of Transvestism, as I described it in the enclosed reprint."[56] But references to S.O.S. type in correspondence were rare, and I found no indication that Benjamin actually used the scale in his decision making. In a spreadsheet of all his trans patients, a column listed patients' "TV-TS type" and what appears to be an intake form likewise has a space to note S.O.S. type.[57] Based on how little the scale came up in correspondence, though, it seems like patients' scale rating served a primarily organizational and research purpose, with little practical clinical relevance. The rating was given after the clinical encounter, based on a conclusion that Benjamin would have come to anyway, because the rating depended on how much someone wanted surgery to begin with. If there were now types of person according to degree of gender dysphoria, those types could be determined in the same way that Benjamin had been assessing patients all along. S.O.S. ratings were an afterthought that justified the recommendations he had been making for the past decade.[58] Nonetheless, as a post hoc attempt to make his practice seem more systematic and scientific, the S.O.S. gave an air of objectivity to Benjamin's decision-making process.

For Benjamin and Belt, larger questions about what sex was and how it worked were distilled into a question of who should and should not be allowed to access surgery. Despite Benjamin's claims to transsexual diagnostic expertise, it was not obvious who should qualify for medical transition, which opened up the possibility for terrible mistakes, which in turn required expert regulation of the process. Assumptions about masculinity and femininity certainly played a role in this process, especially as time went on and gender clinics developed institutionalized screening practices. But in the early days of trans medicine, sorting masculine from feminine paled in comparison to assessing possible risk. This quotidian clinical practice would continue to shape the experiences of trans people attempting to access surgical care for decades to come.

Epilogue

Ultimately, the legal threat that Belt so feared proved a nonissue, and the anticipated lawsuits never materialized (Meyerowitz 2002: 121). But the specter of litigation had a tremendous impact, shaping both the availability of surgery for trans patients and the requirement for psychiatric assessment before a surgeon would operate. For much of the 1950s, Belt was the only urologist in the United States and one of few in the world who would perform trans surgeries. His methods for soothing concerns about retribution thus became effective requirements, leading to selection criteria based on a general sense of a patient's likeliness of regretting their surgery and turning to Belt for revenge. By 1962 his anticipation of legal trouble was enough to make him shutter his trans surgical practice, leaving transsexuals with even fewer options for medical care.

There was another effect of Belt and Benjamin's anxiety: it helped them solidify their own importance and the role of medical expertise in making decisions about trans bodies and lives. Because of the potential for disaster, one needed an expert to make the right choice. To maintain control over who could access surgery, Benjamin and Belt created an anticipated problem that only their careful selection of patients could prevent from happening. Their own track record of happy post-op patients and the actual needs of people who desperately wanted surgery could, in their minds, be justifiably ignored in the face of an anticipated future disaster. This fear of the future had a material legacy as trans medicine coalesced around a model that functioned as if disaster were imminent. Though trans people rarely changed their minds, trans people's changed minds dictated the entire trajectory of trans medicine in the second half of the twentieth century. Practitioners of trans medicine could position themselves as experts precisely because they cast transition outcomes as both possibly good and inevitably bad, with their expertise hinging on a regime of anticipation that came to exist through "simultaneous uncertainty *and* inevitability of the future" (Adams, Murphy, and Clarke 2009).

Trans medicine gained legitimacy and coalesced into a recognized field of expertise throughout the 1970s, thanks in large part to the rise of university-supported gender clinics and research projects that gave clinicians and researchers institutional backing. Positive press coverage and legal victories in favor of trans people further supported a sense of optimism about public and professional acceptance of medical transition (Meyerowitz 2002: 254). This did not, however, result in greater trans self-determination or diminished fears about bad outcomes. On the contrary, clinicians doubled down on limiting access to both hormonal and surgical interventions. What had functioned as informal habits at the height of Benjamin's influence in the 1950s and 1960s became codified as official regulations in 1979, in the form of the Harry Benjamin International Gender Dysphoria Association (HBIGDA) Standards of Care. The HBIGDA Standards continued to foreground possibilities of regret and the need to protect clinicians through a system of "peer review," given the controversial nature of transsexuality itself.[59] That included a psychological evaluation.

Access to transition care has become more available in some respects—though still tremendously limited by expense, ridiculous waiting times, and general lack of access to health care, even if requirements have loosened somewhat—but the approach set in motion by Benjamin, Belt, and the founding members of HBIGDA continues to put clinicians' needs over patients' in a long-standing model of the emotionally unstable trans person likely to regret their transition. Today, anxieties about regret continue to limit access to surgical transitions, whether from efforts by concern trolls to "protect" young people who want to transition or continued requirements for evaluation by mental health professionals before being able to access surgery.[60] As of this writing in spring 2021, a recent spate of successful legislative efforts in the United States and United Kingdom to ban trans youth from accessing medical transition are finally bringing mid-twentieth-century doctors' fears about the illegality of providing trans medical care to fruition.

The transsexual was made transsexual by their desire for surgery but was denied it on the same basis: because they were transsexual, they could not be trusted to have surgery. I highlight this absurdity not merely to point out an illogic but also because doing so makes visible how trans clinical practice has never needed to make sense from trans perspectives. Benjamin and Belt constructed good medicine and transness as mutually exclusive. In their framing, one could not be transsexual and also an expert on one's own needs. There has decidedly been a push for a different kind of good medicine in the years since Benjamin and Belt controlled access to surgery, ranging from the inclusion of nonbinary people in the HBIGDA-descended World Professional Association for Transgender Health's most recent Standards of Care, to informed consent models of accessing estrogen and testosterone. But these efforts continue to frame medicine as possessing a "gate" that needs to be "opened," as though a slight tweak to clinical practice is the solution to the problems that clinical practice has caused, while fears of uncertainty tend to be combatted with insistence that trans people are in fact certain about their gender and bodily desires (Lane 2018; Callahan 2015; shuster 2016). Perhaps, though, medicine is not the right source of knowledge for structuring decisions about the shapes that peoples' bodies can take. Maybe uncertainty is not a dirty word. Maybe if doctors and senators and trans-exclusionary radical feminists on the internet stopped treating hormones and surgery as last-ditch tragedies, we could finally talk about something interesting, like making them free to everyone who wants them.

Beans Velocci (they/them) is a lecturer in history and sociology of science at the University of Pennsylvania.

Notes

1. Elmer Belt to Harry Benjamin, February 22, 1960, series IIC, box 3, folder Belt, Dr. Elmer (1959–1962), Harry Benjamin Collection, the Kinsey Institute for Research in Sex, Gender, and Reproduction, Inc., Bloomington, IN (hereafter HBC).

2. Patient names have been changed in accordance with Kinsey Institute policy. I have maintained original initials to facilitate reference and, when possible, used the same pseudonyms as Meyerowitz 2002.

3. I use "trans medicine" as a shorthand for the clinical apparatus that developed around hormonal and surgical interventions for trans people. While this was not an actor's category, I gesture with "trans" toward the ways that these clinical practices exceeded the highly contingent category "transsexual."

4. Benjamin also treated trans men according to the same principle. Most of his initial patients, however, were trans women. For brevity, this article contends with Benjamin's treatment of trans women specifically, but a comparison of the precise ways that Benjamin's treatment of trans women and trans men differed is a crucial area of further investigation.

5. On the potential for the transsexual to unsettle gender norms, see, among others, Stryker 1994 and Meyerowitz 2002.

6. See also correspondence between Louise Lawrence and Alfred Kinsey, series IB, box 1, folder 1, Louise Lawrence Collection, Kinsey Institute, Bloomington, IN.

7. Belt to Benjamin, December 15, 1958, series IIC, box 3, folder Belt, Dr. Elmer (1958–1959), HBC.

8. Belt to Benjamin, July [n.d.], 1956, series VIB, box 23, folder 34, HBC.

9. While the mayhem statute does not seem to have led to the feared crackdown on trans surgeries, it's worth nothing that in the twenty years leading up to Barry's case, there had been at least two high-profile, nationally reported cases in which San Francisco surgeons had run afoul of the law for using the same kinds of sexualized surgeries that trans people wanted—but in these two cases, coercively for eugenic purposes. See Blue 2009; *Washington Post* 1936; and *Boston Daily Globe* 1936. See Amin 2018 for the eugenic history of the technologies of transsexuality.

10. H. M. Coon to W. B. Campbell, July 19, 1948, box 3, folder B, VB, HBC.

11.   Harry Benjamin to Karl Bowman, n.d., attached to Coon's report, H. M. Coon to W. B. Campbell, July 19, 1948, box 3, folder B, VB, HBC.

12.   Benjamin to Alfred Kinsey, Oct. 4, 1950, File Benjamin, H., Alfred Kinsey Correspondence [digitized], Kinsey Institute, Bloomington, IN (hereafter AKC).

13.   Barry was finally able to access surgery in Sweden in 1953. Benjamin to Kinsey, December 1, 1953, file Benjamin, H., AKC.

14.   Benjamin to Barry, December 27, 1949, series IIC, box 3, folder B, VB, HBC.

15.   Benjamin to Karl Bowman, n.d., series IIC, box 3, folder B, VB, HBC.

16.   Caren Ecker to Benjamin, October 5, [1953], series IIC, box 4, folder E, C, HBC.

17.   Caren Ecker to Benjamin, December 3, 1953, series IIC, box 4, folder E, C, HBC.

18.   The earliest mention of Belt operating on one of Benjamin's patients is in Benjamin to Kinsey, September 22, 1954, File Benjamin, H., AKC. Based on a 1960 letter from Benjamin to Belt, suggesting that Belt experimentally remove only one testicle from a patient and implant the other in the abdomen because "You won't castrate anybody that way," it seems like Belt did not want to perform castrations out of a legal concern. Harry Benjamin to Elmer Belt, July 12, 1960, series IIC, box 3, folder Belt, Dr. Elmer (1959–1962), HBC.

19.   Carlson was by no means an expert on transsexuality. He had, however, treated Belt's daughter-in-law for "puerperal insanity," according to an August 20, 1956 letter from Benjamin, so Belt trusted him. Belt to Benjamin, August 20, 1956, series VIB, box 23, folder 34, HBC.

20.   Benjamin to Belt, May 12, 1958, series IIC, box 3, folder Belt, Dr. Elmer (1958–1959), HBC.

21.   Benjamin to Belt, June 11, 1958, series IIC, box 3, folder Belt, Dr. Elmer (1958–1959), HBC.

22.   Belt to Benjamin, June 12, 1958, series IIC, box 3, folder Belt, Dr. Elmer (1958–1959), HBC.

23.   Belt to Benjamin, December 15, 1958, series IIC, box 3, folder Belt, Dr. Elmer (1958–1959), HBC.

24.   Benjamin to Belt, December 30, 1958, series IIC, box 3, folder Belt, Dr. Elmer (1958–1959), HBC.

25.   Benjamin to Belt, March 3, 1958, series VIB, box 23, folder 34, HBC.

26.   Benjamin to Belt, September 12, 1957, series IIC, box 3, folder Belt, Dr. Elmer (1958–1959), HBC.

27.   Benjamin to F. Hartsuiker, November 24, 1954, series IIC, box 5, folder Hartsuiker, Dr. F, HBC.

28.   Benjamin to Wardell Pomeroy, January 8, 1959, File Benjamin, H., AKC.

29.   Benjamin to Kinsey, December 3, 1954, File Benjamin, H., AKC.

30.   Benjamin to Morton M. Garfield, March 7, 1967, series IIC, box 6, folder N, W, HBC.

31.   Benjamin to B. S., September 29, 1955, series IIC, box 6, folder S, B, HBC.

32.   Carlotta Dorta to Benjamin, March 13, 1965, series IIC, box 4, folder D, C, HBC.

33.   Benjamin to O. S. [Carlotta Dorta], October 16, 1968, series IIC, box 6, folder S, O, HBC.

34.   Benjamin to M. H., May 15, 1956, series IIC, box 5, folder H, M, HBC.

35.   Stephen Wagner to Benjamin, January 8, 1967, series VIC, box 25, folder 7, HBC.

36.   Benjamin to R. W., November 3, 1969, series IIC, box 8, folder W, R, HBC.

37.   Belt to Robert P. McDonald, June 2, 1958, series IIC, box 3, folder Belt, Dr. Elmer (1958–59), HBC.

38.   Benjamin to Belt, June 2, 1959, series IIC, box 3, folder Belt, Dr. Elmer (1958–59), HBC.

39.   Benjamin to Barry, May 31, 1949, series IIC, box 3, folder B, VB, HBC.

40.   Benjamin to Belt, June 11, 1958, series IIC, box 3, folder Belt, Dr. Elmer (1958–1959), HBC.

41. Benjamin to Wardell Pomeroy, June 27, 1957, File Benjamin, H., AKC.

42. Report sent to Daniel Lopez Ferrer by Walter H. Peterson, director of Chicago Psychological Institute, RE: PW, May 21, 1956, series IIC, box 8, folder W, P(H), HBC.

43. Benjamin to Belt, March 3, 1958, series IIC, box 3, folder Belt, Dr. Elmer (1958–1959), HBC.

44. Benjamin to W. J. D., August 18, 1955, series IIC, box 4, folder D., W. J., HCB.

45. Kinsey to Benjamin, January 5, 1955, File Benjamin, H., AKC.

46. Benjamin to Editor of *JAMA*, April 20, 1955, File Benjamin, H., AKC.

47. Benjamin to E. W., June 30, 1958, series VIB, box 24, folder 22, HBC.

48. HB to W. J. D., August 18, 1955, series IIC, box 4, folder D., W. J., HCB.

49. Belt to Benjamin, July 29, 1956, series VIB, box 23, folder 34, HBC.

50. Belt to B. O., September 5, 1956, series IIC, box 6, folder O, B, HBC.

51. Belt to Burton H. Wolfe, March 24, 1969, series IIC, box 3, folder Belt, Dr. Elmer (1965–1971), HBC.

52. Belt to L. W. H, August 29, 1958, series IIC, box 3, folder Belt, Dr. Elmer (1958–1959), HBC.

53. Benjamin to D. M., March 15, 1954, series IIC, box 6, folder M, D, HBC.

54. Benjamin to F. Hartsuiker, February 15, 1954, series IIC, box 6, folder Hartsuiker, F., HBC.

55. Ruth Rae Doorbar to Benjamin, October 18, 1964, series VIB, box 24, folder 43, HBC.

56. Benjamin to J. S., November 24, 1961, series IIC, box 8, folder S, J, HBC.

57. Patient spreadsheet and intake form, series VIE, box 28, folder 20, HBC.

58. See Mol 2005 for a similar process in the relationship between pathological studies and clinical encounters in cases of atherosclerosis.

59. Harry Benjamin International Gender Dysphoria Association, "Standards of Care: The Hormonal and Surgical Sex Reassignment of Gender Dysphoric Persons," February 1979, series VIC, box 25, folder 19, HBC.

60. On affects of regret and future happiness in contemporary conversations about trans surgery, see Chu 2018.

References

Adams, Vincanne, Michelle Murphy, and Adele E. Clarke. 2009. "Anticipation: Technoscience, Life, Affect, Temporality." *Subjectivity* 28: 246–65.

Amin, Kadji. 2018. "Glands, Eugenics, and Rejuvenation in *Man into Woman*: A Biopolitical Genealogy of Transsexuality." *TSQ* 5, no. 4: 589–605.

Barad, Karen. 2007. *Meeting the Universe Halfway: Quantum Physics and the Entanglement of Matter and Meaning.* Durham, NC: Duke University Press.

Benjamin, Harry. 1966. *The Transsexual Phenomenon.* New York: Julian.

Blue, Ethan. 2009. "The Strange Career of Leo Stanley: Remaking Manhood and Medicine at San Quentin State Penitentiary, 1913–1951." *Pacific Historical Review* 78, no. 2: 210–41.

Boston Daily Globe. 1936. "Ann Cooper Hewitt Accuses Two Doctors: Tricked into Sterilization Operation, She Says." August 15.

Bowker, Geoffrey C., and Susan Leigh Star. 1999. *Sorting Things Out: Classification and its Consequences.* Cambridge, MA: MIT Press.

Callahan, Edward J. 2015. "Opening the Door to Transgender Care." *Journal of General Internal Medicine* 30, no. 6: 706–7.

Callon, Michel. 1984. "Some Elements of a Sociology of Translation: Domestication of the Scallops and the Fishermen of St Brieuc Bay." *Sociological Review* 32, no. 1: 196–233.

Canaday, Margot. 2009. *The Straight State: Sexuality and Citizenship in Twentieth-Century America*. Princeton, NJ: Princeton University Press.

Chu, Andrea Long. 2018. "My New Vagina Won't Make Me Happy." *New York Times*, November 24.

Gill-Peterson, Jules. 2018. *Histories of the Transgender Child*. Minneapolis: University of Minnesota Press.

Kessler-Harris, Alice. 2001. *In Pursuit of Equity: Women, Men, and the Quest for Economic Citizenship in Twentieth-Century America*. New York: Oxford University Press.

Kessler-Harris, Alice. 2003. *Out to Work: A History of Wage-Earning Women in the United States*. New York: Oxford University Press.

Lane, Riki. 2018. "'We Are Here to Help': Who Opens the Gate for Surgeries." *TSQ* 5, no. 2: 207–27.

Latham, J. R. 2017. "Making and Treating Trans Problems: The Ontological Politics of Clinical Practices." *Studies in Gender and Sexuality* 18, no. 1: 40–61.

Latham, J. R. 2019. "Axiomatic: Constituting 'Transexuality' and Trans Sexualities in Medicine." *Sexualities* 22, nos. 1–2: 13–30.

Law, John. 2004. *After Method: Mess in Social Science Research*. New York: Routledge.

Manion, Jen. 2020. *Female Husbands: A Trans History*. Cambridge: Cambridge University Press.

Meyerowitz, Joanne. 2002. *How Sex Changed: A History of Transsexuality in the United States*. Cambridge, MA: Harvard University Press.

Mol, Annemarie. 2005. *The Body Multiple: Ontology in Medical Practice*. Durham, NC: Duke University Press.

Murphy, Michelle. 2006. *Sick Building Syndrome and the Problem of Uncertainty*. Durham, NC: Duke University Press.

Pitts-Taylor, Victoria. 2020. "'A Slow and Unrewarding and Miserable Pause in Your Life': Waiting in Medicalized Gender Transition." *Health* 24, no. 6: 646–64.

Sherwin, Robert Veit. 1954. "The Legal Problem in Transvestism." *American Journal of Psychotherapy* 8, no. 2: 243–44.

shuster, stef. 2016. "Uncertain Expertise and the Limitations of Clinical Guidelines in Transgender Healthcare." *Journal of Health and Social Behavior* 57, no. 3: 319–32.

Skidmore, Emily. 2017. *True Sex: The Lives of Trans Men at the Turn of the Twentieth Century*. New York: New York University Press.

Stone, Sandy. 2006. "The *Empire* Strikes Back: A Posttranssexual Manifesto." In *The Transgender Studies Reader*, edited by Susan Stryker and Stephen Whittle, 221–35. New York: Routledge.

Stryker, Susan. 1994. "My Words to Victor Frankenstein above the Village of Chamounix: Performing Transgender Rage." *GLQ* 1, no. 3: 237–54.

Stryker, Susan. 2008. *Transgender History*. Berkeley: Seal.

Valentine, David. 2007. *Imagining Transgender: An Ethnography of a Category*. Durham, NC: Duke University Press.

Velocci, Beans. 2021. "Binary Logic: Race, Expertise, and the Persistence of Uncertainty in American Sex Research." PhD diss., Yale University.

Washington Post. 1936. "Operation Plot Is Told to Court by Ann Hewitt: Heiress Testifies She Was Tricked by Doctors in Examination." August 15.

The Others of the Ravine

DANIASA CURBELO

Abstract In the society and culture of the Canary Islands, ravines (*barrancos* in Spanish) are spaces that contain a wealth of meanings and perceptions attached to a collective imagination. These natural scars that mark and characterize the island's geography represent scenes of dissidence, as will be shown through the spatial and geographic stories of various transsexuals and transvestites who lived in Tenerife between 1970 and 1990; the specific character of their testimonials is situated in a specific context: El Cabo, a barrio in Tenerife, as well as the Santos Ravine (Barranco de Santos in Spanish). The state repression, marginalization, and violence against sexually dissident people during this age will be the main context of analysis. In a brief journey through history, these aspects will be placed in relation to key events from the Francoist dictatorship on the islands, a travel journal of the nineteenth century, and passages from the conquest of the Canary Islands in which the ravines, among them the Santos Ravine itself, take on a relevant importance. Finally, this study will mention the existence of a chapel consecrated to the Virgin of Candelaria in this environment as possibly the most significant crystallization of the otherness of the ravine. This study thereby contemplates reviewing these spaces on the basis of their formation as media in which specific Canary Island subjectivities can be located.

Keywords ravine, Canary Islands, otherness, transvestite, transsexual, indigenous, colonialism

> We've been looking for Dad for three weeks and we still haven't found any-
> thing. . . . Now I know that a squad is what they call a group of men taken to be
> killed at Tanque Abajo, an enormous ravine, sunken by vegetation, where they
> throw away dead animals and the trash from the entire city. Later the men are
> abandoned and left to rot there without their families' knowledge, as the families
> are fooled and told that the men are prisoners.
> —Nivaria Tejera, *El barranco*

*T*he Ravine (*El barranco* in Spanish) is not only the title of a novel originally
published by the Cuban–Canary Island writer Nivaria Tejera (2016), and
considered to be the first Spanish-language novel about the Spanish Civil War; it
is also one of the fundamental spaces for the development of the story offered by

its author. For the eyes of its protagonist—Tejera herself as a young girl—the ravine is a place for her uncertainties and fears as a daughter of a political prisoner of the Franco regime. Her chilling descriptions of the Tanque Abajo ravine show a situation at the beginning of the dictatorship in the Canary Islands that is neither anecdotal nor singular: the abrupt conditions that characterize the vertical ravines of the islands made these areas natural destinations for the execution and, subsequently, mass graves of the regime's political prisoners. Using the ravines in this way was designed to make it difficult for the families—in most cases even still nowadays—to locate the corpses of the victims.

On our archipelago, we don't have rivers. What we do have are ravines that attach themselves like wounds and scars to the landscape of the island, which is volcanic in origin; these ravines are welcome ecosystems for a wealth of vegetal and animal biodiversity. Geographically speaking, they are places of intermittent transit, given that the unevenness in the terrain also fulfills a crucial function in the water cycle of the Canary Islands, especially in the easternmost islands and the ones with a steeper relief: the channels of these ravines drive precipitation down from the high crags and peaks to the sea. However, this very fact can also become a danger to the people living on the island: the rain "runs" at such a high speed through the ravines that it can occasionally cause floods and mudslides. This destructive condition, which has caused fatalities—such as the eight people who died in Santa Cruz de Tenerife, has since been baptized as the Tenerife flood of 2002—is especially worrisome for institutions and authorities. This accident of nineteen years ago entailed economic losses in the amount of 90 million euros (Guerra 2019). For this reason, in 2019 the Tenerife Water Board announced that it had implemented a flood prevention system by placing sensors in seven ravines around the island to detect flooding after a storm. One such device charged with controlling the unpredictable possibility of flooding is located in the famous Santos Ravine. But the city of Tenerife's efforts to control this grand, sixteen-kilometer ravine that "splits the city in half" does not end with flood sensors. The Santos Ravine is embedded in the local imagination as a synonym of danger not only because of its cliff walls with a slope of up to one hundred meters, but also because of what happens within it and what it contains. A ravine is not just a geographic "margin" that borders or traverses a municipality, thus establishing a physical limit. In the Canary Islands, ravines also represent spaces of cohabitation among subjectivities, in part for being "habitually conceived as environments of communal use . . . , as could be the case, for example, of people who use them to do laundry . . . and, as well, their role as a social setting for young people who didn't hesitate to play on their slopes or swim in their pools" (Estévez 2014: 51). Additionally, it is important to note that, in the case of the Santos Ravine, this condition of marginality was mainly represented in the historical existence of cave dwellings located along the sides of the channel that were inhabited by the socially excluded, who posed an uncomfortable problem for the local institutions. Hence "the caves were and continue to be dwelling places for people from low social classes, who have no better place or residence to settle. . . . [They] present and presented awful hygienic and sanitary conditions; but despite that, several caves were occupied and even recognized as legal residences for administrative purposes . . . [and] as yet another neighborhood of the city" (Noriega Agüero 2017).

Although many of these cave dwellings have been gradually abandoned, some continue to exist today in the Santos Ravine, such as the section near the neighborhood of La Verdellada in La Laguna city. The people who live there can be considered as marginal, due to the clandestine atmosphere given by their distance from the urban areas and the mechanisms of civic control established by law enforcement bodies. This is also the case with other spaces that share similar characteristics with ravines—forests, lakes, mountains, and the countryside, among others, as well as spaces created to mimic nature like metropolitan parks and gardens, which are consolidated as territories of dissidence in the form of "cracks" in the normative civic discourse.[1] As an indication of those characteristics and subjectivities that made the Santos Ravine a territory of marginality within the city, it is necessary to mention the now-lost barrio of El Cabo as another space that enjoyed similar conditions, precisely owing to its border with the ravine channel from the Serrador General Bridge to where the ravine joins the sea. Its proximity, and the fact that it is formed by a neighborhood of citadels—communal housing inhabited by working-class or poor families—make El Cabo a place of transcendental interest to this research project. Thus the ravine is not a territory "on the margin" just because of supra-civic ways of life proposed by the cave dwellings, but also because of the occupation of the space by various dissident subjectivities due to their sexual orientation or identity. It is in this sense that I turn to the term *otherness* as a way of uniting the specter of subjectivities that have experienced a condition of marginality or dissidence in relation to a "norm." While it is true that the use of this concept was born in the social sciences as a way to analyze non-Western cultural experiences—and to define an image of said experiences—the process by which this dichotomy is constructed arises from three key modes: difference, diversity, and inequality (Boivin, Rosato, and Arriba 2004: 5). Within gender studies, otherness has also been addressed as a social construct that legitimizes the inferiority of an oppressed group in comparison to another, privileged group; in this case, it was Simone de Beauvoir who made visible the construct of the category "woman" as the other (Cano 2016: 51).

Due to the current lack of a bibliography in the case of the Canary Islands—a lack that demonstrates the urgent need of scholarship to create a narrative of sexual dissidences on the islands[2]—oral history emerges as an invaluable source of information. The testimonials of three transsexual women and one transvestite—Sonia, Marcela, Farah, and Manoli, respectively—natives of Tenerife and between fifty and seventy years of age, contribute enriching material to this investigation that would otherwise have been impossible to acquire. Their testimonials were acquired through conversations by phone and in person in the weeks prior to the writing of this article, and in my initial thinking I asked them to tell me about their memories related to the ravine. I later transcribed their narratives. This proposal led to testimonials marked by economic instability, social exclusion, sex work, violence, and repression, all of which, in my opinion, are a faithful reflection of the social experiences perceived by sexually dissident people who inhabited the area. From another perspective, these four experiences can also define the modes and strategies of survival and resistance that Canary Islander transsexual women and transvestites put into practice within a context of hostility and severity toward sexual dissidence, between 1970 and 1990. The well-known Law of Social Danger and Rehabilitation, with which the Franco regime substituted the previous Law of Vagrants and Thugs, was approved in August 1970 and entailed a hardening of the repressive measures against social dissidence: the law's second article signaled as a danger to the community those subjectivities who "perform acts of homosexuality or who regularly exercise prostitution." For cases of homosexuality, the law prescribed internment in a "reeducation establishment" with the goal of correcting non-heteronormative behaviors. It must be remembered that conceptual and historical analyses have concluded that Francoism's use of the term *homosexuality* also encompassed the experiences of transvestites—and later, transsexuals—which were considered to be a form of extreme effeminacy. As Oscar Guasch and Jordi Mas (2014: 3) wrote, "The popular imagination of the time period defines transvestites as extreme forms of homosexuality in which certain effeminate men try to approximate the stereotypical ways of being a woman." The Canary Island press echoed the Francoist position, and some columnists event went so far as to celebrate it, as was the case of a column titled Lookout (*Mirador*), published in the *Eco de Canarias* (*The Canary Islands Echo*) on November 4, 1969: "It seems that the new law includes as a grave factor of social danger effeminacy in male clothing. . . . In short, that prevailing 'narcissism' among the youth, favored by effeminacy in the use of clothing and a hedonist and materialist sense of life, drunkards, prostitution, etc." (in Ramírez 2019: 124). For the Canary Islander historian Victor Ramírez, "this fact gives a clear measure of the rigid system of gender roles imposed by the regime and which the press, controlled by said regime, took care of spreading" (124), which would have an evident negative repercussion on those experiences that transgressed the parameters of gender expression, as is the case of transvestites and transsexuals. When the Law of Social Danger and Rehabilitation was modified by a legal reform in 1978 because of its incompatibility with the democratic values that started to emerge after Franco's death, the articles that referenced homosexual acts were eliminated. What were not eliminated were those that referenced "the habitual exercise of prostitution and insolent, brutal, or cynical behaviors with evident contempt for social cohabitation [with which] the punitive Francoist categories could, in the new normative context, continue operating as an instrument for the 'delimitation of social elements in moral terms,' with the resulting possibility of including homosexuality within the realm of what was considered asocial or amoral" (Terradillos Basoco 2020: 93). Moreover, the repression of sexual dissidence continued during the transition to democracy under the "public scandal" law until its repeal in 1989, and under the law on social danger until it ended in 1995, which for Juan María Terradillos Basoco (2020) entailed the expansion of sexual dissidence from its Francoist consideration as a "paradigm of danger" in the period of constitutional democracy, with the subsequent legal, political, and social repercussions for those subjectivities branded as "dangerous." The occupation of space and the practices described in the testimonials pose a resistance to the sex-gender binary and cis-normative order, a "regime of domination that positions cis people in a situation of privilege compared to non-cis people, such as trans people,[3] [which] finds its root in the social naturalization of cis elements, through which non cis identities appear to be 'strange' or 'abnormal' and, therefore, able to be pathologized and dominated" (Bodenhofer González 2019: 101).

The political and social environment of these decades having been described, the testimonials of these four sexually dissident people, each over fifty years old, will broaden the complex contextual framework of the age with their intimate and affective lived experiences. Their epistemological value, therefore, would lie in the very nature of "experience," while feminist epistemologies have denoted the importance of incorporating such experiences in social research beyond their being conceived as merely an object of study, in that they are capable of "bearing witness to forms of domination and oppression that produce subalternate subjects . . . , twice made subalternate by the power of foreclosure deployed by the knowledge itself" (Trebisacce 2016: 289). In this sense, the sociologist Dorothy Smith (2012) would point to how "the tool of experience was designed to create an alternative to the dehumanized subject of the knowledge of the established social science discourse" (in Trebisacce 2016: 289), with which we can affirm that "Experience was a resistant invention, a strategy of dispute; it functions in the way of a chemical indicator, as Foucault would say, to make visible not clear substances this time, but rather naturalized powers that produce subalternates for us, at the same time as they deny us. It was, as well, and because of this, a corrosive force of these powers" (Trebisacce 2016: 289).

From this point on, the testimonies of the four people who have wanted to share with me their experiences in the aforementioned ravine will be introduced. The conversations were later transcribed by me for use in this article.

1) Sonia, transsexual woman born in 1952:

I was born in the home of my grandmother Carmen, which was at the end of Miraflores Street, at the beginning of the 1950s. Afterwards, I was raised in a single-story house in the neighborhood of El Cabo; I lived there for many years, close to what is now Buenos Aires Avenue. Next door to this house there was a citadel, but it wasn't the only one. There are still some standing today. The first citadel that I knew was on Miraflores Street, underneath my grandmother's house, and it had an inn and a bar. I went there many times and that is how I got to know poverty well. It was the first time that I saw someone pick fleas off another person. I remember the heyday of the ravine from when I was eight years old, and it was marvelous: green, with running water, and ducks. . . . Once I grew up, I was always there.

In the eighties the whole area near the ravine was made up of brothels. Indecent people, to put it that way, lived there. There were also gay bars and a boarding house. Under the Serrador Bridge, in the ravine, was where we all would go to "squat" and "satisfy our vices" because no one would discover you from above due to how dark it was. As an adult I never went to the caves, but when I was little, I did, and I remember that married couples lived there; but because later in the brothel they met upstairs, I never went. I know of transvestites that stayed there, as well as drug addicts who went to the ravine to use. The biggest police raids of the time took place there and they happened every five minutes. The mortuary room was also there, and there was a bridge that crossed the ravine—it was short, gorgeous, and made of forged iron. Besides the ravine, we also squatted in the brothels in El Cabo, like the one belonging to Marcela. There was a bar called El Laurel that led to San Sebastian Street; Marcela reigned over it for a few years, and before her it was Luisa, may she rest in peace. We would meet there almost every night. During Carnival we would all pass through El Laurel to get dolled up, have a drink, and then each of us would go her own way.

When I was young, my grandmother Carmen took me to the hermitage of the Virgin of Regla, across from what is now the Auditorium, and later I went with my mother because it was a tradition in the neighborhood. And this hermitage is where the most gays, trans people, and lesbians in Santa Cruz gather, even today, every eighth of September for the festivities. Even the waitress of the Virgin is a transsexual woman named Chani. On that day a mass is held, followed by a procession to the Market of Africa, and we make an offering of flowers. We always meet many of the people who lived with us in El Cabo before they tore it down."

2) Marcela, transsexual woman born in 1955:

Forty or fifty years ago, all of the transsexuals and gay men were in the Santos Ravine. Prostitution took place in every dark corner. Fifty years ago water ran in that ravine from one side to the other, in the top part there were ponds called *ñameras*, and down below, in the bottom part, was the prostitution area. Anywhere with a dark corner was a good spot to do it. The same thing happened on the stairs of the Serrador Bridge, which crosses the ravine and connects the center of Santa Cruz with the neighborhood.

El Cabo was made up of three alleyways, then in the back was the alley with the whorehouses. There were some ten or twelve houses, and each one bore the name of the woman who ran them: Mercedes's House, Juanita La Banana's House, La Pepa's House, . . . mine was Marcela's House, which was La Gallega's House before that. I took over the house in the eighties until the town hall awarded us compensation because they were going to tear down the neighborhood to make way for the construction of the Tenerife Space for the Arts. There were also alternative bars that were open all night and all day for clients who wanted to have sex. Before, there used to be a tiny bridge in the ravine that led to the mortuary room, and while people were holding a wake for the dead, the gays were fucking below. There were fights, and the police were always around. Underneath the Serrador Bridge, they found several women who were murdered, a little ways beyond the mortuary room.

Next to El Laurel bar there was a boarding house where all the older whores stayed, and they later went to the houses in the alleys to squat. El Cabo was a barrio of brothels that had only two alleys to the side and one behind, which was a "runway" of whores, clients, gay men . . . that's what there was. It was like a red-light district similar to Miraflores. All these brothels had been there since the beginning of the century.

And during Carnival people were always looking for places to have sex, between two cars or in a doorway, because people were not connected to anything. The four stairs of the Serrador Bridge were a brothel during Carnival, and even though there was a fear of being seen, the surroundings of the ravine were always favorable places because they were darker than the rest of Santa Cruz. We would always meet in the thicket of the ravine to have sex; it was the best place.

3) Farah, transsexual woman born in 1966:

I began to frequent the area of El Cabo in 1982, at sixteen. I was friendly with the transvestites my age and of the time and with the former "glories" that were around the area. I also knew young boys who were thieves, hashish dealers, and clients of prostitution. I established some affective and sexual relationships with some of the men who frequented the area, and I had at least two serious relationships—as serious as they can be when you're with a man who knows that you're a prostitute and doesn't care. My last relationship of this type helped me leave prostitution. In reality it was a subject that was hurting me, and I wasn't enough of a delinquent to steal, or the types of clients were disgusting and the rates were ridiculous.

I have fun memories most of all of my transvestite companions and how much we used to laugh, despite living in such a tragedy as prostitution. We did everything, from singing flamenco to helping whichever of us was in a tight spot at the time, be it economic or personal. I also have many memories of our rela tionship with the people who worked in the Market of Africa and the neighbors of the barrio. The Santos Ravine was a place to be respected, aware of its dangers, and there, if you were in good company, and felt safe, you had the chance to do things that were forbidden, like smoking joints and doing drugs.

Prostitution was safe if you went to one of the brothels that I remember, one of which was Marcela's, although I never frequented it; or dangerous if you decided, or had no other option, to get in a car with a stranger. You risked getting beaten up or being killed. I abandoned prostitution and the barrio at the same time between 1987 and 1989.

4) Manoli, transvestite born in 1955:

I lived in a cave dwelling in the Santos Ravine for a few years in the eighties. It wasn't my cave, but rather belonged to a partner that I had at the time, and I stayed there every two or three days. There were people living there permanently, people with problems, without family. . . . We were a community in which everyone respected everyone else. When I found pieces of furniture that had been thrown away, I took them to the cave. For bathing there was a wooden room and we would bathe with the water that we collected. When it rained, the water would run through the ravine, and crossing it was a hassle: you either got your legs wet or you jumped from stone to stone, running the risk of falling. When they built the sports center below the Viera y Clavijo Park, they gave the people who were living there a house in Añanza. Now the majority of caves are empty and can be seen from the Galcerán Bridge.

We used to "squat" in the corner of Miraflores Street or in El Laurel, although I always went at night. El Laurel is a tiny bar with a small counter, and almost all of us would go there to get dressed and do our makeup. Across the way there was a bar where we would have lunch. I worked the street only a little; rather, I went more to be with the other girls. I would approach guys and if I could, I would take their wallets. And if I liked him, I would go with him to Marcela's brothel or to the stairs of the Serrador Bridge. Sex cost one thousand peseta, although most of them would only give you five hundred. Many *magos* from the north would come to see us.[4]

One time a few of us went to Madrid to get chest surgery, but in the end I didn't do it because I thought, "And if my life changes what will I do with these two melons?," even though back then I was quite a lady. Later, when I began to work at Candelaria Hospital in the nineties, I introduced myself as "a gay man" to avoid any problems. Afterward I was in jail for a year and a half, and I came out with a very different appearance. It was a very hard time that radically changed my life. Fortunately, I was able to get back my job at the hospital. Now I look at myself in the mirror and I see an effeminate man, and because of that I can't say that I'm a transsexual woman. But neither am I a man because I don't look or act like one. When I go to clothing stores, my eyes are drawn to the women's clothes, even though later I don't buy any or I return them. I'm on an "intermediate ground" between woman and man, but I wouldn't change anything about what I am. I'm very happy as I am, and I will die being happy this way.

These four oral testimonials confirm that the Santos Ravine was a territory on the margins of civil order and functioning governed under repressive structures, not just because of its ideal conditions for putting into practice subalternate sexual encounters—monetized or not—but also because of its proximity to the old barrio of El Cabo. Just as the interviewees mention, "the depth of the ravine made it into the ideal hideout for brawls, fights, and other turbid affairs and goings-on" (Noriega Agüero 2017), among which said subalternate sexual encounters would stand out. The transsexual women and transvestites who for years occupied thickets, stairs, and dark corners embodied the "danger" that the ravine generated by virtue of its being a wild space, added to its confrontation with the standards of representation of gender and sexuality of the time. The borderline conception formulated by Guasch and Mas (2014) contemplates a rereading of the transvestite condition as a supra-binary gender experience prior to the use of the term *transsexuality*, which has been banished from trans discourses in Spain not only because of its pejorative connotation but also because of the legalization and medicalization of gender transitions from the eighties onward. Ultimately, the experiences of these four people were marked by two determining axes: inhabiting a space halfway between natural and urban like that of the Santos Ravine, and living transgressive or even supra-binary gender experiences. Curiously, both dimensions share the concept of transit or the flowing of water and mud or being between sex and gender categories. In the same way, this conjunction between space and dissident practices cannot be decoupled from concrete physical places like brothels or venues like El Laurel, meeting places for the transvestite and transsexual community of Santa Cruz de Tenerife prior to and during the eighties, and the annual celebration of Carnival, one of the greatest sociocultural events of Tenerife (figs. 1 and 2). Therefore, the ravine, a "breach" that splits the capital in two, becomes a place that creates a sense of discomfort for the repressive institutions and a sector of society.

It must be said that the Santos Ravine and barrio of El Cabo of today are radically different from that in the 1990s, as described in the testimonials. For a city like Santa Cruz, the elimination of this bothersome marginality so close to the center and consumer areas inevitably required remodeling the famous ravine and expelling the residents of El Cabo and other barrios like Los Llanos, Las Torres, and San Sebastian. The Cabo-Llanos Plan, which entailed the rehabilitation of the old quarter near the mouth of the ravine, was an ambitious urban project that commenced in the beginning of the nineties with the purpose of expanding the capital, but which hid a main interest in increasing the value of the ground that they would name the Golden Mile of Santa Cruz. When the economic crisis halted this plan, large construction projects like the Tenerife Auditorium, several skyscrapers, and the contemporary art center known as the Tenerife Space for the Arts (TEA) mentioned by Marcela had been finalized. In the year 2002, almost parallel to the urban remodeling, construction began on the last section of the Santos Ravine to build a new parallel road with the purpose of decongesting traffic and adjusting the ravine mouth to prevent possible flooding. Its final section was transformed into an immense and diaphanous "drain" as vegetation was substituted for hard pavement. It is not outlandish to affirm that the Cabo-Llanos Plan entailed a political strategy of social sanitization by vacating the famous barrio and, therefore, the ravine. José Antonio Ramos Arteaga (2019: 84–85) writes: "The organic territorial relationship that for centuries articulated the continuity between the port, markets and spaces of civic anomie—vacant lots, cave dwellings in ravines and mountain foothills, streets like Miraflores, or small stigmatized city blocks like the one displaced by the current TEA building—has now been scorched." However, the problematic conditions ascribed to the Santos Ravine appear to date back centuries. Cave dwellings are mentioned in a "1797 register of parishioner residences" where "certain people, possibly sexual workers" (87), lived. One of the most significant and explicit historical registers about the existence of monetized sexual practices in Santa Cruz de Tenerife dates back to the beginning of the nineteenth century—though we can't discard the existence of other registers of greater antiquity. Using notes he wrote in his journal during a visit in 1800 to Canarias as part of a scientific campaign, French cartoonist and natural scientist Jacques-Gérard Milbert wrote "Picturesque Journey to the Island of Tenerife," among other appreciations. He noted,

Figure 1 (left). Carnival 1974 in Santa Cruz de Tenerife. Left to right: Manoli, Marcela, and Luisa. Personal collection of Luisa Martín.

Figure 2 (below). Carnival night at El Laurel (ca. 1970s). Left to right: an unknown person, Manoli, Sonia, and Luisa. Personal collection of Luisa Martín, given before her death to Daniasa Curbelo.

> The foreigner who sees the population of Santa Cruz and its surroundings for the first time experiences astonishment and disgust in equal measure. . . . Half a league from the city, in a place of repellent aridity, surrounded by sulfur-colored rocks eroded and calcinated by a devastating sun, where one can find an aqueduct whose waters feed an old windmill, we can find some volcanic caves converted into a shelter for those repulsive priestesses of Venus. The entrance to the cave is closed by a torn mat, while an old blanket, or any other rag strewn about on the floor, serves as the voluptuous bed where the men go in search of pleasure. These horrific lairs, which being far from the city serve as the setting for debauchery between the women prostitutes, is where the soldiers of the garrison and the sailors from the port go to do their repugnant orgies. . . . Nevertheless, the Santa Cruz prostitutes, given to the most vile debauchery, have not banished, however, their religious sentiments. (Milbert 1800, quoted in Ledesma Alonso 2020).

Although it is difficult to determine with clarity the exact locations of the caves mentioned by Milbert, given that he situates them in an arid landscape half a league from Santa Cruz, I would venture to contemplate two possible settings based on the data and characteristics cast by his description. One of them is Vallesco, a small barrio constructed in the side of another ravine close to Santa Cruz. Even though people didn't start to inhabit this area until the second half of the nineteenth century, given its arid and rocky landscape, famous caves converted into houses, and distance to the capital—some three kilometers that roughly equal the half league mentioned by Milbert—Valleseco approximates the place where the practices detailed by the Frenchman took place. The other possible setting is the Santos Ravine itself, owing not only to its already-mentioned natural features and inhabited caves but also to an account of a "windmill erected there, of which a channel-aqueduct remains today beneath the cut in the ravine known as Black Man's Jump" (Noriega Agüero 2017), next to modern-day Viera y Clavijo Park, a spot that is also found about a half league's distance from the center of the city. Although we cannot confirm the exact location of the caves described, I will mention the relevance of some of the concepts employed by Milbert to refer to the sexual practices that took place in said caves—such as "repulsive priests of Venus," "repugnant orgies," and "vile debauchery"—and how this language constructs an image of repudiation that is embedded as yet another annex to the discourse that is already starting to form around what is or is not civic on the islands under Eurocentric colonial parameters. In this way, we can see that the ravine is defined as an indomitable space that the authorities have tried to control, delineate, possess, and vacate, becoming, like any other place surveilled and accosted by a power represented in public institutions, into a place of dissidence. This is reminiscent of the fifteenth-century conquest of the archipelago, which bore witness to important confrontations with a colonial order installed through the process of territorial conquest that began in 1402 and officially ended in 1496 after decades of battles between the indigenous *Imazighen* (Berbers) and European conquerors. Many of these battles took place in ravines, as these spaces were inhabited by and known to the former. One of the most famous anticolonial battles on the island of Tenerife took place in the Acentejo Ravine on May 31, 1494, in the town of La Matanza (literally, "the slaughter" or "massacre"), which takes its name from the massacre of the invading troops of the Spaniard Alonso Fernández de Lugo at the hands of the indigenous Guanche people, who were very familiar with the terrain, which provided them an advantage in the battle. To this day, hundreds of people still go to this ravine each year to commemorate the indigenous victory in a festive environment, which has made the Canary Islands a symbol of colonial resistance. Many historical accounts of the conquest mention "the way in which these indigenous people will repel the habitual entrances into their lands of the conquest-ambitious Europeans, repeatedly underline the ferocity with which the indigenous people defended themselves" (Gil Hernández 2015: 85). One such account describes a battle:

> The Christians, both the Portuguese and the Canary Islanders, were able to follow them so skillfully that, when the shepherds began to enter the ravine, our people were already close to them; and thus, suddenly, they entered the ravine in such a way that the shepherds were forced to climb the rocks of the crags, whose ruggedness was quite astonishing; but much more admirable was the agility with which the Canary Islanders walked along the crags. (López Ulloa quoted in Gil Hernández 2015: 86).

The mouth of the Santos Ravine is considered to be the precise spot where Alonso Fernández de Lugo set up his main camp in 1494, and which would later become the seed for the city of Santa Cruz (Rumeu de Armas 1975). It is fitting to highlight the fact that the ravine's name is subject to the tension between indigenous and colonial, given that there are expert voices, such as that of the philologist Alejandro Cioranescu (1975), who affirms that it took its name from Diego de Santos, a colonist who owned properties near its mouth. In contrast, the historian Juan Bethencourt Afonso maintains that the ravine's toponym originated from the existence on its margins of a cave with Guanche idols, possibly denominated "saints" by the Christian order imported with the colonial enterprise, which would make it into an ancient sacred space or place of indigenous worship (Cuscoy 1968). In this way, the fact that many Canary Island ravines have been the settings for the events and practices mentioned here could imply a conception of these places as spaces that crystallize resistance. This includes resistance against different hegemonic or repressive power structures, depending on the context and time period, such as the European colonial enterprise installed through the conquest of the islands, the Franco dictatorship, or the binary sex-gender and cisnormative order. Therefore a rereading of the concept of ravine would also be tied to sexual dissidence in the form of the close ties that Santos Ravine maintains with the past of the transvestite and transsexual community of Tenerife at the end of the twentieth century. Finally, I would like to mention a case that, in my opinion, acquires a radically different resignification when placed into context with the information and contemplations presented in this essay. The history of worship of the Virgin of Candelaria also reveals indigenous-colonial tensions in that the myth of her appearance recounts that she was found by two Guanche shepherds in the mouth of the Chimisay (Güímar) Ravine at the end of the fourteenth century, even before the start of the conquest in 1402. For a large section of the island's population, this constitutes a "syncretism that fused the worship of Chaxiraxi, Mother of the Son (who according to some versions corresponds to the Amazigh deity Tanit) with Catholic worship" (Pérez Flores 2017: 145). However, it must be remembered that the transformation and manipulation of indigenous worldviews can form part of the strategies put into effect by the colonial enterprise to introduce a new civic-religious order. Although the official worship of this divine figure is found in the Basilica of Candelaria, almost twenty kilometers from Santa Cruz de Tenerife, in the Santos Ravine there exists a cave where people pay homage, extra-officially or counterhegemonically, to the same image of *La Morenita*, which is the name by which the Virgin of Candelaria is known on the Canary Islands due to her dark skin. This "other" Virgin of Candelaria is preserved in a small chapel built in 1931 by a resident named Antonio Hernández within a cave of the ravine as a show of gratitude for a supposed miracle worked by the Virgin, curing his health after he fell from a height of twenty-eight meters at age eight. Antonio's family house was a cave dwelling that was eventually made into a hermitage and that "with the passage of years . . . became consolidated as a place of worship, especially every month of August, when people celebrate the festival of Candelaria" (Gonar 2020). The most significant element of this other figure lies in the space where its worship is performed, given that, as we have confirmed, it lives together with dissident and marginal subjectivities and realities that form the human landscape of the Santos Ravine: inhabitants of the cave dwellings, drug addicts who frequented the ravine, gay men who went cruising, and transsexual and transvestite women who found in its mouth the ideal space to have sexual encounters with clients and lovers. The presence in the Santos Ravine of the Virgin of Candelaria, an archetype of femininity, and her borderline condition of worshiping in a cave rather than a basilica, dialogues closely with the experiences of those transsexual women and transvestites who frequented its vegetation not to work miracles but to live their sexualities, circumventing social repression thanks to the clandestine protection offered to them by the ravine.

Ultimately, this environment is subject to continuous transformation, due as much to natural causes (mudslides and rains) as to social causes (remodeling and urbanization). However, the experiences documented here allow the Canary Island population to recognize those stories that do not deserve to be buried by the collapses and undergrowth of memory.

Daniasa Curbelo was born in Tenerife, graduated in fine arts from the University of La Laguna in 2017, and has participated in different exhibitions and meetings on and off the island, collaborating in editions and promoting several artistic and audiovisual projects such as the direction of the documentary *Memorias Aisladas* (2016) and the publication *Entre Líneas* (2017). Their work is linked to their positionality and lived experience as well as to concrete problems, constituting themselves and transiting, from a transfeminist, anticolonial, and dissident perspective, within the indefinite frameworks of interdisciplinary. In 2020 Curbelo received the Emma Goldman Snowball Award from the Dutch FLAX Foundation for international commitment to equality and feminist movements. In 2021 Curbelo received a master's degree in gender studies and equality policies at the University of La Laguna.

Notes

1.   On this topic we can mention the practice of cruising, the pursuit of sporadic sexual relationships between men in public spaces, as an example of a clandestine practice that proposes a counternarrative to the heteronormative order that defines and regulates sexual pleasure. For more information, I recommend the reading "Geografía, homosexualidad masculina y cruising en Tenerife (Canarias, España)" ("Geography, Male Homosexuality, and Cruising in Tenerife [Canary Islands, Spain])" by Francisco Javier Dóniz-Páez (2015).

2.   To date, the Canary Island researcher and doctor of Spanish philology José Antonio Ramos Arteaga has been the foremost theorist on sexual dissidences on the Archipelago, a topic he addresses in "La posibilidad del (contra)archivo queer en Canarias: Roger Casement y los cuerpos colonials" ("The Possibility of the Queer (Counter)Archive in the Canary Islands: Roger Casement and Colonial Bodies") (2017), written in collaboration with Carlos Laiño Domínguez.

3.   In this case, the concept of "trans" functions as an umbrella term to refer in an overall way to the set of experiences and gender-dissident identities known according to the context and the age as transsexuality, transgenderism, and transvestitism.

4.   In Tenerife, the term *mago* or *maga* is used in a derogatory or caricature-like way in urban areas to describe people native to or living in rural towns.

References

Bodenhofer González, Canela. 2019. "Estructuras de sexo-género binarias y cisnormadas tensionadas por identidades y cuerpos no binarios: Comunidades educativas en reflexión y transformación." *Revista punto género*, no. 12: 101–25. revistapuntogenero.uchile.cl/index.php/RPG/article/view/56250.

Boivin, Mauricio. Ana Rosato, and Victoria Arriba. 2004. *Constructores de otredad: Una intro- ducción a la antropología social y cultural.* Editorial Antropofagia. antroporecursos.files .wordpress.com/2009/03/bolvin-m-rosato-a-arribas-v-2004-constructores-de-otredad .pdf.

Cano, Julieta. 2016. "La 'otredad' femenina: Construcción cultural patriarcal y resistencias fem- inistas." *Asparkía: Investigació feminista*, no. 29: 49–62. www.e-revistes.uji.es/index.php /asparkia/article/view/2341.

Cioranescu, Alejandro. 1975. "Los primeros pobladores de Santa Cruz de Tenerife." *Anuario de estudios Atlánticos*, no. 21: 61–94. anuariosatlanticos.casadecolon.com/index.php/aea /article/view/301/301.

Cuscoy, Luis Diego. 1968. *Los Guanches: Vida y cultura del primitivo habitante de Tenerife.* Santa Cruz de Tenerife, Canary Islands: Cabildo Insular de Tenerife.

Estévez, Fernando. 2014. *Atlas de Patrimonio Cultural Inmaterial de Canarias: Elementos del Ámbito de los "Conocimientos y prácticas relacionadas con la naturaleza y el universo" de la isla de Tenerife.* Memoria del proyecto. La Laguna, Canary Islands: Fundación General Universidad de La Laguna.

Gil Hernández, Roberto. 2015. "Los guanches: Conquista y anticonquista del archipiélago canario." PhD diss., Universidad de La Laguna. riull.ull.es/xmlui/bitstream/handle/915/18167/Gil %20Hern%C3%A1ndez.%20Los%20guanches%20conquista%20y%20anticonquista %20del%20archipi%C3%A9lago%20canario.pdf.

Gonar, Humberto. 2020. "La 'otra' Virgen de Candelaria." *El día*, August 8. www.eldia.es/santa -cruz-de-tenerife/2020/08/09/virgen-candelaria-22362767.html.

Guasch, Oscar, and Jordi Mas. 2014. "La construcción médico-social de la transexualidad en España (1970–2014)." *Gazeta de antropología* 30, no. 3: article 6. www.gazeta-antropologia .es/?p=4619.

Guerra, Dalia. 2019. "Siete barrancos de Tenerife contarán con sensores de alerta contra inunda- ciones." *El día*, November 28. www.eldia.es/tenerife/2019/11/29/siete-barrancos-tenerife -contaran-sensores-22522416.html.

Ledesma Alonso, José Manuel. 2020. "Descripción de Santa Cruz de Tenerife, del dibujante francés Gérard Milbert en 1800." *El día*, June 14. www.eldia.es/santa-cruz-de-tenerife/2020/06/14 /descripcion-santa-cruz-tenerife-dibujante-22391178.html.

Noriega Agüero, Miguel A. 2017. "Las cuevas del barranco de Santos." *La prensa* (suppl.), *El día*, October 21. www.asotavento.com/2017/10/las-cuevas-del-barranco-de-santos/.

Pérez Flores, Larisa. 2017. "Islas, cuerpos y desplazamientos: Las Antillas, Canarias y la descolo- nización del conocimiento." PhD diss., Universidad de La Laguna. www.academia.edu /40429799/ISLAS_CUERPOS_Y_DESPLAZAMIENTOS_LAS_ANTILLAS_CANARIAS_ Y_LA_DESCOLONIZACI%C3%93N_DEL_CONOCIMIENTO.

Ramírez Pérez, Víctor. 2019 *Peligrosas y revolucionarias: Las disidencias sexuales en Canarias durante el franquismo y la transición.* Colección Alongues. Las Palmas de Gran Canaria, Canary Islands: Fundación Canaria Tamaimos.

Ramos Arteaga, José Antonio. 2019. "En la ciudad emboscada." In *¡Autonomía! ¡Automatización! Dispositivo para el fomento del pensamiento crítico contemporáneo en TEA*, edited by Tenerife Espacio de las Artes, 84–85. Santa Cruz de Tenerife, Canary Islands: Tenerife Espacio de las Artes. www.academia.edu/42842481/_Autonom%C3%ADa_Automatizaci %C3%B3n_Volumen_III.

Ramos Arteaga, José Antonio, and Carlos Laiño Domínguez. 2017. "La posibilidad del (contra) archivo queer en Canarias: Roger Casement y los cuerpos coloniales." *InterAlia: A Journal of Queer Studies*, no. 12: 230–40. interalia.org.pl/media/12_2017/interalia_12_2017_hispanic.pdf.

Rumeu de Armas, Antonio. 1975. *La conquista de Tenerife (1494–1496)*. Santa Cruz de Tenerife, Canary Islands: Cabildo Insular de Tenerife.

Tejera, Nivaria. 2016. *El Barranco*. Edición de Antonio Álvarez de la Rosa. Biblioteca Atlántica. Santa Cruz de Tenerife, Canary Islands: Consejería de Turismo, Cultura y Deportes.

Terradillos Basoco, Juan María. 2020. "Homofobia y ley penal: La homosexualidad como paradigma de peligrosidad social en el Derecho penal Español (1933–1995)." *Revista de estudios jurídicos y criminológicos*, no. 1: 63–102. dialnet.unirioja.es/servlet/articulo?codigo=7482239.

Trebisacce, Catalina. 2016. "Una historia crítica del concepto de experiencia de la epistemología feminista." *Cinta moebio*, no. 57: 285–95. scielo.conicyt.cl/pdf/cmoebio/n57/art04.pdf.

The Collective Scene

Transvestite Cabaret during the End of Francoist Spain

IÑAKI ESTELLA

Abstract This article offers an analysis, though necessarily fragmented and incomplete, of *travesti* cabaret during the 1960s and 1970s in fascist Spain. It explores in particular the cabaret shows of travestis in Barcelona, as well as the admiration and recognition that they produced. The study focuses on the political capacities that privacy and closed spaces generated in an environment of dictatorship, albeit through a certain presence of the public as audience. From this analysis follows a problematization of the conception of the public as the ideal location for politics, particularly the street, as well as their possibilities for resistance. This essay seeks a reassessment of intimate spaces for sharing experiences that ultimately affect and condition the necessity of public representation.
Keywords travestis, cabarets, Spanish dictatorship, oppression, public sphere, performance

The repression of homosexuality during the Franco regime has become the subject of much academic reflection, particularly since the fiftieth anniversary of the first demonstration for "homosexual liberation" in Barcelona in 1977. This process of recovering the history and memory of the era has focused on the repressive capacity of the law and the terrible effects that it had on the detained and imprisoned (Subrat 2019; Mora 2015; Platero 2015). The flood of publications in this vein, however vital, also attributes an absolute repressive power to the Francoist state, both through its laws and its imposition of a state biopolitics—to borrow a term that Michel Foucault found inadequate in the context of the Spanish dictatorship—that generalized the dictatorship's reach across the total population. However, as some scholars (Rosón 2016) have begun to suggest, research on the possibility of resistance in the heart of the Franco regime is necessary and is something that this essay will elaborate on, taking as a basis for analysis the complex and paradoxical space of the cabaret in 1960s and 1970s Barcelona: a space crossed by a dominant state heterosexuality but in which several travestis made a career as figures admired inside and outside the walls of the bar.

TSQ: Transgender Studies Quarterly ∗ Volume 8, Number 4 ∗ November 2021 **498**
DOI 10.1215/23289252-9311088 © 2021 Duke University Press

This research is important in that it illustrates modes of alternative sexual socialization produced during the Franco regime that escaped the Francoist ideology itself, meaning that the imposition of fascist dogmas was not as total and absolute as it has often appeared. The homosexual liberation protests of July 26, 1977, attended by a larger number of travestis, revealed an outburst and public exhibition of a social practice born of what had previously only been possible due to a shared, private intimacy in the cabaret. In this regard, Judith Butler's (2015: 25) reflections on the right to appear in the street, the primary scene of the revolt, as "bodily demand for a more livable set of lives" are important, both then and later in the revolts that took place around squares (Sol in Madrid, Tahrir in Egypt) in 2011. However, we must also consider how the confluence of bodies in the street was actually formed, especially in a situation of military dictatorship like Franco's Spain, in which the mere fact of public visibility could have life-and-death implications. In this regard, James Scott's (2003) reflections, offered in an anti-Foucauldian reading, speak to the development of zones of privacy in times of repression as places that ferment resistance so as to avoid public repercussions and their potentially lethal consequences. In a certain way, resistance generated in intimate or private conditions can be considered an essential prerequisite for their later public expression; it is behind closed doors where alliances and private identities are forged so that, when the time comes, travestis decide to risk going public together. This essay addresses the first of these moments through the example of Barcelona's cabaret scene.

The reconstruction of the history and memory of repression in Spain has been especially productive in generating political prototypes that become the cultural models of the era of dictatorship. In this process, it is easy to assume that anyone whose subjectivity does not mirror that of the resistant archetype were therefore a reflection of its opposite, Franco's ideology (which, to be clear, was not monolithic either). One of the best examples of this assumption is the exhibition *Ocaña, 1973–1983: Acciones, actuaciones, activismo* (*Actions, Performances, Activism*), held at the Palau de la Virreina in 2011. Ocaña, a marginal artist both during his lifetime and posthumously, long illegible by any institutional artistic measure (Aliaga 2018), was recovered, thanks to this exhibition, out of oblivion and into the Parnassus of contemporary Iberian creativity. Ocaña is now hailed as one of the most important performers in the history of recent art, the discipline in which this article is written. As Rafael Mérida Jiménez (2018: 9) explains, today Ocaña is the recipient of all manner of tribute: documentaries, archives, websites, crowdfunding to restore his works, and even a brotherhood of *Beata Ocaña* (*Blessed Ocaña*), who make him a devotional subject. While it is true that this process of recovery could be sensed prior to the exhibition at the Virreina, what is astonishing is the speed and intensity with which the process unfolded. In just under five years Ocaña was transformed from an anecdote in the national history of art to the embodiment of the resistance of cross-dressers during the Franco regime. This fast-paced recovery has also been tried, albeit with less success in my opinion, with Copi, an Argentine cartoonist, writer, and performer based in Paris who was close to Ocaña (Mérida Jiménez 2016: 117). Copi was the subject of another exhibition in the the Virreina center in 2017, which makes Virreina a major institution in the recovery of trans history in Catalonia.

From the perspective of cultural studies, Brice Chamouleau (2017: 112) has already laid out the problem with involving this new narrative epic of Ocaña and his friends in the exhibition catalog: they forget a range of marginal social practices in favor of centering one ideal model of resistance. The fact that historiography has attended to some of these practices while others are ignored constructs a pioneer narrative on top of a model of forgetting that smooths over the story of resistance. In these narratives, the tactics of collective protest are rooted in the figures of individual resistance, as in the description of Ocaña's relevance in the exhibition catalog, allowing the anti-Franco revolt to adopt the structure of a genealogical tree hiding outdated epistemologies under the wrapping of activist commitment. Consequently, these narratives say very little about the relation of individuality to collective political practice. That these travesti practices of the 1960s and 1970s also occurred at a time when queer theory had not yet formally emerged invites us to think that the boundaries of gender and transgender defined spaces other than those that have dominated the debate since the 1990s.

In one of the most relevant entries in the Virreina exhibition catalog on Ocaña, Paul B. Preciado (2011: 107) describes Ocaña's actions documented in one of the most famous records of the *cantillanero* artist, the film *Ocaña, un retrato intermitente* by Ventura Pons (1978):

> "While walking among people, Ocaña borrows from a passerby a stroller with a child that allows the eccentric couple (Ocaña dressed as a woman alongside Camilo, dressed in pure white) to perform for a moment the heterosexual family, the symbolic nucleus and cell of reproduction of the national-Catholic political sex norm. This could have been a mere performative repetition if it were not for Ocaña then pulling up his dress, exposing his buttocks and penis, at which point the owner of the stroller snatches the child and his means of transport, bewildered."

The quote is relevant because it presents several main ideas at the core of the reading displayed in the exhibition catalog, based on occupying the public sphere in a manner that Ocaña imprinted with his "little plays" (*teatrillos*), as he liked to call his street performances. Ocaña's occupation of the public sphere is important for Preciado because it frames his performances as a history of the activist work that would later be developed by collectives, like *Act Up* who denounced the AIDS epidemic of the 1980s, or even the movement to rescue urban space by activist groups like *Reclaim the Streets* that, during the 1990s in England, threw improvised raves to prevent car traffic. This idea has circulated more recently thanks to Germán Labrador (2017: 309), who associates Ocaña's performances with the political renewal of spatiality in the era of Spanish political transition. The "performative disobedience of sex and gender" Preciado sees in the film is grounded in how the action takes place in the public domain, where the reaction of rejection frames the detail of the scene. It is in this context that the figure of the passerby snatching the cart from the artist acquires its depth by revealing the dominant norms of the public sphere and the rupture that Ocaña's presence seems to generate within the common sense of Francoism, "revealing his political, sexual antagonism and gender" (Preciado 2011: 105).

Without a doubt, Preciado understands Ocaña's performance as "the maximum horizon of what historically and sociologically embodies a radical political subversion" (Chamoleau 2017: 120). In this horizon of subversion, even basic political demands are overshadowed by the performance in the street. But more important, it seems that his judgment rests on a reading of the images that is challenged by any careful viewing of them: Preciado's description of the fragment of the Pons film is overtly exaggerated (something very common in many contemporary historical and artistic analyses, which tend to be very knowledgeable but neglect visual analysis).[1] First, Ocaña shows his penis not when dragging the stroller, but rather in the previous scene (fig. 1). The passerby carrying the stroller, who gives it to the artist (fig. 2), is an older woman and not a man as implied by Preciado (likely it was the child's grandmother). And, finally, Preciado's description of the "outburst" in reaction to the stroller is an exaggeration. The older lady does not touch the cart but rather, without being seen due to the crowd, grabs Ocaña's right arm from behind. This action provokes the artist to move in a direction that opens the visual space to reveal a younger person (probably the child's parent) who appears next to the artist and the lady (fig. 3).

The violence that Preciado accords the scene fades in its description here, but it repeats the distortion that has gripped the figure of Ocaña more generally (Mérida Jiménez 2018). Other recognized voices in the field of gay film studies, like Alberto Berzosa (2014: 170), would agree with us that the scene is crucially a premeditated and detailed recreation of the type of performances that Ocaña had already pursued in the Ramblas neighborhood of Barcelona. In fact, it is difficult to see the tension that Preciado describes, not only because the performance was prepared in advance (as Joan Bufill clarified in an article in the magazine *Star* in 1978, the year the film was released) but also because it was received by a "loyal

Figure 1. Ocaña showing his penis in *Ocaña: Intermittent Portrait* (dir. Ventura Pons, 1978, min. 3:33). Courtesy of Ventura Pons.

audience" (170) and "nobody comes out scared" (Chamouleau 2017: 123); the atmosphere is, in essence, festive. The filmic scene, in this more convincing interpretation, seems to represent a familiarity by which the grandmother is presenting the father or mother of the child to a performing character who is being filmed in the street in broad daylight, followed by a crowd. A rite of acceptance and mutual family recognition is implicit.

If we are right, and because of absences in Preciado's passage there is reason to think so, the scene would shift from an example of the pervasiveness of Francoist ideology in all spheres of society (particularly in the figure of the grandmother, who in Preciado's reading encapsulates this logic) to one that shows the obvious popularity of a transvestite who is treated like family. And this would allow us to think that the Franco regime was unable to penetrate every sphere of social life, that despite its power it could not make everyone submit to its narrow views, even in public acts of collective recognition. Again, Chamoleau (2017) has emphasized how taking a critical snapshot of Francoist subjectivity can highlight the emergence of new sexual identities, which prevents us from noticing the modernization of heteronormativity against which transvestites clash without necessarily emulating old fascist blemishes. Between the lines we can see the

Figure 2. Grandma giving Ocaña the stroller (out of frame) in *Ocaña: Intermittent Portrait* (dir. Ventura Pons, 1978, min. 3:50). Courtesy of Ventura Pons.

generalization of the model of Francoist identity, such as that in Preciado's example, which facilitates an understanding of political transition in terms of instinctual release and liberation, preventing a more developed social reflection and class analysis (122). The result is a conception of the transitional political process that resolves into the model of contemporary Spanish democracy. Nothing is further from reality, if we consider the Vagrancy Act, the massacres of Vitoria and Montejurra in 1976 (for which there have still been no legal consequences), or the Atocha murders in 1977. The simple enumeration of these facts reveals very clearly how far from exemplary the democratic process was during this transitionary period. And the reference is relevant because of the enormous literature that makes the transvestite a main figure of that transition (Picornell 2010).

Francoism was unable to control all spaces, some of which were closed but not completely private. This conclusion can be found in *Lejos de los árboles* (dir. Jacinto Esteva, 1972), a portrait of a Spain marked by deep contrasts during the early 1960s to early 1970s. In one of the last moments of the film, we witness a scene located in the Copacabana, a place today occupied by the Barcelona Wax Museum and which toward the end of the sixties broke with state expectations by hosting some of the first performances by transvestites. Far from what we would associate

Figure 3. The grandmother calls Ocaña's attention to introduce him to the child's father in *Ocaña: Intermittent Portrait* (dir. Ventura Pons, 1978, min. 4:00). Courtesy of Ventura Pons.

today with the stereotypical image of the cabaret, the images in Esteva's film more closely resemble the link between flamenco and the lumpen proletariat that has been called the *flamencocamp* (Navarro 2014). After a cathartic movement in which the dancers move around the film camera in ecstasy, Margarita, one of the resident transvestites, appears. Her outfit deserves attention not only for having newspapers attached to her precarious clothing but also for being at odds with the most common image of the transvestite today; an open shirt tied at the waist clearly reveals her flat chest. The tight-kneed pants open in shreds at the ankles, allowing a form of movement akin to twirling a skirt (fig. 4). In the film, after a few steps that begin this movement of the pants/skirt, the dancer's crew sets fire to the newspapers on her costume, turning it into a fireball that consumes itself, and then falls to the ground in a frenzy. In a clearly spontaneous gesture, Margarita extinguishes the flames by dancing on them.

The image, as well as its process of artistic canonization, are interesting, given the time that they were recorded, sometime between the late sixties and early seventies; this reveals how certain transvestite practices could be carried out before a cheering audience. Transgression of the sexual norm, in fact, is not only represented in the figure of Margarita: Esteva's camera is also trained on

Figure 4. Margarita spin dancing to move the tatters of his trousers in *Far from the Trees* (dir. Jacinto Esteva, 1972, min. 1:29:50). Courtesy of Filmoteca de Catalunya.

one of the attendees who appears in public in several moments; another assistant, probably an artist as well, appears with makeup or a wig, walking among the audience. What is most striking in these images is the complicit indifference of the public to the fact that some of the transvestite practices they were watching were prohibited by law and repressed by law enforcement. In fact, law enforcement is visible in the scene at the Copacabana shortly before the dance performed by Margarita. However, they do not act against the transvestites or those who seem to challenge the sexual and gender order, but rather against one of the spectators wearing a tie—a symbol of technocrat heteronormativity—who started a fight and was removed from the venue by *los grises* (the armed police corps).

The clothing Margarita wears in Esteva's film scene deserves our attention, since clothing is what forms the basis of a transvestite reading. In this case, we find a characteristically masculine piece of clothing (pants) to which certain modifications are made so that, when put into practice (spinning on herself), it appears feminine. Margarita likely could not directly sport women's wear because of the dominant prohibitions of the era, prohibitions that, on the other hand, did not prevent other artists from wearing women's clothes in the Copacabana. Even so, transvestites had been forced to wear masculine clothes since the 1950s, but this did not prevent the drag queens or transvestites from being clearly recognizable in the cabaret. The art critic Sebastián Gasch (1972: 155), linked to the Catalan historical avant-garde, illustrates this in his *Memorias de un sesentón* when he says,

> At the end of our war, the transvestites, forced by the authorities, stopped dressing as women and adopted men's clothing. Most of them appeared on stage in a flowery shirt with very wide sleeves and black pants very tight to the legs. During the decades that we are commenting on [1950s] Mirko, dressed in this guise, was eternal in the posters of the Molino. She was the undisputed *starlet* of the program and her performances were received with clamorous applause.

This passage reveals several facts that are important. The first is that the prohibition on dressing as a woman could be circumvented with outfits that implied a certain degree of feminization, without explicitly embodying it. It is important to note that, despite the masculine clothing, the lines between masculine and feminine remained porous. Mirko, in Gasch's recollection, continues to be a star and a transvestite despite wearing men's clothing, resulting in an ambiguity that is clearly out of date, owing to both the breakdown of watertight subjectivities and the procedure for generating that stardom. Second, the passage emphasizes the recognition by an audience of the artist—Gasch speaks of the applause that greeted Mirko's work—which was typical of the cabaret, as we will return to later.

What Fernando López Rodríguez (2016) has written about the use of female attire by male flamenco dancers, a growing trend in the second decade of the twenty-first century, is interesting here, as it can help us understand the transgressive nature of Margarita in the Copacabana of the 1970s. According to López Rodríguez, flamenco is an eminently masculine dance; even the presence of women in these shows has a phallic character. Hence the use of feminine objects (polka-dot dress or a fan) does little to effect feminization of flamenco, "given the masculine values that govern the entire choreography: technical virtuosity, speed, rigidity, heavy weight" (284). According to this author, feminization has to do with the adoption of fragility, a fragility that is used in the movement that makes flamenco itself overflow and question its own limits to shift into another style yet to be defined. This nonconformity is what López calls "queer" (284–85).

It is not easy to adapt these ideas to Margarita's performance. Her outfit is at once both male and female owing thanks to its parody of rags, a DIY bricolage that fails to hide a certain improvisation on the part of its creator. Her dance is clearly masculine, which can be seen in certain gestures (when she extinguishes the fire by dancing over it) and in the courage of being set on fire, but it lacks technical virtuosity, being rather a parody not so much of women (it does not comply with the registration of the feminine fragility that López Rodríguez describes) as of flamenco. In any case, the result does not correspond to a standard flamenco show, being a mix of parodic flamenco, circus show, and amateur entertainment.

That feminization depends not only on clothing, as López Rodríguez clarifies, is also exemplified by Margarita. A photograph of Joan Colom taken in the *Barrio Chino* in Barcelona offers a similar interpretation: the men's clothing (a woolen jacket, striped trousers, and lace-up shoes) and Joan of Arc haircut (the historical symbol of a warrior woman) can barely hide his characteristically feminine pose, all of which has attracted the attention of a gentleman in a suit in the background of the photograph (fig. 5). The image seems to repeat itself in the same manner: the feminization of the male body, essential in the consideration of the transvestite, did not depend so much on the use of certain clothes but on what was actually done with them, that is, on their modifications. Moreover, the clothes also depended on the gestures that were developed with the artist's body in a public space.

The scene of the Copacabana in Esteva's film is also relevant because it exemplifies the nature of what was permissible to an audience behind closed doors. The public sphere has undoubtedly been one of the master concepts in art history since the 1990s, exactly the time when Preciado's critical theory makes its appearance. According to this historiography, for which the ancient notion of the monument has been germinal (the monument being the space where the idea of public sculpture converges with models of art for the public sphere), the street is taken to be the principal space where any notion of the public can reside. Theories of the public sphere, from those of Jurgen Habermas to Alexander Klage and Oskar Negt, have held particular influence in the discourse on contemporary art, limiting itself to a conception of the street as the epitome of the public. This has also provided for an easy expansion of the notion of the public sphere in the claims that generally conclude in various modalities of direct action.[2] It is in this context that the concatenation that Preciado makes between the *little plays* of Ocaña and ACT UP must be understood. As we can see, this reading marginalizes other models of the public, whose existence does not depend on open spaces and explicitly political organizing.

It was necessary to wait for the translation of Michael Warner's book *Publics and Counterpublics* into Spanish in 2008 to gather an understanding of

Figure 5. Joan Colom, *Untitled (Man Climbing Sidewalk)*, from the series *The Street* (1960). Vintage copy, ca. 1960. Gelatin-silver bromide on baryta paper, 9.05 × 3.94 in. Reina Sofia Art Center Museum. Autric-Tamayo Family Donation, 2018. Reina Sofia Museum Photographic Archive.

the public sphere that would depart from the concept of the street. However, the conditions under which the translation was undertaken deserve some attention. It is important to recognize that the Museum of Contemporary Art of Barcelona (MACBA), then the epicenter of activist interpretation of the public sphere, was one of the institutions responsible for that edition, which conceptualized the visitors to the museum as a kind of counter-public. However, the translation does not maintain the general tone of Warner's original, dedicated to the production of a homosexual subculture, something rather unlike the international and eminently mass audience strolling like tourists through the museums of the world. Spanish reading audiences had to wait until 2012 for a partial translation undertaken in Mexico that maintains this central aspect of the original text. The chapter cowritten with Lauren Berlant, "Sex in Public," is still untranslated into Spanish and addresses police raids on cruising bars in lower Manhattan at the end of the 1990s, then in the process of being gentrified and, in any case, a radically different kind of space from what is found in a museum. As we can easily see, the notion of the public (or counterpublic) addressed by Warner includes a public sphere that cannot be assimilated into the space of the street or open political manifestation in urban space. Warner addresses a mode of public production that is configured through a range of different modes, including the similarity of tastes and interests, the coincidence of confined space in a bar, a theater, or other shows taking place on the stage—for example, a cabaret like the Copacabana.

Clearly, Warner points to a space of mediation where the private, according to bourgeois conventions (the expression of sexual orientation, for example), already has a public dimension, making sexuality a matter of overcoming any private-public distinction. Warner calls collectivities formed in this way counterpublics, precisely to establish a distance from a hegemonic notion of the public that he clearly connects to the Enlightenment tradition. For Warner (2012: 69–70), counterpublics are important for various reasons, but especially because they allow us "to elaborate common worlds, to make the transposition of shame to honor, from concealment to the exchange of points of view with other generalized ones." For our purposes it becomes necessary to highlight the use of the term *transformation*, from which the transvestite synonym *transformista* is derived, to refer to the public expression of intimacy. On this point he adds: "The styles of embodiment that are learned and cultivated, and the affects of shame and disgust that surround them, can be tested and in some cases reassessed. The visceral private meaning is not easy to change on the part of oneself, by an act of free will. It can only be altered through exchanges that go beyond self-expression, to the construction of the collective scene" (71). Warner's words represent a radical inversion of the typical reflection on the space of politics. Shared intimacy and privacy are understood as conditions that fear transforms into an autonomous value, into a reason for shared pride. The street plays no role in Warner's analysis becoming, as we understand him, a useless arena. The street likewise was not the epitome of political expression for transvestites in the context of 1970s Barcelona. Some transvestites even questioned the tactics deployed there. The second edition of the magazine *La pluma*, released in 1978 from the Coordinadora de Collectius per l'Alliberament Gay (CCAG), which had links to Ocaña, is a clear example of how the place of transvestism in society had become an issue that transvestites addressed in a plurality of ways. Luis, one of the transvestites interviewed in that issue, using unfiltered language, evaluated the different modes that were made public:

> This topic is quite broad because they (gay transvestites) hurt you a lot as a transsexual or transvestite who feels like a woman and people in that sense take one thing for another, and all, what you need to see are these people who are in their mind living normal lives but have their derivations, I mean there are crazy clichés, etc. All this is closely linked. . . . Now as you understand, a gentleman or a lady who looks down the Ramblas at a homosexual who dresses as a woman and goes sissy, one already has the concept and not everyone looks at everyone with the same eye. . . . Yes, of course, you have to see that there are also people who will admire you and that also depends on the place where you are. You go to the Ramblas and of course, you cannot expect anything else from a worker who goes with his wife for a walk, right? And then you go to any cafeteria or any pub in the upper part and they already know that you are a transvestite or a transsexual and I think they even admire you, right? Because they know that you have taken a step forward towards what you have wanted to be and they see that you know how to behave. I have always believed that if you behave like people they will never have to reproach you for anything, you will always be a transsexual. (CCAG 1978: 9)

In the context of the political transition out of fascism, Luis reveals a reversal of the values that structure Preciado's text: street theater such as Ocaña's almost seems to be referring to or popularizing a certain image of the travesti that Luis rejects, reminding us that homosexual discourse is far from monolithic (Mira 2004: 24). In bars and pubs, on the contrary, admiration is produced, confirming the "transformation of shame into honor" that Warner describes.

The Copacabana, the Molino, the Barcelona de Noche, the Gambrinus, the Dickens, and the Espigón or EA3, to name just some of the cabarets that featured transvestite shows in Barcelona in the 1960s and 1970s, could also be spaces that hosted counterpublics in the same sense that Warner understands the term. Cabaret was certainly a place of abuse but also of mediation and protection through which some transvestites could receive the admiration of a public sheltered by the intimacy of this unique space.

Meanwhile, in other cultural spaces such as the cinema, censorship was undoubtedly practiced, especially regarding homosexuality (Melero 2014: 195). The opposite situation is the one that Gasch (1972) portrays again when pointing out the admiration that the transvestites provoked in the public with the example of Mirko. As he points out in a reading of Mirko's *Memorias de un sesentón*,

> Mirko, a wonderful dancer who resisted everyone's jokes and sang as in his best days, when he was king and lord of La Criolla, still added a very personal style to his performance and wore the dust from Calle del Cid on his heels.
>
> . . . Mirko was the first to make fun of himself. He kept his appearance even at the risk of losing his prestige. And, suddenly, it took over the public. The thing was superiorly intelligent. Intelligence also has its seduction. (155)

The passage reveals how Mirko's show might have been an object of ridicule, but the artist could turn that into a center-stage attraction. This is a typical cabaret maneuver, as the stage forms a space in which the dialogue between artist and spectator is direct, establishing a game in which both try to make each other uncomfortable and expose themselves.

Even so, mockery has been, according to authors such as Víctor Mora, an essential resource in the presence of homosexual, transvestite, or trans characters in the mainstream Spanish cinema of the 1970s such as *Mi querida señorita* (dir. Jaime de Armiñán, 1970) or *No desearás a la vecina del quinto* (dir. Ramón Fernández, 1970). According to Mora's (2015) analysis, the emergence of the homosexual in film is the result of a moment of openness that, far from being disruptive, was useful for Francoism in reinforcing the legitimization of male identity. Following Mora, in these films the homosexual appears as an isolated character, without a partner and without a community, who is ultimately made an object of derision. This semantic and physical disconnection from the social flow makes it possible to isolate the image of the homosexual presented in these films, ensuring a distance that prevents contact with homosexuality, exactly what the "law of social dangerousness" and its prison sentences were pursuing off-screen.

In the example above, in which Gasch addresses Mirko's performances, we see how mockery and humiliation, in effect, reaffirm the scheme with which Mora analyzes these films. However, it would be wrong to think that this was purely humiliating because, according to Gasch, in the end it is the artist who, responding in kind, has the audience in the palm of his hands; this feat is a response to the attitude of mockery that equalizes the relationship between artist and spectator, something Gasch comes to label as seductive.

One of the best examples in which a transvestite cabaret performer was greeted with social admiration is Johnson, another famous artist of the Molino, known to leave no doubt about his homosexuality onstage, with his masculine clothes and short hair juxtaposed against thick makeup and endless lashes. This juxtapositional style, as we noted with Mirko, created a character who passed masterfully between masculine and feminine. Gasch (1972: 173), in the space of a few sentences, moves from linking this characterization to the masculine and feminine identity, to once again embodying another male stereotype:

> The artist is wearing a tuxedo. We have already said it. But by art of *birlibirloque*, we find ourselves before a lady with an abundant bust and wasp waist, with a microscopic umbrella, dressed in satin and lace and feathers in her oversized hat. And thanks to the stimulus that the artist causes to our imagination, we find ourselves in front of a Don Juan with a top hat, a stiff and very tall collar, a cinnamon-colored coat somewhat longer than our jackets, a little stick and a monocle with a black ribbon.

The admiration for this character reached such a point that the Barcelona Wax Museum opened its doors in 1973 with a wax reproduction of Johnson. This figure was accompanied by others that made up the section "characters of the moment," which was combined with other thematic sections. The figure represented an implicit recognition at the important public level in an institution like a museum, and on one occasion his figure was apparently even mistaken for that of US President Lyndon B. Johnson.

This admiration for the performing transvestite could be found in spaces as publicly charged as a museum, in particular a wax museum, a must-see destination for the average tourist. But it was also found in other places with less cultural and social significance. The underground cartoonist Nazario (2016: 43), spectator and participant in the transition out of fascism in the Barcelona of the era, describes in his memoirs other, more shadowy types of places that were also traversed by an unexplained social hierarchy:

> In the middle of all those faggot bars, *Las Cuevas* was like a relic. An *old-fashioned drag queen*, as he said. But there was no need for anyone to say anything, because the ages of Juanito, the owner, and most of the artists exceeded the *critical ages*. That gloomy room was frequented by a quite heterogeneous public. . . . Sometimes whores would appear there accompanied by their pimps, small groups of gangster-looking men and some men who looked like tough Galician or Basque sailors who ended up drunk, chanting a song that some of the stars had reserved for such occasions. . . . The mature transvestites did not live fully in drag, but they

had their performances assured in that place, which placed them in a certain category halfway between the transvestite divas signed by Barcelona de Noche or
El Molino; the amateurs who performed their free performances on weekends
at the Dickens, the Breakwater or the EA3, and the *old glories* who exhibited
their decadence at the Bodega Bohemia.

It is quite likely that Nazario is describing a moment after the death of the dic-
tator, but it is still important because it reveals in the first place that transvestite
practices had a broad social framework. In the same way, this passage alludes to a
past yet to be narrated, one that has been denied in favor of an epic story that
excludes the *juanitos* and artists of "critical ages," not to mention local bars whose
presence in the discourse is nonexistent and whose disappearance through the
sieve of history is inevitable. The diversity of spaces and generations, of identities
and positions of Nazario's recollection, makes the violation of the norm in these
places precisely the norm.

In some cases, cabaret could become a refuge. Pierrot (2006), commen-
tator, writer, and participant in the scene, recalls in his *Memorias trans* an event in
which the protagonist was Madame Arthur, the famous Valladoid *travesti*, one
of the first to star in shows of this type. Apparently, after one of these numbers,
Madame Arthur had no time to change before rushing to a performance of a
colleague at another location. After being stopped on the way by the police,
Madame Arthur served three months in jail. This suggests that local shows and
cabaret were a safe haven because they suspended the rules that applied outside.
Being hunted from bar to bar without the right clothes could, however, lead
to jail.

The cabaret was a mixed and undefined space that seemed to suspend state
legislation, as well as the dominant sexual norms outside its doors. Cabarets were
spaces that harbored the desire to see and voyeuristically control, but they also
went on to influence renowned artists like Joan Brossa, Mestres Quadreny, and
Antoni Miralda (Estella and Rosón 2018). They were an informal but nevertheless
highly complex space, in which domination intersected with the will to survive,
a cocktail which could produce combinations that now seem impossible. It is
probably this constitutive ambiguity of the cabaret that has allowed it to be read
in one approach as a carefree space, as highlighted in *Varietés* (Doctor and Juan
Sánchez 2015). This book is not only dedicated to Alaska, the resident diva of
the Movida, but it is also the introductory text to more than two hundred photographs, in which we can read a defense of variety shows that looks down on the
effects of their lightheartedness: "Long live the frivolity, the light, the unimportant,
the capricious, and the ephemeral, that however illustrate many things about an
era and some artists who for whatever reason did not become what they dreamed
of" (12).

Siegfried Kracauer (2006: 257), speaking of shows in the Weimar Republic in his essential reference on the cabaret imaginary, indicates how phenomena that are banal in appearance are the ones that hide the most original essence of an era. No doubt this was the case with the cabaret of transvestites in the context of the 1960s and 1970s in Barcelona, a space showing the ambiguities of regulation, where both shame and its transformation into honor took hold in a way in which privacy acquired an essentially public dimension.

Iñaki Estella is a professor in the Department of Art History at the Complutense University of Madrid. Specializing in art from 1945 onward with a focus on intermediate art and performance practices, Estella is linked to Fluxus and its empresario and a practitioner of transvestism at the end of his life, George Maciunas. Estella's publications include *Fluxus* (2012), *George Maciunas: History, Bureaucracy, and Collectivity* (2020), *Llámalo Performance* (as coeditor, 2015), and the first four volumes of *Disagreements: On Art, Policies, and the Public Sphere in the Spanish State* (2004–7).

Acknowledgments

I would like to thank Sergio Ferrero's helpful assistance in obtaining the film stills for this essay.

Notes

1. To a large extent, it was his involvement in the research project "*Desacuerdos*: On Political Art and the Public Sphere" (MACBA 2004–7) that led to his rise when an interview of him appeared in the accompanying volumes of *Desacuerdos* (Carrillo: 2005). His presence in this project was expanded with a workshop that he organized at Arteleku in 2005. His relationship with the museum grew further when, between 2014 and 2015, he became jointly responsible for its research program. His exit from the museum was controversial, inappropriate, and related to the censorship of the exhibition *The Beast and the Sovereign*, which also resulted in the removal of the museum director. In 2017 he was the director of the public programs held in Athens and Kassel within the context of *Documenta 14*, the most important call for international contemporary art since the Second World War (Marzo: 2014).

2. In this regard, it is also interesting to consider the relevance that activism has had at MACBA, an institution that, as we have seen, has had a relationship with Preciado. This link can be traced even to 2000 with the workshop "De la acción directa como una de las bellas artes."

References

Aliaga, Juan Vicente. 2018. "El arte contaminante: Apuntes sobre Ocaña en el contexto artístico español." In *Ocaña: Voces, ecos y distorsiones*, edited by Rafael M. Mérida Jiménez, 15–32. Barcelona: Bellaterra.

Berzosa, Alberto. 2014. *Homoherejías fílmicas: Cine homosexual subversivo en España en los años setenta y ochenta*. Madrid: Brumaria.

Bufill, Joan. 1978. "Untitled." *Star*, no. 38: 62–66.

Butler, Judith. 2015. *Notes Toward a Performative Theory of Assambleism*. Cambridge, MA: Harvard University Press.

Carrillo, Jesús. 2005. "Entrevista Beatriz Preciado." In *Desacuerdos: Sobre arte, políticas y esfera pública en el Estado español*, edited by Jesús Carrillo, Iñaki Estella, and Lidia García Merás, 244–61. MACBA: Barcelona.

CCAG (Coordinadora de Collectius per l'Alliberament Gay). 1978. "Mesa redonda: Los travestís y los transexuales toman la palabra." *Pluma* 2: 9–12.

Chamouleau, Brice. 2017. *Tiran al maricón: Los fantasmas queer de la democracia (1970–1988)*. Madrid: Akal.

Doctor, Rafael, and Juan Sánchez. 2015. *Varietés*. Madrid: La Fábrica.

Estella, Iñaki, and María Rosón. 2018. "El cuerpo en la transición: Sexualidad, feminismo y el estríptis de Christa Leem." In *Arte y transición*, edited by Juan Albarrán, 133–56. Madrid: Brumaria.

Gasch, Sebastián. 1972. *Memorias de un sesentón*. Barcelona: Dopesa.

Kracauer, Siegfried. 2006. *Estética sin retorno*. Murcia: Colegio Oficial de Aparejadores y Arquitectos.

Labrador, Germán. 2017. *Culpables por la literatura: Imaginación política y contracultura en la transición española (1968–1986)*. Madrid: Akal.

López Rodríguez, Fernando. 2016. "Meter el dedo en la llaga: La fragilidad en el baile flamenco." *Daimon: Revista internacional de filosofía*, suppl. 5: 279–85.

Marzo, Jorge Luis. 2014. "La exposición *La bestia y el soberano* en el MACBA: Crónica de un cortocircuitos anunciado." *Anuario del Departamento de Historia y Teoría del Arte* 26: 11–20.

Melero, Alejandro. 2014. "Representación de la homosexualidad en el cine de la dictadura franquista." *Zer* 19, no 36: 189–204.

Mérida Jiménez, Rafael. 2016. *Transbarcelonas: Cultura, género y sexualidad en la España del siglo XX*. Barcelona: Bellaterra.

Mérida Jiménez, Rafael. 2018. "Las mil y una noches de Ocaña." In *Ocaña: Voces, ecos y distorsiones*, edited by Rafael Mérida Jiménez, 9–14. Barcelona: Bellaterra.

Mira, Alberto. 2004. *De Sodoma a Chueca: Una historia cultural de la homosexualidad en España en el siglo XX*. Madrid: Egales.

Mora, Víctor. 2015. "La popularización del arquetipo homosexual en la comedia cinematográfica del tardofranquismo." *Dossiers Feministes*, no. 20: 337–51.

Navarro, Alicia. 2014. "Oh *La criolla*, sitio flamenco, lumpen y canalla." *Encendiendo la mecha* (blog), March 26. pieflamenco.com/oh-la-criolla-sitio-flamenco-lumpen-y-canalla/.

Nazario. 2016. *La vida cotidiana del dibujante underground*. Barcelona: Anagrama.

Picornell, Mercé. 2010. "¿De una España viril a una España travestí? Transgresión transgénero y subversión del poder franquista en la transición española hacia la democracia." *Feminismos*, no. 16: 281–304.

Pierrot. 2006. "Memorias trans 2°. Diario digital transexual." carlaantonelli.com/memorias-trans2 -7.htm.

Platero, R. Lucas. 2015. *Por un chato de vino: Historia de travestismo y masculinidad femenina*. Barcelona: Bellaterra.

Preciado, Paul B. 2011. "La Ocaña que nos merecemos: Campceptualismos, subalternidad y políticas performativas." In *Ocaña, 1973–1983: Acciones, actuaciones, activismo*, edited by Pedro G. Romero, 13–33. Barcelona: Institut de Cultura and Palau de la Virreina.

Rosón, María. 2016. *Género, memoria y cultura visual en el primer franquismo*. Madrid: Cátedra.

Scott, James. 2003. *Los dominados y el arte de la resistencia*. Navarra: Txalaparta.

Subrat, Piro. 2019. *Invertidos y rompepatrias: Marxismo, anarquismo y desobediencia sexual y de género en el Estado español (1868–1982)*. Madrid: Editorial Imperdible.

Warner, Michael. 2008. *Públicos y contrapúblicos*. Barcelona: MACBA.

Warner, Michael. 2012. *Públicos y contrapúblicos*. Mexico City: Fondo de Cultura Económica.

Mariela Muñoz

Citizenship, Motherhood, and Transsexual Politics in Argentina (1943–2017)

PATRICIO SIMONETTO and JOHANA KUNIN

Abstract Mariela Muñoz became the first transsexual widely socially recognized as a mother in Argentina. She emerged as a leading figure during her struggle to recover legal custody of three of her children, which had been previously annulled by a judge. Moreover, in 1997 she became the first transsexual recognized as a woman by the state. This text analyzes the making of Mariela Muñoz's motherhood repertoires to redefine political, social, and intimate citizenship. It argues that her politics were paradoxical, in that she appealed to traditional meanings of womanhood such as fulfilment through motherhood and the duty of care for others. On the other hand, these uses of key cultural symbols displaced the imagined margins for *travestis* and *transexuales* and helped her enjoy popular support.

Keywords transsexual, motherhood, kinship, citizenship, Argentina

I t's August 1993. Outside a police station, fifty people wait in support of their friend and neighbor. It's been a month since Mariela Muñoz was imprisoned, accused of child abduction and forgery. She is the mother of seventeen foster children that adopted her as their mother.[1] Suddenly, Mariela leaves the building and joins the crowd. A cameraman push through them to get a clear shot of the first well-known Argentine transsexual mother. Mariela hugs one of her elder daughters and her grandson, and presents them to the TV cameras: "Here is my family." Mariela is covered in tears, she cannot stop crying. The journalist asks her how it feels to be free, and she replies, "I am happy because I am a lady, a mother and a grandmother. I am thankful for everyone who supports me" (Muñoz 1993a).

Mariela Muñoz became the first transsexual widely socially recognized as a mother in Argentina.[2] She emerged as a national leading figure during her struggle to recover legal custody of three of her children, which had been previously annulled by a judge. Moreover, in 1997 she became the first transsexual recognized as a woman by the state.

TSQ: Transgender Studies Quarterly * Volume 8, Number 4 * November 2021 **516**
DOI 10.1215/23289252-9311102 © 2021 Duke University Press

This text analyzes the making of Mariela Muñoz's motherhood repertoires to redefine political, social, and intimate citizenship.[3] By establishing connections with maternal discourses and practices as a key axis of female citizenship in Argentina, we show how her maternal politics challenged the cis-straight-male neoliberal project, creating paths for social recognition for transsexual people.

We argue that, as local and regional accounts of mothering and maternity in Argentina carried much symbolic weight, Mariela's maternal politics socially legitimized her as a *transsexual* citizen on a broad scale. Her politics were paradoxical. On the one hand, she appealed to traditional meanings of womanhood such as fulfilment through motherhood and the duty of care for others. On the other hand, these uses of key cultural symbols displaced the imagined margins for transsexuals and helped her enjoy popular support. By placing herself in the cultural core of womanhood, Mariela achieved rights such as social recognition as a mother and a woman. Her politicization of care was also a criticism of the neoliberal patriarchal project in that she claimed to protect children abandoned by the state. However, her use of these cultural symbols also may have echoed conservative discourses that rejected abortion and socially sanctioned biological "bad mothers."

This article dialogues with the literature on kinship, politics, and cis-heteronormativity. It remarks how trans* kinship challenges the relationships between nature and social roles (Fernández Romero 2020; Platero Méndez and Ortega Arjonilla 2017). Recent literature has studied gay and lesbian homo-parenting (Biblarz and Savci 2010); trans-parenting and queer mothering practices (Manning et al. 2015); and multiparent families (Gibson 2014). The few existing studies on trans-parenting usually focus on technologically assisted reproduction as a main entry point to this area of study (James-Abra et al. 2015; Israel 2005). This emphasis on biological reproduction can be explained by the greater access to these procedures in the global North, in contrast to the long history of informal circuits of child fostering practices in Latin America, that is to say the practices of circulating children to be raised by non-biogenetic parents, linked to the question of mutual-help networks (Fonseca 2002; Bowie 2004), and to the community-based maternal practices of the travesti and transsexual community in Argentina (Wayar 2020). Muñoz's story contributes to rethinking this field by looking into repertoires of kinship production and into the cultural meanings of trans-parenting* that go beyond biological reproduction.

The study of Muñoz's struggle also helps reconceptualize feminist perspectives. It challenges the limits of cis-gendered and antimaternal feminisms by showing how agendas that were initially considered conservative could lead to social transformation. It demonstrates that, even guided by traditional repertoires and without a long-term political strategy, widely visible intimate politics in specific times have shifted normative boundaries. Moreover, this political struggle highlights how a central cultural symbol such as motherhood can be appropriated by social agents as unexpected as transsexuals and can create potent identifications to try to break through the cis-heterosexual regime.

This article is organized in three sections. First, a brief biography of Mariela Muñoz is introduced. Second, we analyze the symbolic power of motherhood as a driving force for women's agency in Argentina and as a hallmark of Mariela's politics. Third, it describes Muñoz's maternal political repertoires in the remaking of citizenship.

A Brief Biography of Mariela Muñoz

Mariela Muñoz was born in Lules, Tucumán, in 1943.[4] She grew up in a rural, poor working-class family who worked in the sugarcane harvest. Like many others, her family migrated to work in the emerging industries. They moved to Quilmes, an industrial suburb in the Buenos Aires metropolitan area, where her father became a cook in a textile factory.

In 1958 she renamed herself Mariela. In the beginning, her parents tried to "correct" her manhood by taking her to doctors and brothels. Nonetheless, after several attempts, her father decided to raise her as Mariela.

As a teenager, she was responsible for taking care of her six siblings and worked as a babysitter. When she was sixteen, she became a fortune teller and read tarot cards. Some years later, she founded an informal social shelter for children and single mothers. She created an extended family of twenty-three children and several grandchildren, many of whom came, like her, from Argentina's poor northern provinces in a quest for a better life and ended up living in the poor suburban neighborhoods of Buenos Aires.

In 1981, like other transsexuals who tried to circumvent the Argentine legal prohibition of genitalia-related surgeries, she traveled to Chile to have gender-affirmation surgery. There she had her ID forged. She also married her partner Jorge, a bricklayer.

Mariela was legally recognized as a male citizen; consequently, she was unable to legally adopt.[5] To achieve her desire to become a mother with Jorge, she made an arrangement with two poor women who were pregnant. She promised them that if they did not have an abortion, she would raise their children. Both the mother of twins and, some time later, the mother of a little girl registered themselves at the hospital with Mariela's forged documents, which made Mariela their legal mother. In 1993 the mother of the girl accused her of abduction and document forgery. Judge Pedro Entío ordered the imprisonment of Mariela and her husband, their children were taken from them, and the children's birth certificates were annulled. Mariela was sentenced to one year in prison. She started a long struggle, which garnered international recognition. In 1995 she appeared before the International Tribunal on Human Rights Violations against Sexual Minorities (ILGHRD and CUAV 1995) in New York where she stated: "[The little girl's] mother started to blackmail me. First she demanded money. Then a lot and a house. She threatened to abuse me. When I bought a car for the kids, she demanded it in exchange for the girl. When I refused, she reported me to the police. . . . I was arrested and taken to the police station . . . the next morning, the police took away Maira and the two twins." Although Mariela won social popularity, the children were never returned to her custody.

However, Mariela never gave up and kept fighting other battles. In 1997, after years of legal struggle, a judge gave an order to rectify Mariela's birth certificate, recognizing her gender as female. That same year Mariela announced her participation in the primary election of the Justicialist Party,[6] but after her house was attacked by gunfire, she gave up her candidacy. Mariela continued participating in politics and in the media. She was an advisor for the National Institute against Discrimination. She spent her last days in the home of one of her sons, and after several strokes, she died in 2017.

Motherhood and Citizenship in Argentina

There were many historical moments when the agency of Argentine women was focused on maternalist repertoires, which placed them as leading actors who did not necessarily aspire for the subversion of gender norms. Thanks to strategic maternalisms, women made political gains while achieving visibility and certain degrees of legitimacy, like Mariela.

In Argentina since the nineteenth century, cis-women were challenged to exercise patriotic motherhood by providing virtuous citizens to the nation (Di Liscia 2008). Although motherhood has been linked to female subordination, maternity was politicized and used as a central argument in the demand for women's rights. At the turn of the twentieth century, Argentine feminists appealed to a supposed "feminine nature" to demand that the obligation to reproduce the species should have as a counterpart the recognition of rights. They reformulated femininity and motherhood within the ideology of their complementarity and equivalence (or superiority) with respect to men (Nari 2004). Moreover, they claimed that cis-women mothers would radically transform politics and society by introducing maternal thought and morality that made them superior to men. Both self-sacrifice, which implied care for others—mainly "those most in need" such as the elderly, children, cis-women, and workers—and the ethics of responsibility, which had previously been based in the private sphere, were extended to the public arena (Biernat and Ramacciotti 2013).

Argentina's history has several examples of female agency and conservative sexual division of labor coexisting. During Peronism, María Eva Duarte de Perón

(Evita) exalted female participation by forging an impressive mobilization of cis-women to rally support for her husband's government. Cis-women's suffrage, so strongly sought by socialist feminists, was achieved by Peronism in 1947. The government promoted women's work as an option to contribute to the family's economy, without neglecting their supposed maternal and conjugal responsibilities (Barrancos 2010).

The state terrorism imposed between 1976 and 1983 meant the forced disappearance of thousands of militants, torture, prison, sexual abuse, forced exile, and child appropriation. In this context, the Mothers of Plaza de Mayo questioned the government about the whereabouts of their children and other family members and became an extraordinary civil force (D'Antonio 2018). Appealing to blood ties as a guiding principle of collectivity, they have struggled for the recognition of their demands during and after the last Argentine military dictatorship. Even if their collective action was born from the sexual division of labor (caring for their children), their actions broke that same division: they left the domestic sphere and confronted the de facto rulers. They took back the maternal values that the state urged them to practice in their private lives and brought them into the political sphere (Zarco 2011).

Motherhood politics and contentious actions deployed by the relatives of the victims were consolidated as key cultural symbols of social movements in postdictatorial democracy. While policymakers still imagined the mother-child bond as the target of the increasingly scarce social policies due to the neoliberal agenda, mothers emerged as public figures of street protests and civil society (Adair 2019). Repertoires of motherhood have legitimized cis-women's voices and demands for food assistance, subsidies, and housing. They have also become a platform for protest and for making cis-women's needs visible in relation to their situation of material poverty. However, this voice usually becomes legitimate only when it is compatible with the forms of femininity accepted by state social programs.

Between the neoliberal heyday of the 1990s and its consequential crisis in the early 2000s, mothers became public actors in social movements such as those in the workers' takenovered factories and the unemployed workers' movement (*piqueteros*).[7] Their political discourse was articulated around the need to defend the factories and their families, "since taking care of the factory is taking care of their children" (Álvarez and Partenio 2010)

Since the 1980s, the gay, lesbian, feminist, and travesti movements participated in the reshaping of postdictatorship citizenship. These movements struggled against the legal codes that since the 1930s empowered policemen to deploy violent practices against sexual dissidents during both civil and military governments. In the 1990s gay movements such as the Argentine Homosexual

Community and Gays for Civil Rights (1991–96) employed the language of familism to face the material consequences of HIV/AIDS by proposing a civil union bill (Bellucci 2010).

Family-oriented and maternal discourses were an important source of not only public power but also community care practices. "Travestis motherhood" was an extended practice in northern Argentina. It involved an alternative construction of bonds and kinship to achieve shelter and care that was initially neglected by travestis' nuclear families (Wayar 2020). They bonded through shared experiences such as migration, rejection, police violence, poverty, and sex work (Berkins et al. 2015). Travesti/trans* kinship has been conceptualized as a project of care that contrasted with cis-heterosexual violence (Wayar 2020). Even if new conceptualizations of travesti motherhood emerged in the last decades, the efficacy of Mariela's discourse survived. In 2013 Florencia de la V, a famous trans* TV actress and host, answered the critics of a conservative journalist who accused her of not being a woman, holding her ID and breaking into tears while she presented herself as a "proud Argentine woman and mother" (Florencia de la V 2013)—just like Mariela two decades before.

Mariela Muñoz's Repertoires of Motherhood and the Remaking of Citizenship

The court's involvement forced Muñoz to begin a public struggle as a mother in a difficult scenario for travestis and transsexuals. They have suffered from long-term violence such as police persecution and social exclusion. Still today their life expectancy is only thirty-five years (Berkins et al. 2015). Their daily life was tough, and they could be stopped by a police officer while out for groceries and be accused of being scandalous in the street, or just for being dressed in clothes "contrary to their sex." One of the most important leaders of the travesti/trans* movement in Argentina, Lohana Berkins (2003: 65), described this life as a "daily stage of siege."

Within this context, Mariela deployed a public political maternalism that inscribed her transsexual experience in the discourse of familism. On TV Mariela presented herself as a "symbol of Argentine mothers," creating a link with social and political discourses that highly appreciated motherhood.

Although Mariela lost custody of the children, she was able to win a level of grassroot support that was unprecedented in times of conservative neoliberal politics. As a TV journalist expressed in 1993: "Mariela has won the support of the majority of society. It is not clear if these displays of affection come because there is more respect for the transsexuals or if it is Mariela's maternal instinct. The truth is that she is popular, her neighbors gave her their support, and they even composed a song for her" (in Muñoz 1993b).[8] Mariela articulated the paradoxical meanings of motherhood to inscribe herself in social, valorized notions of womanhood related to caregiving. If the Argentine state tried to prevent children's informal fostering practices (Pérez 2020) through the reinforcement of the biological mother's caring role, Mariela took advantage of the social association between motherhood and womanhood to get support for a different type of family, one not based on biological ties. She sutured her condition as a mother with her woman embodiment, pushing beyond what was considered the biological limits of gender and kinship.

We recognize seven principal practices of her maternal repertoire: 1) pointing out the care of her foster children; 2) shading her sexuality; 3) marking her desired motherhood, 4) performing emotionally charged agency; 5) emphasizing motherhood as a condition for being a woman; 6) taking motherhood beyond the feminist, lesbian, and gay agenda; and, finally, 7) transforming motherhood into a metaphor of social policies to critique the neoliberal project. First, her primary practice was highlighting the care she provided for her children. Mariela referred to care as an innate duty of women and mothers, an idea that she would express throughout her life. "My children are my best lawyers"—Mariela would repeat to exalt her parenting skills—"I had been a good mother: they turned out to be good and honest men and women" (ILGHRD and CUAV 1995). Mercedes, who lived with Mariela since she was four years old until she was eighteen, said: "She is a great mother, she treats us so well, she gave us all she could, she forced us to study, she has taught us to respect and to be respected" (in Muñoz 1993b). In 1997 she said on TV, "I am proud to have been raised by Mariela. I also have my biological mother, but I have a better relationship with Mariela" (in Muñoz 1997). Enrique Sanchez was born in the province of Chaco, worked in a brick factory since he was nine years old, and migrated to Buenos Aires to escape poverty. Raised by Mariela, he later said, "I see Mariela as a woman, and I will continue seeing her like that, as a mother" (in Muñoz 1993b).

It is difficult to find stories that deny that Mariela was what was considered a "good mother." A police report states that "the children were raised excellently and there are several proofs that the couple loved them."[9] The social approval was due to the confluence between parenting practices related to education and moral norms: the fact that her children were straight, employed, working-class people and had their own families helped legitimize her motherhood. While Mariela was pushing the norm of motherhood beyond biology, she was at the same time affirming its conservative dimensions—the price she had to pay to be recognized as a woman and a mother.

Second, Mariela publicly deemphasized her sexuality to embody what was expected from a mother. In several interviews she repeated, "When I had to choose between my children and a man, I chose my children" (ILGHRD and CUAV 1995), as a mechanism to distinguish herself from the press's sexualization of transsexuals' bodies. In contrast with the exultant figures of travestis, Mariela's modest clothes erased the eroticism from her body by covering breasts and legs, her appearance converging with what the public expected from a mother.

This distinction allowed her to break down narratives that mocked trans-sexuals and to create narratives far from sex work, revues, and police stations. Her performance allowed her to be recognized as a female, a rare accomplishment for many transsexuals (Audras 2016). Mariela questioned the press for calling her a "travesti mother" and for accusing her of being involved in international child trafficking. She stated, "The Argentinean public was not fooled, I received empathy from everyone. I became the symbol of Argentinean motherhood" (ILGHRD and CUAV 1995).

Mariela refused to reduce her life to her sexuality: she embodied the fig-ure of the mother as a nonsexual subject. When asked by journalists about her life before the gender-affirmation surgery, she defined herself as a virgin: "I did not know how I could have pleasure. I have never had sex before. My husband was my first man" (Muñoz 1993b). Mariela's invoking of the virginal body consti-tuted a reappropriation of the Catholic idea of immaculate conception. Her vir-ginal body interacted with cultural icons such as the virgin of Lujan, whose figure represents Argentine nationhood and is revered in public celebrations. It was also linked to other maternal figures with no mediation of biological reproduction, such as Evita, whose rhetoric elevated her as the mother of the workers and of those in need.

Third, Mariela distinguished herself from the biological mothers of her children by emphasizing her maternal desire. Her explanation about the arrange-ment with their biological mothers pointed out that she helped them to avoid an abortion. She said, "I met a woman who was pregnant and did not want children. I asked her not to have an abortion. She in turn asked me to take care of her baby after birth. Another pregnant woman who did not want children allowed me to adopt her twin babies. She gave birth in a hospital where she was registered under my name" (ILGHRD and CUAV 1995).

Abortion has been restricted in Argentina until 2020. It is estimated that 450,000 abortions were performed in Argentina in clandestine clinics or by people with no medical training, causing hundreds of deaths (Amnesty International Argentina 2018). Several testimonies show that people considered Mariela's par-enting a better option than abortion, as one of her neighbors declared, "I ques-tioned myself, if it was better to have these children aborted before birth or to have Mariela raise them" (in Muñoz 1993b). Even if Mariela never expressed opposi-tion to abortion, her use of its social rejection helped her win a wide range of popular support. In 1993 a journalist noticed that even if some priests spoke in public against Muñoz, a lot of Catholics valued her duty as a mother (in Muñoz

1993b). By performing a "good mother," Mariela created a strong identification with a wider public; however, this performance was accompanied by an unwanted though effective demonization of her children's biological mothers, who were portrayed as "bad mothers," and by her "heroic" avoidance of abortion. This may have been the reason she was not especially supported by Argentine feminists. Moreover, the complete absence of the media's discourses about biological fathers highlights the naturalization of the maternal "duty" of women to raise their children. In 1993 Mariela was invited to appear on the famous TV talk show *Almorzando con Mirtha Legrand*, whose host was an icon of the Argentine neoliberal and conservative era. Mirtha Legrand openly supported her: "She always surprises me, because when you think of gays, travestis [you think of] people with irregular lives. [But] this woman has dedicated herself to take care of children, to educate them, to feed them, and it is admirable" (in Muñoz 1993a). In contrast with narratives focused on transsexual sexuality, some journalists and a wider public expressed empathy for Mariela's maternal calling (Giberti 1997). The same year on TV, a psychologist stated that Mariela was a mother because "she adopted her children, it is not enough to give birth, you have to choose them" (in Muñoz 1997).

Fourth, Muñoz performed emotionally charged motherhood repertoires. In 1993, as Mariela left the police station breaking into tears, a journalist asked her, "The cry of a mother?" (in Muñoz 1993c). Mariela cried a lot in public, and every time she spoke about her children she became visibly overwhelmed. Rafael Fredda, former president of SIGLA (Society of the Integration of Gays and Lesbians in Argentina) remembers that at the beginning he thought it was a strategy she used to gain respect as a mother. However, when he became her friend, he noticed that there was an expression of "true feeling."[10] Even if crying was a valuable practice, it was a symptom of her suffering expressed by an expected body language to be performed in public by women. In the negotiation of Mariela's motherhood, crying was understood as a way of showing her "real love for the children" (in Muñoz 1993b).

In contrast with the alleged male rationality, women's complaints have been represented as emotional and inevitably guided by "maternal love." In 1993 Mariela wrote a letter from jail: "I want to express my anguish because they have taken my children away from my arms, knowing that I can't provide them with the love they need. I want you to understand my feelings as a woman and a mother" (*El popular* 1993). By highlighting sadness, love, pain, and crying, she publicly reaffirmed her bond with her children. Moreover, the metaphor of the theft from her arms activated the image of child appropriations denounced by the Mothers of Plaza de Mayo.

Fifth, she created a chain of meanings in which womanhood was expressed by becoming a mother. As the relationship between womanhood and motherhood was at the core of Argentine gender culture, Mariela's social acknowledgment as a mother helped her achieve a broader recognition as a transsexual woman. Muñoz was the first transsexual to get legal recognition of her self-perceived gender. While the judge's decision was based on the constitutional ban on discrimination, Mariela's popularity was decisive. After this recognition, different journalists valued Mariela's attitude as a "good woman" and "mother." When Mariela visited Legrand's TV Show, the host held Mariela's national identity document and said, "This is amazing, it is a revolution. Congratulations, here you have the document where it says that you are a lady" (in Muñoz 2000). Mariela's recognition on national TV as a lady by the national icon of traditional upper-class conservative femininity was a starting point to imagine a potential new citizenship that could integrate transsexual experience under normative rules.

Mariela had a long path affirming her gender. In 1981 Mariela traveled to Chile to obtain gender-affirmation surgery, a practice that was forbidden in Argentina.[11] However, coming back after the change was difficult. Several attempts to get her identity documents to reflect her gender-affirmation surgery were denied. Mariela presented herself as a woman and downplayed her trans-sexual identity. When she described her relationship with her husband and children, she insisted that she did not tell them about her being a transsexual before pursuing the surgery. Mariela popularized the theory of the "incorrect body," a mainstream narrative in the 1990s and early 2000s with which some transsexuals legitimated their demands for gender-affirmation treatments (Wayar 2020). As one of her neighbors declared, "She is a woman in the body of a man. A small piece of meat does not define her sex" (in Muñoz 1993b).

In 1997 a court ordered the state to rectify Mariela's birth certificate to recognize her gender as female, on the basis that the state could not violate the constitutional principle that banned discrimination. Mariela's petition was part of a wider strategy of transsexuals and travestis that included organizing demon-strations and presenting lawsuits demanding access to surgery and modification of legal documents. Muñoz, along with other activists, cleared the way for a long struggle of the Argentine trans* movement that in 2012 achieved the enactment of the Gender Identity Law, which recognizes self-perceived gender and mandates private and public health systems to provide free gender-affirmation treatments (Theumer 2020).

Sixth, Mariela took motherhood beyond the feminist, lesbian, and gay agenda, although she created tensions with part of this agenda. On the one hand, Mariela's case was at odds with the denaturalization of women's role as caregivers, as promoted by lesbian and feminist movements. On the other hand, Mariela's story was closer to the gay movement's familist rhetoric in its quest for civil union recognition (Vespucci 2014). In contrast to the traditional press, lesbian, gay, and feminist publications gave scarce visibility to Mariela's struggle.[12] Fredda high-lighted that some of the leaders felt uncomfortable with Muñoz's discourse and insisted that she changed it.[13] Maria Luisa Peralta, who participated in Lesbianas a la Vista (Visible Lesbians) since 1996, remembers, "In the 1990s, motherhood was not a popular topic among feminist groups. Lesbians had an agenda for those who had sons and daughters of their previous straight marriages, they were at risk of losing their children for being lesbians. But the topic of lesbian motherhood [that also implied adoptive mothers like Mariela] did not emerge until the end of the decade."[14]

Travestis and transsexuals faced several obstacles in their quest to be included in lesbian and gay politics, as some of the latter believed that the presence of the former would delegitimize their goal of inclusion in the wider society. Lohana Berkins (2003: 61) described how they had to fight for their visibility. Although the travestis and transsexuals contributed money for demonstrations, some refused to name them on pamphlets and banners.[15]

In 1996 SIGLAS's newspaper highlighted the difficulties of working with Mariela in light of the "debates between travestis, transsexuals and feminists."[16] As Berkins expressed, some cisgender feminists refused to recognize the travesti movement and forbade their participation in the National Women's Gathering.[17] Moreover, Peralta remembers that Mariela did not have a feminist perspective about gender roles; she was considered "quite traditional for publicly advocating for women's fulfilment through motherhood."[18] Even if some lesbians supported her, Mariela's agenda was considered a threat to their quest for the right to access legal abortions.

Finally, Mariela's participation in traditional party politics transformed her struggle to perform motherhood into a metaphor for social justice and a criticism of the neoliberal project. In 1997 she became the first transsexual candidate to run in an election by participating in the Peronist primaries as a contender of the official candidate Hilda Beatriz González "Chiche" Duhalde, a conservative Peronist woman who created a system of social policies based on women's participation during the 1990s.

Mariela challenged the Peronist establishment in the context of a party leading the neoliberal project. After two administrations, the Peronist Carlos Menem deeply transformed Argentina: he disassembled the social state, promoted the deindustrialization, privatized state-owned companies, and created macroeconomic policies that tied Argentina's currency to the US dollar. Under the United States' influence, the government became a global example of neoliberalism by reaching new economic heights and promoting financial stability. However, the collateral effects of these politics created a crisis: in 1995 unemployment was 18 percent, and poverty quickly increased to 50 percent of the country's population (Masson 2004).

Mariela stated, "I only agree with stability, but there are several social inequalities" (*Crónica* 1997a). She appropriated Peronist narratives by highlighting that she wanted to "continue with the example of Eva Perón, my idol. I want to do something for the people that need me. I have always been supportive, I have raised seventeen children and that too is social policy" (*Crónica* 1997a). Her reference to Evita as an icon of social justice was again in line with her paradigm of women's responsibilities for the care of those most in need, in this case as the "female face" of the state. Mariela performed her motherhood as a symbol of the failures of the male economic regime: taking care of abandoned children and mothers without any social protection (Biernat and Ramacciotti 2013). After Mariela criticized the irregular conditions in which the primaries were taking place, her house was attacked by gunfire. She then decided to give up her candidacy (*Crónica* 1997b). She continued participating in politics, running again as a candidate for parliament in the 2000s, but never succeeded. Even if her participation was not the main factor for the transformation of citizenship, Mariela's transsexual politics, and her uses of maternity and caregiving in the frame of the neoliberal regime's crisis, helped pave the way for the future emergence of travesti and transsexual rights.

★   ★   ★

Mariela Muñoz's struggle for social recognition as a mother and woman faced the daily marginalization of poverty and cis-sexism. By deploying a wide maternal political repertoire, giving political value to care and amplifying the margins for transsexual social recognition, she participated in redefining intimate citizenship. Mariela's maternal citizenship paradoxically combined traditional notions of womanhood—such as fulfilment through motherhood—with the expansion of socially accepted boundaries for travestis and transsexuals. Through her agenda, she criticized the male-dominated neoliberal project by valorizing care as social politics while at the same time channeling the popular rejection of abortion.

Her trajectory defied the limits of cis-gendered and antimaternal feminisms and showed how demands that could be initially considered conservative can lead to unexpected public support and legitimation of a marginalized community. Mariela was not, then, necessarily the victim of patriarchal rule but a political subject with agency that fought for her rights. She struggled to create a new horizon in the frame of a very conservative society in which transphobia and discrimination were, and still are, prevalent.

Mariela's story, unlike many studies of care, is evidence that caring or mothering does not necessarily hinder women's possibilities. Mariela's maternalist and caregiving repertoires are alternatives within the local symbolic limits of what is intelligible and possible. Those repertoires have political validity and force, not because the feminization of care or maternalism in any of its forms are natural, but precisely because that is how they are perceived. Therein lies their power. Their agency cannot be noticed unless it is based on situated knowledge and in nonmetropolitan-centric views or academic or political desires of Northern feminisms.

Patricio Simonetto has a PhD in social and human sciences from Quilmes University (Argentina). He holds a Marie Skłodowska-Curie Individual Fellowship at the Institute of the Americas, University College London. He is a research assistant at the National Council of Scientific and Technical Research (Argentina). He specializes in the social history and culture of sexuality in Latin America and is the author of *Money Is Not Everything: The Purchase and Sale of Sex in Argentina in the Twentieth Century* (2022); *El dinero no es todo: La compra y venta de sexo en la Argentina del siglo XX* (2019), and *Entre la injuria y la revolución: El Frente de Liberación Homosexual en la Argentina* (2017).

Johana Kunin has a PhD in social anthropology from École des Hautes Études en Sciences Sociales, France, and from the Advanced Social Studies School, San Martin National University, Argentina. She is a CONICET Postdoctoral Fellow. She researches the relationship of environment, care, and gender in pesticide-based agricultural production in the Argentine Pampas. She is a social anthropology lecturer at IDAES/UNSAM and coordinator of the Situated Motherhoods and Motherings Study Circle at UNSAM.

Acknowledgments

We are thankful for the contributions of Thomas Shalloe, Maria Audras, María Luisa Peralta, and Rafael Fredda. This research is funded by the MSCA project 886496.

Notes

1. In 1993 Mariela fostered seventeen children, but she raised twenty-three in total until her death.
2. Mariela Muñoz defined herself as a transsexual woman. Beyond its use as a medical term since 1949, *transsexual* was used in Argentina to define people who accessed biotechnological procedures to affirm their gender beyond the one assigned to them at birth. During the 1990s, transsexual became a political identity that defined those who argued that they were trapped in the "wrong body" and articulated a wider demand for state recognition and access to gender-affirmation surgeries, which were banned in Argentina. Transsexuals distinguished themselves from *travestis*, a political and social identity that designated a wider group of people who didn't adjust themselves to the male/female binary and usually did not undergo genital gender-affirmation surgeries.
3. Here we address the notion of "intimate citizenship" to examine rights, obligations, recognitions, and respect around those most intimate spheres of life (Plummer 2011).
4. Lules is a town in northwestern Argentina that in 1947 registered twelve thousand citizens.

5. Argentina has allowed child adoption regardless of the adopter's sexual orientation or gender identity since 2010, after the sanction of the equal marriage law.

6. The Partido Justicialista (PJ) is the political party that represents the ideas of Juan Domingo Perón's governments (1945–51; 1951–55; 1973–74), also known as "Peronism."

7. In the early 2000s, in response to workplace closures, a wave of workers factory takeovers occurred in Argentina. Workers occupied factories and created cooperatives under their management.

8. We translated the TV show transcriptions.

9. Intelligence Police Department of Buenos Aires Province (DIPBA), Mesa DS, no. 35333, 1993.

10. Rafael Fredda, pers. comm., July 27, 2020.

11. In 1944 decree no. 6216 prohibited any intervention that led to women's sterilization without considering any treatment to conserve reproductive organs. Another law, passed in 1967, explicitly stated that it was forbidden to practice any surgery that modified the "sick's sex, except ones allowed by a justice authorization" (Farji Neer 2017).

12. Gays for Civil Rights (GAYDC) and the Society for Lesbian and Gay Integration in Argentina (SIGLA) gave explicit support in their magazines. See Gauna 1993.

13. Rafael Fredda, pers. comm., July 27, 2020.

14. Maria Luisa Peralta, pers. comm., August 20, 2020.

15. In 1995, after three demonstrations, the pride demonstration changed its name to "Gay, Lesbian, Travesti, Transsexual, and Bisexual" in recognition of their participation (Alvarez 2019).

16. Rafael Fredda and Fotografía Alejandro Correo, "Organizaciones," NX, no. 31, 1996, p. 28+, archives of Sexuality and Gender, Buenos Aires.

17. The *Encuentro Nacional de Mujeres* or National Women's Gathering convenes thousands of women annually since 1985. The meeting rotates locations throughout Argentina every year, and participants usually save up and fundraise to attend.

18. Maria Luisa Peralta, pers. comm., August 20, 2020.

References

Adair, Jennifer. 2019. *In Search of the Lost Decade: Everyday Rights in Post-dictatorship Argentina.* Oakland: University of California Press.

Álvarez, María Inés Fernández, and Florencia Partenio. 2010. "Empresas recuperadas en Argentina: Producciones, espacios y tiempos de género." *Tabula rasa*, no. 12: 119–35.

Amnesty International Argentina. 2018. *Aportes al debate sobre derechos sexuales y reproductivos.* amnistia.org.ar/wp-content/uploads/delightful-downloads/2016/09/Medici%C3%B3n-de-abortos-Clandestinos.pdf.

Audras, M. 2016. *Amor a paso gigante.* Argentina-France. Independent production.

Barrancos, Dora. 2010. "Mujeres en la Argentina: Un balance frente al Bicentenario." *Revista de trabajo* 6, no. 8: 323–31.

Bellucci, Mabel. 2010. *Orgullo: Carlos Jáuregui, una biografía política.* Buenos Aires: Emecé.

Berkins, Lohana. 2003. "Un itinerario político del travestismo." In *Sexualidades Migrantes: Género y Transgénero*, edited by Diana Maffía, 59–68. Buenos Aires: Scarlett.

Berkins, Lohana, Renata Hiller, Aluminé Moreno, and Ana Mallimaci. 2015. *Cumbia, copeteo y lágrimas: Informe nacional sobre la situación de las travestis, transexuales y transgéneros.* Buenos Aires: Ediciones Madres de Plaza de Mayo.

Biblarz, Timothy J., and Evren Savci. 2010. "Lesbian, Gay, Bisexual, and Transgender Families." *Journal of Marriage and Family* 72, no. 3: 480–97.

Biernat, Carolina, and Karina Inés Ramacciotti. 2013. *Crecer y multiplicarse: La política sanitaria materno-infantil. Argentina 1900–1960.* Buenos Aires: Biblos.

Crónica. 1997a. "Mariela Muñoz candidata." June 24.

Crónica. 1997b. "Mariela Muñoz se retira de la elección." July 25.

D'Antonio, Débora. 2018. "Redes de denuncias políticas y jurídicas por violaciones a los derechos humanos en el plano internacional: El rol de las Madres de Plaza de Mayo (Argentina, 1976–1983)." *Travesía: Revista de historia económica y social* 20, no. 2: 15–44.

Di Liscia, María Herminia Beatriz. 2008. "Mujeres en los movimientos sociales en Argentina: un balance del último siglo." *Cadernos de estudos Latino-Americanos,* no. 6: 141–80.

El popular. 1993. "Madre transsexual." May 24.

Farji Neer, Anahí. 2017. *Travestismo, transexualidad y trasgeneridad en los discursos del Estado Argentino: Desde los edictos policiales hasta la ley de identidad de género.* Buenos Aires: Teseo.

Fernández Romero, Francisco. 2020. "'We Can Conceive Another History': Trans Activism around Abortion Rights in Argentina." *International Journal of Transgender Health* 22, nos. 1–2: 1–15.

Florencia de la V. 2013. "El descargo de Flor de la V." Telefe, November 18. YouTube video, 8:44. www.youtube.com/watch?v=cNyYLY7QQqc.

Fonseca, Claudia. 2002. "Inequality Near and Far: Adoption as Seen from the Brazilian Favelas." *Law and Society Review* 36, no. 2: 397–432. doi.org/10.2307/1512182.

Gauna, Patricia. 1993. "Entrevista a Mariela Muñoz." *Confidencial,* no. 9: 3. América Lee, Centro de Documentación e Investigación de la Cultura de Izquierdas, Buenos Aires. americalee.cedinci.org/wp-content/uploads/2017/07/ConfidencialArgentina_n9.pdf.

Giberti, Eva. 1997. "Mariela Muñoz, el derecho a la diferencia." *Clarín,* May 27.

Gibson, Margaret F. 2014. *Queering Motherhood: Narrative and Theoretical Perspectives.* Bradford, ON: Demeter.

ILGHRD (International Gay and Lesbian Human Rights Commission) and CUAV (Community United Against Violence). 1995. *The International Tribunal on Human Rights Violations against Sexual Minorities.* New York City, October 17. outrightinternational.org/sites/default/files/188-1.pdf.

Israel, Gianna E. 2005. "Translove: Transgender Persons and Their Families." *Journal of GLBT Family Studies* 1, no. 1: 53–67.

James-Abra, Sarah, L. A. Tarasoff, D. Green, Rachel Epstein, Scott Anderson, Stu Marvel, L. S. Steele, and L. E. Ross. 2015. "Trans People's Experiences with Assisted Reproduction Services: A Qualitative Study." *Human Reproduction* 30, no. 6: 1365–74.

Manning, Kimberley, Cindy Holmes, Annie Pullen Sansfacon, Julia Temple Newhook, and Ann Travers. 2015. "Fighting for Trans* Kids: Academic Parent Activism in the Twenty-First Century." *Studies in Social Justice* 9, no. 1: 118–35.

Masson, Laura. 2004. *La política en femenino: Género y poder en la provincia de Buenos Aires.* Buenos Aires: Centro de Antropología.

Muñoz, Mariela. 1993a. "1993—Mirtha Legrand—Mariela Muñoz." Videos SIGLA. YouTube video, 8:27. youtube.com/watch?v=kcr3eBHARrY.

Muñoz, Mariela. 1993b. "DiFilm—Mariela Muñoz—Transsexual (1993)." ArchivoDiChiara, January 4, 2015. YouTube video, 4:53. www.youtube.com/watch?v=R3A4R1R7RF4.

Muñoz, Mariela. 1993c. "Mariela Muñoz sale en libertad 1993." DeFilm, October 20, 2018. YouTube video, 2:38. www.youtube.com/watch?v=hQgiypIJnFs.

Muñoz, Mariela. 1997. "1997—Fte a fte—Mariela Muñoz concejala." Videos SIGLA. YouTube video, 9:59. www.youtube.com/watch?v=QSjni-kDIok.

Muñoz, Mariela. 2000. "2000—Mirtha Legrand—Mariela Muñoz." Videos SIGLA. YouTube video, 9:57. www.youtube.com/watch?v=09kKzlivSdY.

Nari, Marcela M. A. 2004. *Políticas de maternidad y maternalismo político: Buenos Aires, 1890–1940*. Buenos Aires: Editorial Biblos.

Pérez, Inés. 2020. "Domestic Workers' Experiences of Motherhood in Mid-twentieth-century Buenos Aires." *Women's History Review* 30, no. 2: 208–22.

Platero, R. Lucas, and Esther Ortega Arjonilla. 2017. *Investigación sociológica sobre las personas transexuales y sus experiencias familiares*. Madrid: Transexualia.

Plummer, Keith. 2011. *Intimate Citizenship: Private Decisions and Public Dialogues*. Seattle: University of Washington Press.

Theumer, Emmanuel. 2020. "The Self-Perceived Gender Identity." *Interventions* 22, no. 4: 498–513.

Vespucci, Guido. 2014. "Una fórmula deseable: El discurso 'somos familias' como símbolo hegemónico de las reivindicaciones gay-lésbicas." *Sexualidad, Salud y Sociedad (Rio de Janeiro)*, no. 17: 30–65.

Wayar, Marlene. 2020. *Diccionario travesti de la T a la T*. Buenos Aires: Página 12.

Zarco, Abril. 2011. "Maternalismo, identidad colectiva y participación política: Las Madres de Plaza de Mayo." *Revista punto género*, no. 1: 229–47.

Trans-, Translation, Transnational

COLE RIZKI

As I sat to write this introduction as *TSQ*'s new translation section editor, I realized that *translation*, when framed as a semiotic process, may appear at first glance as a misnomer for the intellectual and epistemic work that I hope this section can perform. Much of the intention behind the translation section has been "to decenter the Northern, white, anglophone bias" of trans studies by including work-in-translation (Stryker 2020: 303). To continue this important project and expand on its aims, this section now also invites short reflections that develop alternate genealogies for the field through knowledge formations and disciplines that do not reproduce the imperatives of US American studies, which has largely overdetermined trans studies' field imaginary. In other words, this will require recognizing trans studies for what it has often been to date: an unmarked area studies formation that takes US American studies as its unspoken center. While trans studies has indeed aimed to address questions of empire, racialization, and political economy, for example, it has repeatedly done so through critique that prioritizes the US nation-state and its transnational histories. This section thus invites short reflections that interrogate trans studies' material, institutional, and disciplinary boundaries, working at the rub where critical area studies and trans studies meet.

At its most colloquial, like trans, translation has often been thought in terms of horizontal movement, a movement across, from one language to another. Susan Stryker, Paisley Currah, and Lisa Jean Moore's (2008: 14) theorization of *trans-* instead underscores verticality or the ways in which trans- "becomes the capillary space of connection and circulation between the macro- and micropolitical registers through which the lives of bodies become enmeshed in the lives of nations, states, and capital-formations." When figured as a trans- operation, translation illuminates the enmeshment of knowledge formations at the micro and macro levels. Such an understanding of translation aligns with feminist elaborations on "cultural translation," which, as Claudia de Lima Costa (2014: 20)

TSQ: Transgender Studies Quarterly ★ Volume 8, Number 4 ★ November 2021 **532**
DOI 10.1215/23289252-9311116 © 2021 Duke University Press

writes, "is premised on the view that any process of description, interpretation, and dissemination of ideas and worldviews is always already caught up in relations of power and asymmetries between languages, regions, and peoples." This section seeks work on cultural translation as a "trans" operation, examining micro-level acts of interpretation, description, and dissemination as they are mediated by relations of power and asymmetry at both the micro and macro level.

Reflections on cultural translation might foreground "the relationalities and attachments that different analytical categories have as they travel [that] will greatly influence their ability to translate" (21). This is particularly important with concepts such as gender, sexuality, and race. As Neferti X. M. Tadiar (2016: 173–74) cautions, "gender, race, sexuality" as "analytical lenses" have become "nearly Kantian categories"—their arrangement and deployment predetermined by the disciplinary expectations of scholars working within the US academy. Tadiar warns that "you are seeing only as far as these imperial shores will allow: the familiar forms of life that an 'American grammar' of power and marginality, visibility and invisibility, identity and difference, normativity and nonnormativity, being and becoming can help you make out." She goes on to ask, "When we do the critique that we do so well, do we not employ the grammar of the police? . . . Do not we communicate and traffic in the particular colonial, capitalist, real abstract codes of social and subjective being that make up an American grammar?" (176). This is to put pressure on the commensurability of cultural, political, and social arrangements of knowledge. It is also a reminder, as Macarena Gómez-Barris (2017: 126) writes, to recognize when and how "local vernaculars of struggle" might get "run through the machine of North American theories, abstracting from local conditions of possibility and constraints" as a form of extractivism. Such cautions are not a call to abandon the work of cultural translation or to abandon these categories but rather to recognize them as particular arrangements of knowledge and experience, as modes of perception and forms of reading that forge grids of intelligibility and regulate epistemological economies.

As Stryker, Currah, and Moore (2008: 14) ask, "How might we move between the necessary places of identity where we plant our feet and the simultaneous imperative to resist those ways in which identities become the vectors through which we are taken up by projects not of our own making?" Such productive investments in and failures of identity as lived formation along with reflections such as Tadiar's and Gómez-Barris's that highlight the geopolitics of disciplinary grammars suggest that if we are to translate concepts such as *trans*, *brownness*, and *gender* among others, we must attend to the material, political, and cultural frameworks that freight such concepts and with which they travel. Likewise, refusing to translate formations like *brownness*, for example, or *travesti* might also do political work. Such refusals have the potential to generate other forms of proximity, other forms of "being-in-common," to invoke José Esteban Muñoz's (2020: 2) formulation, in excess of geopolitical borders. Translation's refusal, as a critical mode of accompaniment and care, can signal a commitment to copresence as affiliation that does not collapse, meld, or erase ways of organizing experience.

This is certainly not to suggest that concepts and theories as arrangements of knowledge are not taken up or intervened in different ways across multiple geopolitical borders. Translation does not generate isomorphic meaning effects, nor are concepts and meaning passively received but rather appropriated and ascribed anew within contexts of power. I draw attention here to the ways that we may wish to attend carefully to mediation and the ways that certain knowledge formations and modes of critique travel south while others may not travel north. Commensurability and incommensurability of ways of being in and knowing the world are at stake. Material and ideological conditions matter. The task at hand thus "demands mapping the dislocations and continual translations" of trans theories and concepts "as well as the constraints [that] mechanisms of mediation and technologies of control impos[e] in the transit of theories across geopolitical borders" (de Lima Costa 2014: 24). This section seeks work that performs such mappings and attends to the mechanisms of mediation and technologies of control central to understanding how theories and concepts move through the world.

Such mechanisms of constraint are also material. Textual translation, as labor, holds great consequence. It not only governs who gets cited but also foregrounds the uneven material conditions of knowledge production under which we all labor—to the benefit of some and the exclusion of others. It signals the labor of scholars whose primary language is not English who must translate their work (or pay for such services) in order for their research to appear in journals published by presses (like this one) that will not publish work in other languages. As Sonia E. Alvarez, Kia Lilly Caldwell, and Augustín Laó-Montes (2016: v) suggest, without the work of translation and the circulation of work-*in*-translation, it is impossible to forge the "feminist, pro-social justice, antiracist, postcolonial/decolonial, and anti-imperial political alliances and epistemologies" that translation, as trans- operation, has the power to effect. This section will thus continue to invite work-in-translation that cultivates feminist, antiracist, post/decolonial, and anti-imperial epistemologies as well as reflections that address the political economies of translation.

National and regional political, ideological, and theoretical currents similarly impact the ways that conceptual apparatuses do and do not translate, pushed or carried along in transit. For example, the continued centrality of socialism as a viable mode of politics as well as the import of Marxist theory to feminist, queer, and trans and travesti studies throughout Latin America might differently shape the theoretical, conceptual, and political genealogies of trans studies and its critical moves. The repeated and violent collapse of financial markets in the region during the 1980s, 1990s, and early 2000s due to neoliberal economic policies further underscores the imperative of attending to articulations of class and labor. At the same time, trans and travesti theory as it emerges from Latin America's Southern Cone and its diasporas centers class and revolution as, in part, grounded in recent experiences of leftist resistance to dictatorship. Such incommensurability with a US context—politically, historically, perhaps even theoretically—is productive and, on the other hand, points to how attention to class struggle has largely failed to translate meaningfully into US trans studies.

Some of the questions this section asks include: How does *trans* as a geopolitical knowledge formation travel, get received, reshaped, and refused outside the US academy and in the global South? What kinds of feminist, antiracist, post- and decolonial global south genealogies might unfold through translation or its refusal? What are the material conditions of the circulation and translation of trans knowledges, cultural formations, and political claims? How do we analyze this circulation, from its material conditions of inception, contexts of production through to its movement and recombination? How do material, political, and cultural frameworks affect how trans theory travels (or cannot)? What kinds of counterpractices or countertranslations might we mobilize? How do geopolitical and scalar categories such as province, state, island, archipelago, region, nation, ocean, or global south or north facilitate (mis)recognitions or mediate knowledge formations?

This section seeks work (three thousand words or less) that pays deep attention to how transcultural, transregional, and transnational flows of ideas, subjects, capital, and resources impact the field of transgender studies—its constitutive categories, critical vocabularies, institutional boundaries, and disciplinary commitments. This includes theoretical reflections, meditations on artistic and aesthetic practices, and writing on activist projects that change how we conceive both translation and our field(s). In addition to featuring such reflections, the section will also continue to publish work in translation. I invite work by academics, artists, and activists working across disciplines in and from the global South as well as work by scholars with deep area training.

Translation, as Anjali Arondekar and Geeta Patel (2016: 154) suggest, is "a choreography from which one might commence, rather than a conversion that occludes or wraps up its trajectories." Translation as choreography, as the art of composition, unfolds new ways of being and knowing in proximity and in difference. At the same time, untranslatability and (mis)recognition might also serve as points of departure, fueling new arrangements of knowledge, vulnerability, and care across geopolitical borders, while we remain attentive to the ways in which the incommensurable continues to structure our field(s).

Cole Rizki is assistant professor of Spanish and affiliate faculty of women, gender, and sexuality at the University of Virginia. His research and writing focus on the entanglements of transgender cultural production and politics with histories of state violence and terror throughout the Americas. His scholarship appears in journals such as *TSQ*, *Radical History Review*, and *Journal of Visual Culture*. He is coeditor of *TSQ*'s special issue "Trans Studies en las Américas" and editor of *TSQ*'s Translation section.

References

Alvarez, Sonia E., Kia Lilly Caldwell, and Augustín Laó-Montes. 2016. "Translations across Black Feminist Diasporas." *Meridians: Feminism, Race, Transnationalism* 14, no. 2: v–ix.

Arondekar, Anjali, and Geeta Patel. 2016. "Area Impossible: Notes toward an Introduction." *GLQ* 22, no. 2: 151–71.

de Lima Costa, Claudia. 2014. "Lost (and Found?) in Translation: Feminisms in Hemispheric Dialogue." In *Translocalities/Translocalidades: Feminist Politics of Translation in the Latin/a Américas*, edited by Sonia E. Alvarez, Claudia de Lima Costa, Verónica Feliu, Rebecca J. Hester, Norma Klahn, and Millie Thayer, 19–38. Durham, NC: Duke University Press.

Gómez-Barris, Macarena. 2017. *The Extractive Zone: Social Ecologies and Decolonial Perspectives.* Durham, NC: Duke University Press.

Muñoz, José Esteban. 2020. "The Brown Commons." In *The Sense of Brown*, edited by Joshua Chambers-Letson and Tavia Nyong'o, 1–7. Durham, NC: Duke University Press.

Stryker, Susan. 2020. "Introduction: Trans∗ Studies Now." *TSQ* 7, no. 3: 299–305.

Stryker, Susan, Paisley Currah, and Lisa Jean Moore. 2008. "Trans-, Trans, or Transgender?" *WSQ* 36, nos. 3–4: 11–22.

Tadiar, Neferti X. M. 2016. "Ground Zero." *GLQ* 22, no. 2: 173–81.

Dedicated to the Last Pearl

Jojo "Josefina Larina Queen of the Congolina" Gilbert, of the Pearl Box Revue

HARRISON APPLE

Jojo came into my life when I threw the One More Time ball in October of 2013, an evening dedicated to septuagenarian drag legends who wanted to come out looking glamorous after more than thirty years out of the spotlight. While I was busy making arrangements in the background for the evening, scurrying around in my thrift store dyeable heels and brocade skirt suit, she caught me by the arm, pulled me to her side, and told me that, especially for me, she was singing "My Funny Valentine." Jojo was the last living member of the Pearl Box Revue, a 1970s stage show managed by Lucky LaBaker and Bobby Lopez out of Buffalo, New York. We

Figure 1. Jojo poses in her apartment, wearing a shake dancer dress and platinum wig, in the late 1960s. This picture is part of the Jojo Gilbert Collection at the Pittsburgh Queer History Project.

became fast friends. I was her captive audience, with her teaching me when I do and don't look glamorous, giving advice on the finer points of pleasure that come with removable dentures, and her encyclopedic knowledge of stage show monologues. Elsewhere I've talked about Jojo and her contemporaries as troubling the field of oral history, in which the interview is taught as a pristine and unadorned event. But Jojo's life was about getting more. To her dying day, she spoke in stage patter. And like the movement of images across a scrapbook page, that rhythm is how she taught me to share her memory.

Harrison Apple is an oral historian, reluctant community archivist, and PhD of gender and women's studies with a minor in information from the University of Arizona. Their dissertation, "A Social Member in Good Standing: Pittsburgh's Gay and Lesbian Afterhours Social Clubs," weaves the oral history of club owner and gay would-be mafiosa "Lucky" with urban history of race and sexuality in Pittsburgh to reconstruct the meaning of "membership" to these after-hours queer discos. In their work to rediscover records of club activity beneath layers of complex and intentionally opaque documentation, they simultaneously lean toward betraying the archival profession by preserving materials in place, even as they are imminently deteriorating. Apple's writing has been published in *Archivaria*, *TSQ*, Outhistory.org, and the *Introduction to Transgender Studies* (2019).

Button Rhetorics

K.J. RAWSON

Buttons are strange historical objects. After they are retired from their honored place on a backpack or jean jacket (or perhaps rescued out of the junk drawer), scores of buttons have found their way to queer archives where they are proudly claimed as valued queer heritage artifacts. Buttons rarely have attributed creators and usually lack specific dates (aside from, say, political campaign buttons). Buttons are designed to be worn or posted, to be mobile through space and often transient in time. We rarely know who wore them or for how long, why they mattered, or

Figure 1. Genderpress, Mirha-Soleil Ross, and Xanthra Phillippa MacKay, "TS's against Racism," the ArQuives Digital Exhibitions n.d.; see also "TS's against Racism" button n.d.

what effects they may have had. In other words, we are often left talking about how fun they are, but they remain obstinately vague historical objects despite our efforts to pin them down (sorry, I couldn't resist).

The "TS'S AGAINST RACISM" button pictured above—attributed to Mirha Soleil-Ross and Xanthra MacKay's genderpress—is now part of an extensive Soleil-Ross collection held at the ArQuives: Canada's LGBTQ+ Archives. It has been photographed and made available on the ArQuives' website and is additionally linked to the Digital Transgender Archive ("TS's against Racism" button n.d.). Like the original button that these digital surrogates seek to represent, the photograph of this button has been reproduced and circulated. The date the button was created is noted as the 1990s, an imprecision cultivated by the very nature of buttons.

This simple, round button appears to be small, though it is admittedly difficult to tell from the digital reproduction, and, unfortunately, I have never held it in my hands. It includes only three words: "TS'S AGAINST RACISM," with the word *racism* repeated twice. It is described online as being "purple," though it certainly seems pink in the photo. In either case, we can agree that it's a queer hue.

The main text is in a shadowy font that becomes legible as the letters appear to pop off the button, casting black shadows in their relief. Behind the main text, the word *racism* is repeated in the largest font that will fit on the button, italicized, as if it is perpetually active and running across the background. *Racism* is written in white, a nod to the specter of whiteness that enables the presence of racism and renders it legible.

In three short words, this button manages to cohere a group identity with a plural noun (*TS'S*) against a shared concern (*racism*). While the in-group term *TS* is abbreviated, *racism* is spelled out fully and repeated twice, ensuring that there is no ambiguity. The button identifies the wearer as TS and invokes an unseen community of other TS people with a shared antiracist position. This button functions as a form of rhetorical activism that brings together a marginalized identity group (TS'S) to take a stand against an ideology that harms others and, certainly, TBIPOC people.

Though it would be hard to fit *transsexual* on a small button, it is likely that graphic design was not the only motive for using the *TS* abbreviation here. As was common in trans community discourse in the last few decades of the twentieth century, many buttons in this collection used *TS* as a shorthand for *transsexual*, *TV* for *transvestite*, and *TG* for *transgender* (Button Collection n.d.). This shorthand had many benefits, including creating group identity through shared language, quickly distinguishing among various trans identities, and, perhaps most importantly, keeping cis folks unaware of trans community building happening in their midst without any spoken words.

Buttons may be transient objects with little monetary value, but their contributions to queer community building and activism secure their place in the archival record.

K.J. Rawson is associate professor of English and women's, gender, and sexuality studies at Northeastern University. He is also the founder and director of the Digital Transgender Archive, an award-winning online repository of trans-related historical materials, and he is the cochair of the editorial board of the Homosaurus, an international LGBTQ linked data vocabulary. His work is at the intersections of the digital humanities and rhetoric, LGBTQ+, and feminist studies. Focusing on archives as key sites of cultural power, Rawson studies the rhetorical work of queer and transgender archival collections in both brick-and-mortar and digital spaces. He has coedited special issues of *Peitho* and *TSQ* and coedited *Rhetorica in Motion: Feminist Rhetorical Methods and Methodologies* (2010). Rawson's scholarship has appeared in *Archivaria, Enculturation, Peitho, Present Tense, QED, RSQ, TSQ,* and several edited collections.

References

ArQuives Digital Exhibitions. n.d. digitalexhibitions.arquives.ca/items/show/737 (accessed June 28, 2021).

Button Collection. n.d. Digital Transgender Archive. www.digitaltransgenderarchive.net/catalog ?f%5Bcollection_name_ssim%5D%5B%5D=Button+Collection (accessed June 9, 2021).

"TS's against Racism" button. n.d. Digital Transgender Archive. www.digitaltransgenderarchive .net/files/1v53jx176 (accessed June 9, 2021).

Rebels, Criminals, Pioneers
Jack Starr and Friends in the QPA Queer Photo Archive

JENNI OLSON

With the purchase of this black-and-white, 5 × 8 in. newswire photo of Jack Starr in 2017, I began my journey into creating my small but very cool QPA—Queer Photo Archive, which features an array of other gender-nonconforming, trans, and queer pioneers (please visit *TSQ*Now* at www .tsqnow.online to see more images and info). This particular photo also prompted me to embark on an ambitious exploration into the life of this amazing person. Days and nights of research (especially looking at newspaper accounts of the era) yielded a decades-long account of the life of a gender rebel who was repeatedly arrested over the course of the 1920s, 1930s, and 1940s for wearing men's clothing. There were numerous aliases—Jacques Moret was the other most popular one, but Jack Starr was the most enduring. Jack's exploits unfolded primarily in Montana. In the repeated front-page accounts of the various arrests and trials, Jack comes across as an adventurer, a ladies' man, a cultured musician, and an unrepentant rascal often in trouble with the law. There are repeated mentions over the years of Jack's female companions, and a wildly entertaining list of occupations: bootlegger, bartender, blackjack dealer, truck driver, longshoreman, shipyard steamfitter, and riveter.

I was blessed with the opportunity in 2019 to work with the amazing writer-directors Stephen Kijak and Kimberly Reed to tell a little bit of Jack's previously untold story in the Scout Productions LGBT history series, EQUAL—which is now airing on HBO Max and stars the fabulous Theo Germaine as Jack. I'm also currently working on a film treatment about Jack in hopes that even more people might be inspired by the courage of this century-old role model.

During the fall of 2020 as guest curator for Karen Tongson's awesome Butch Hair Quarantine Instagram account, I had the opportunity to share a selection of my QPA photos and research and to reflect a bit about my great affection

TSQ: Transgender Studies Quarterly * Volume 8, Number 4 * November 2021   **542**
DOI 10.1215/23289252-9311158   © 2021 Duke University Press

for all these heroic criminals. Much of the contemporaneous coverage of their stories conveys a surprising warmth and friendliness toward these subjects—all arrested for the crime of passing as men.

We don't know that Jack or any of these folks would have identified as trans in our contemporary understanding of that identity. Since Jack actually lived as a man for a considerable period of time, it certainly feels appropriate to embrace him as a trans man forefather. The passing sojourns of the other folks in my QPA photo collection seem to have been briefer; in my research I have not been able to track them beyond the newspaper coverage to know what happened to them in the end.

I strongly identify with gender-pioneering heroes like Jack, imagining that if I had lived in those very rigidly gendered times, this likely would have been the best option available to me. In my own

Figure 1. Jack Starr, January 8, 1944. Courtesy of the author.

gender journey (which has included a period of time on testosterone and in which I have mainly identified as a butch dyke), I continue to ponder the mystery of being different. Gender-nonconforming, butch, trans, AFAB, masculine of center. Words may fail us. But these pictures are worth a thousand words.

Jenni Olson, one of the world's leading experts on LGBT cinema history, is an independent writer and nonfiction filmmaker based in Berkeley, California. Her reflection on the last thirty years of LGBT film history appeared in *The Oxford Handbook of Queer Cinema* (2021). Jenni's work as a film historian includes the Lambda Award–nominated *Queer Movie Poster Book* (2005). She is a former codirector of the San Francisco International LGBTQ Film Festival, the oldest and largest queer film festival on the planet. She holds a BA in film studies from the University of Minnesota and is currently an independent consultant in marketing and digital film distribution. A 2018 MacDowell Fellow, Jenni is now in development on her third feature-length essay film, *The Quiet World*, and an essayistic memoir of the same name.

A Most Unusual Volume

Ms. BOB DAVIS

Jessica Helfand, senior critic in graphic design at Yale University and author of *Scrapbooks: An American History* (2008), says, "When you feel an increased sense of vulnerability, what can you do to steel yourself against the inevitable tide of human suffering but to paste something in a book? It seems silly, but on the other hand, it's quite logical" (Gambino 2009).

Vulnerable certainly describes the people who, in the mid-twentieth century, created the contemporary LGBTQ+ community. One notable manifestation of that vulnerability are the scrapbooks of trans-related photographs and ephemera lovingly compiled by a trans woman named Denise in the 1960s and 1970s. Denise's scrapbooks were donated to the Louise Lawrence Transgender Archive (LLTA) by Taryn Gundling, professor of anthropology and transgender studies at William Paterson University. Denise gave them to Taryn sometime around 2008 at a support group meeting in central New Jersey. Denise, who was over eighty at the time, considered them her contribution to transgender history.

Four years of research confirmed Denise's place in New York City's early trans community. She identified as a heterosexual transvestite and was the cover girl for issue number 7 of Virginia Prince's *Transvestia*, January 1961. She knew Susanna Valenti and stayed at Susanna's Chevalier d'Eon Resort, where some weekends were set aside for trans women to live in their preferred gender.

There are six scrapbooks with thousands of clippings from newspapers, magazines, supermarket tabloids, transgender contact magazines, and programs from female impersonator shows, a labor of love that must have taken hundreds of hours to complete.

One scrapbook is smaller than the others and more unusual. Denise took E. Carlton Winford's oversized 1954 book *Femme Mimics: A Pictorial Record of Female Impersonation* and used it as a scrapbook. She pasted white paper over its pages, covering the original photos and text. Then she pasted articles and photographs from 1960s female impersonator magazines, like *Female Mimics* and

Figure 1. Denise pasted clippings over the text of *Femme Mimics: A Pictorial Record of Female Impersonation,* by E. Carlton Winford (1954), turning it into a scrapbook.

Female Impersonator, over the blank pages. She scrapbooked about fifty pages this way, then she stopped using the blank sheets and started pasting the clippings directly over the book's text, so fragments of the original book are visible between Denise's clippings, like a palimpsest, layer upon layer of text and photos. Antiquarian book dealer, historian, and curator Gerard Koskovich labeled it "the strangest example of transgender folk art I've ever seen" (pers. comm., January 7, 2018).

Four of Denise's scrapbooks confirm another of Jessica Helfand's observations about scrapbooks: "Everybody made scrapbooks a hundred years ago, and people didn't worry about getting it right. They just made things, and they were messy, incomplete, and inconsistent. To me, the real therapeutic act is being who you are" (in Gambino 2009).

Denise's scrapbooks can be viewed online at the Digital Transgender Archive site (Denise n.d.). The Louise Lawrence Transgender Archive (n.d.) has created an online exhibition of Denise's scrapbooks with more information about Denise and her circle of cross-dressing friends.

Ms. Bob Davis, MFA, founder and director of the Louise Lawrence Transgender Archive, served two terms on the GLBT Historical Society board of directors, one as secretary. She has presented four papers at three different Moving Trans History Forward conferences presented by the chair in transgender studies at the University of Victoria. She presented her paper "Glamour, Drag, and Death: HIV/AIDS in the Art of Three Drag Queen Painters" at Queering Memory 2019, a conference presented by Archives, Libraries, Museums, and Special Collections (ALMS) in Berlin. Ms. Bob has been capitalizing on her advanced age, contributing "For as Long as I Can Remember . . ." to *Glimmerings: Trans Elders Tell Their Stories* (2019) and "The View from Now" to *TRANScestors: Navigating Transgender Aging, Illness, and End of Life Decisions* (2020). She teaches music at Napa Valley College.

References

Denise. n.d. Scrapbooks. www.digitaltransgenderarchive.net/catalog?utf8=%E2%9C%93&f%5B institution_name_ssim%5D%5B%5D=Louise+Lawrence+Transgender+Archive&q= scrapbooks (accessed June 9, 2021).

Gambino, Megan. 2009. "The Cherished Tradition of Scrapbooking: Author Jessica Helfand Investigates the History of Scrapbooks and How They Mirror American History." *Smithsonian*, May 13. www.smithsonianmag.com/arts-culture/the-cherished-tradition -of-scrapbooking-135493660/.

Helfand, Jessica. 2008. *Scrapbooks: An American History*. New Haven, CT: Yale University Press.

Louise Lawrence Transgender Archive. n.d. lltransarchive.org (accessed June 9, 2021).

Drag Attack

The Celebration of the Posthuman Transvestite in the Spanish Party Underground

ANDRÉS SENRA

Figure 1. Drag Attack Event, featuring Vurdalak DJs and The Kinky Team, by Tatu Vuolteenaho (2014).

Halfway between a transformation that performatizes the most stereotyped becoming of women and the drag queen as a mythical being, a demigoddess of nightlife, in which transformation rarefies the concept of identity toward other possible genders, Tatu Vuolteenaho (1968, Yivieska), a Finnish transvestite-drag queen, organized a series of underground nighttime parties called Drag Attack from 2013 to 2019 in various gay clubs in Spain. Tatu's happening parties proposed a precarious, do-it-yourself crossdressing that reclaims the figure of the monster in a shift that goes beyond the subversion of gender binaries to embody a subversion of humans, invoking nonbinary beings that refer to magical, queer, and posthuman figures in relation to art history, pop culture, and recent thought. According to

TSQ: Transgender Studies Quarterly ★ Volume 8, Number 4 ★ November 2021 **548**
DOI 10.1215/23289252-9311186 © 2021 Duke University Press

Tatu Vuolteenaho, "Drag queen, drag king, drag freak . . . drag can be anything. We question gender, beauty, race, and condition to the point where spectators can start to wonder whether they are looking at a real human being."

The peculiar aspect of Drag Attack is that it was also proposed as a horizontal collaborative experience of strange community cross-dressing in which the participants cross-dressed in accordance with the concept of each event, in a context such as the commercialized consumption of the pink market. In this way, participants queered the homonormative gay spaces of the nighttime scene. The capacity to transform into a strange other is collectively performatized through body makeup and clothes, playing with the idea of vague, degenerated nonbinary identities and personifying aliens, cyborgs, hybrids, witches, or other queer beings that, on other occasions, refer to seraphim, tetramorphs, and ectopic-eyed archangels with undefined identities. While the gender embodied by the transformations of Tatu Vuolteenaho and the participants frequently passes to a second plane, all the characters performatize, independently of their possible gender, the monster-feminine in a vindication of this minority other as a subversive strategy of binarism. The monster-feminine in Drag Attack, far from being a universal neuter, is a form of being in the world, of being by being drag. Drag here is embodied as the capacity to transgress the very concept of identity. This performative work allows us to rethink the category of the monster from a postgender, posthuman, and queer perspective, as a "deformation and malformation" of the normative mind-body canon. Queering gender refers to the idea of the monster in such a way that the monster is queer par excellence. It is, in its potential threat to humans, what is supposed by a questioning of liberal humanism and its gender binarism. Tatu Vuolteenaho reclaims the drag queen and the transvestite as witches, as gender-dissident beings, performatizing and embodying a queer witch, the fairy as a witch, sister of desires, pleasures, and orgies that accompany cis-women witches in the covens of popular esoteric imagination. Music, dance, altered states of consciousness, desire, and pleasure were conjured in community meeting spaces for the celebration of the other and the electronic fits and outburst of Drag Attack.

Andrés Senra has a degree in philosophy from the Universidad Nacional de Educación a Distancia (2018) and a degree in biological sciences from the Complutense University of Madrid (1993), and he is a PhD candidate in the philosophy program at the University of Salamanca. He is also an artist, researcher, and teacher of the bachelor of arts at the Universitat Oberta de Catalunya. In his latest artistic research works, he has addressed issues such as recent Spanish economic and cultural emigration, the archive as a work of art, and the political and affective history of the LGTBIQ+ community in Madrid, work for which he received in 2013 a research grant from the National Museum Centro de Arte Reina Sofía for the project Archivo queer?

Transformers

DIEGO MARCHANTE

Figure 1. Diego Marchante "Genderhacker," *Curro* (2010). Transformers series.

TSQ: Transgender Studies Quarterly ★ Volume 8, Number 4 ★ November 2021
DOI 10.1215/23289252-9311200   © 2021 Duke University Press

Figure 2. Diego Marchante "Genderhacker," *Curro's Revelation* (2010). Transformers series.

En esta imagen, vemos a Curro, un joven novillero que encarna el estereotipo del torero: héroe nacional, símbolo de poder, coraje y bravura española. Y nos hace toda una revelación. Deconstruye uno de los estereotipos más castizos del nuestro contexto, y al mismo tiempo, subvierte el propio álbum familiar, ya que desafía la prohibición en la niñez de acudir con traje de campero a las fiestas populares.

Esta serie fotográfica forma parte de *Transformers*, un proyecto artístico que visibiliza el travestismo de las lesbianas *butch*, los *drag kings* y los trans* masculinos. Vidas que deconstruyen la afirmación de que la masculinidad no es performativa, un imperativo cultural que mantiene que esta masculinidad es un privilegio único de los hombres. Vidas que resisten a las estrategias de normalización y construcción del género a través de la performance (*drag king*) o del propio cuerpo (transgénero). A través de una serie de fotografías realizadas en 2010, subvierto algunas de las masculinidades heroicas que circulan en España. A través de herramientas cómo la parodia y el travestismo desestabilizamos los planteamientos binarios de género que dominan los cuerpos e intentamos superar las rígidas categorías que suponen lo masculino y lo femenino. Este proyecto, en consecuencia, trata sobre el constante deslizamiento pendular entre la representación y la identificación de los cuerpos. La mezcla entre el travestismo en el escenario y la masculinidad fuera de él sugiere que la línea entre lo *drag* y lo transgénero se confunde permanentemente. En mi caso, pudiendo elegir la opción de vivir la masculinidad de una manera más orgánica e integrada en la vida cotidiana.

* * *

In this image, we see Curro, a young steer (bull) handler, who embodies the stereotype of the Spanish bullfighter: a national hero and a symbol of power, courage, and Spanish bravado. And he makes quite a revelation: he deconstructs one of our most contextually pure-blooded Spanish stereotypes, while at the same time subverting the family photo album as he openly defies the childhood prohibition of attending village parties in a traditional country suit.

This photographic series is part of *Transformers*, an artistic project that makes visible cross-dressing among butch lesbians, drag kings, and trans* masculine individuals. These are lives that deconstruct the assertion that masculinity is not performative, that is to say, a cultural imperative that preserves masculinity as a privilege reserved solely for men. These are lives that, be it through performance (drag king) or their very own bodies (transgender), resist strategies of normalization and gender construction. Using a series of photographs taken in 2010, I subvert some of the heroic masculinities that circulate within Spain. Through the use of tools such as parody and cross-dressing, I destabilize the binary perspectives of gender that dominate bodies and attempt to overcome the rigid categories that signify masculinity and femininity. This project, therefore, addresses the constant pendular swinging between the representation and identification of bodies. The blending of cross-dressing onstage and masculinity off-stage suggests that the line between drag and transgender becomes permanently muddled. In my case, this means being able to choose to live my masculinity in a more organic way, integrated into my daily life.

Diego Marchante ("Genderhacker") is a transfeminist activist, transmedia artist, and lecturer with a doctorate in fine arts from the University of Barcelona, where he is professor of audiovisuals and gender studies at the Faculty of Fine Arts. In 2011 he published *Archivo T*, an archive of social movements and artistic practices that have addressed gender issues in the Spanish context from a queer and transfeminist perspective. His work has been exhibited at Center of Contemporary Culture of Barcelona (CCCB), Museum of Contemporary Art of Barcelona (MACBA), and National Museum Art Center Reina Sofía (MNCARS). In 2020 his project *Gendernaut: Queering the 90's* was selected for the MNCARS's Our Many Europes—Europe's Critical 90s project, organized by the network of European museums l'internationale.

Catalan Scenes

FRAU DIAMANDA

Figure 1. Photograph by Cecilia Gamarra, 2013. Design by Diego Posada, 2020.

En el baño, va desplumándose de vestuario post show. Público de bar queer la ha despedido de escena entre ovaciones y rechifles. Ya de civil, se mezcla con los habituales del lugar. Travesti Rubia 1 muy mona la felicita y se hace íntima entre copas y cotilleo. La invita a fumar afuera. Salen y continúan cotilleo ameno entre risas y humo de tabaco frente a gran gato gordo de metal que las ignora. De pronto, Travesti Rubia 2 sale muy pedo y puesta, exigiendo un mechero. Se acerca y se le concede fuego. Mira a su rival rubia y soltando insultos intenta buscar pelea. Siamesas rubias se miran directo y quieren arrancarse los ojos. La Fray, muy diplomática, trata de evitar la masacre de uñas y mechas y con argucias se lleva del brazo a Travesti Rubia 1 rumbo al Moog. Por el camino fuman porro para calmar los nervios y se adentran en la Rambla que es un mar de guiris pedos y chillones en pleno Sant Joan; se deslizan abriéndose paso entre mar de cuerpos y lenguas del mundo entero. Les lleven MADREs, GUAPAS y OLÉs por doquier y hasta algún aguerrido les da un pellizco en la teta l vuelo. Aun así lograron llegar a spot de chico rubio que reparte sellos de ingreso for free al antro techno.

TSQ: Transgender Studies Quarterly ∗ Volume 8, Number 4 ∗ November 2021   **553**
DOI 10.1215/23289252-9311214   © 2021 Duke University Press

Con sendas muñecas selladas, ambas ya hacen cola donde se les invita a vino cutre de botella de plástico que es repartido entre la peña por chica rumana entusiasta y amistosa. Una vez dentro, cubil techno retumba a beats hiper-acelerados y decibeles malsanos. Abundan los tíos monísimos y ambas pactan con coque de manos no pelearse por ninguno: pacto de hermanas cazadoras en plan de ligue de la noche, prestas a diseñar sus propias rutas de caza.

* * *

In the bathroom, she plucks off her postshow wardrobe. The audience in the queer bar bade her farewell from the stage amid standing ovations and whistles. Now in street clothes, she intermingles with the bar's regulars. Blonde Transvestite 1, very cute, congratulates her, and the two get cozy over drinks and gossip. Blonde Transvestite 1 invites her outside for a smoke. They go out, continuing their pleasant gossip between laughs and tobacco smoke in front of a large, fat, metal cat, which pays them no mind. Suddenly, Blonde Transvestite 2 comes out, very drunk and dolled up, demanding a lighter. She approaches and lights her ciga-rette. She looks at her blonde rival and, spitting insults, tries to pick a fight. Blonde Siamese twins glare at each other, each wanting to rip out the other's eyes. Frau, a diplomat, tries to prevent a massacre of nails and highlights; cunningly, she drags Blonde Transvestite 1 by the arm toward the club. Along the way they smoke a joint to calm their nerves and plunge into La Rambla, which is a sea of foreign-ers, drunk and shrieking in the middle of Sant Joan. They slither through the sea of bodies and tongues from all around the world. OH MY GODs, HOTTIESs, and OLÉs rain down on them from all sides, and one daring man even gives their tits a quick pinch on the fly. Even so, they manage to arrive at the spot where a blond boy is handing out free entrance stamps to the techno club.

With their wrists duly stamped, they join the line of people clamoring for free, cheap wine from a plastic bottle, which is distributed to the crowd by an enthusiastic and friendly Romanian girl. Once inside, the techno den booms with hyperaccelerated beats and unhealthy decibel levels. There are cute guys all around, and the two girls shake hands in a pact not to fight over any of them: a pact between two sister hunters on the prowl for a one-night stand, each ready to plot her own route for the hunt.

Frau Diamanda is a transvestite audiovisual artist, translator, writer, drag performer, inde-pendent curator, cultural agent, DJ, and occasional actress from Peru living in Barcelona since 2016. She took the Independent Studies Programme at the Museum of Contemporary Art Barcelona from 2017 to 2018.

Femme4Femme: Remembering Cousin Robert

LINDSEY SHIVELY

Figure 1. Cousin Robert, top row, fifth from the left. Unknown San Francisco location, possibly Finocchios, unknown year.

Cousin Robert was part of the Castro drag scene for seven decades before he died in 2019 at age ninety. He was born in the city and was a regular at Twin Peaks, back when the windows were covered up to protect from vice raids and angry locals. He lived way up on 17th Street, and I wonder how he managed to climb that steep hill in strappy heels. Robert told me that he always passed, so he didn't need to change out of his look before leaving the bar.

TSQ: Transgender Studies Quarterly ★ Volume 8, Number 4 ★ November 2021   **555**
DOI 10.1215/23289252-9311228   © 2021 Duke University Press

As the only other queer in our biological family, I inherited his photo album when he died. These photos connect me to a legacy of San Francisco queer life before AIDS, ghosts smiling from blurry photos of the performance stage at Finocchios.

So many transsexuals and drag queens kept scrapbooks and photo albums that were tossed by relatives when they died. If Robert Rossi had died in the plague with the rest of his chosen family, maybe that is what would have happened with these photos too. Instead I was able to claim them and am honored to share them with you, beloved queer and trans community. Here is Cousin Robert and our unknown ancestors.

Lindsey Shively is a queer librarian living in the Bay Area, where her family has lived their participation in the colonization and genocide against Ohlone and Bay Miwok people, seven generations ago.

Samantha Hudson

IRA TERÁN

The transvestite identity is created on the margins of imperialist bourgeois society, in the nonpayment of narratives (and consumptions) naturalizing the sex-gender system. For this reason, the transvestite carries the social punishment of turning her identity into her work. In the transvestite we find the radicality of our trans genealogy, the half diaries of the bastard daughters of the night. The transvestite life is a life of community tenderness, in which new ways of reproducing life flourish—of lives marked by the system as surpluses—beyond the heteronormative nuclear family. Such care springs from the precariousness and loneliness that history etches on the skin of those who distance themselves from inflicted masculinity, belonging to the dispossessed class. Today the wounds of the transvestite body are named as parody. I speak here with the transvestite Samantha Hudson, an emerging singer, performer, and artist in the

Figure 1. Samantha Hudson. Photograph by Felipe Longoni. Courtesy of Samantha Hudson.

TSQ: Transgender Studies Quarterly * Volume 8, Number 4 * November 2021   **557**
DOI 10.1215/23289252-9311242   © 2021 Duke University Press

underground transvestite scene in Spain, about the trans-exclusionary discourse that exiles trans femininity and transvestism from the analyses around compulsory femininity, ignoring the naturalizing, rather than natural, character of gender.

Ira: Feminine people who have been assigned the category "man" at birth, inhabit a broken masculinity, they are "non-men." This term was popularized in the 1970s by the Radical Queens collective. In their manifesto they declared, "Both roles (masculinity and femininity) are inventions of the oppressor, both are oppressive for the one who accepts them" (Mecca 2009: 114). Transvestites are traitors to hegemonic masculinity, and their femininity is laboriously their own. This femininity is lived from an ambivalence between the oppression that is historically contingent in it and the liberation of the power to express itself as the system has never allowed. Survivors of a system that correctively violates them daily with the intention of assimilating them to the social reproduction of the system, which educates them that what they are and the way they express themselves is not right. In no way is the experience of transvestite femininity a pantomime of compulsory femininity, but rather a manifestation of it outside its naturalized context. Considering all these debates that run through feminism, what is your relationship with femininity? What would you say to colleagues who argue that cross-dressing is misogyny?

Samantha: I relate completely to femininity, in fact, I have the contradiction of forcing myself to perform a more masculine appearance only to be desired by the male gaze. I do not understand that whoever seeks the abolition of gender is taking a position against people who disagree with the roles that have been imposed on them, who consider that their ways of being can be explained only in a parody key. It is necessary to contextualize transvestism historically as the only way that transfeminities had to express a femininity that was not allowed to them. They imitated song divas, yes, but because they couldn't be and construct themselves as themselves in their temporal context. Furthermore, the imitation of referents is called parody only when it does not naturalize gender. Through this ridicule, on the one hand, the transvestite subjects are dehumanized and, on the other, their dissidence is distorted, preventing anyone from being able to value their existence as an argument against what is established.

Ira Terán is a Spanish marxist and transfeminist activist with a BA in English from the University of Zaragoza. Her research tackles queer social reproduction and utopian trans politics.

"Can We Be Visible in This Culture without Becoming a Commodity?"

An Interview with Disclosure Director Sam Feder

LAURA HORAK

Abstract In this interview, *Disclosure* director Sam Feder discusses the ambivalence of representation for trans people, their determination to hire as many trans people as possible on set, and how *Disclosure* evolved into the form it takes today.
Keywords transgender, representation, documentary, Hollywood, film history, television history

S am Feder was fifteen when they began creating media. He bought a manual black-and-white film camera, a Pentax K1000, for a photography class and began making photo essays about neglected children and racism in Brooklyn, where he lived. In high school they became an HIV activist creating photo essays about Black and Brown HIV+ gay men adopting kids born HIV+, and in their early twenties, they bought their first digital video camera, the SONY PC1. Soon after, they turned their lens toward the trans community. Since then, Feder's celebrated feature-length documentary films have captured crucial moments of trans history in the making. *Boy I Am* (2006), codirected with Julie Hollar, explored tensions in dyke communities around trans men coming out, with appearances by Dean Spade, Imani Henry, and Jack Halberstam. Their next feature-length film, *Kate Bornstein Is a Queer and Pleasant Danger* (2014), profiled the groundbreaking trans activist following the release of her memoir. But it was not until his most recent film, *Disclosure* (2020), which explores how trans people have been represented in Hollywood and how trans actors, directors, and critics have been shaped by their experiences with these representations, that Feder has crossed over from the indie world to mainstream recognition. *Disclosure* premiered at the Sundance Film Festival in January 2020, but because of the COVID-19 pandemic, all its subsequent festival screenings were canceled or moved online. Netflix licensed the film

TSQ: Transgender Studies Quarterly ∗ Volume 8, Number 4 ∗ November 2021 **559**
DOI 10.1215/23289252-9311256 © 2021 Duke University Press

for distribution and released it online on June 19, 2020. In this interview, Feder talks about the ambivalence of representation for trans people, their determination to hire as many trans people as possible on set, and how *Disclosure* evolved into the form it takes today. This interview is a condensed and edited version of two interviews I conducted with Feder—an online "master class" hosted by the Aesthetica Short Film Festival on November 5, 2020, and a one-on-one Zoom conversation on February 16, 2021.

Laura Horak: *First off, congratulations on the meteoric success of* Disclosure, *from premiering at Sundance to being distributed by Netflix—it's really incredible to see this film find the audience that it deserves. Tell us the story of how* Disclosure *came into being. When did you get the idea? What were the first steps that you took?*

Sam Feder: On June 9, 2014, Laverne Cox was on the cover of *Time* magazine (Steinmetz 2014). She was the first openly trans woman to be on the cover. She was wearing this beautiful blue dress, looking defiantly down at the camera, and the text on the cover read "The Transgender Tipping Point." When I saw that, many of my feelings and thoughts converged, and I felt that a film about it had to be made.

But I'm not a trained historian, I'm not a trained archivist. However, there were two films that deeply influenced my relationship to the media, so I began to consider making *Disclosure*. Those films were *Ethnic Notions* (1986) by Marlon Riggs, which looks at the representation of Black people in film, and *The Celluloid Closet* (1995), which looks at gay and lesbian representation in film. I wanted to see what that history looked like for trans people, especially at this moment, because when that cover story of Laverne on *Time* magazine hit the newsstands, trans people had barely been acknowledged, let alone celebrated in the mainstream. On one hand, I was thrilled, because we all need to be seen. But I also became really concerned because whenever a marginalized community gets mainstream attention, backlash ensues, and especially when all the public knows about that community has been deeply distorted by media. The community of trans people I knew were and continue to be disproportionately underemployed, lacking access to safe housing and health care. Meanwhile, media is reporting that trans people are experiencing a success because Laverne is on TV? There was more to the story than what the public was seeing. And I wanted to tell that story.

LH: *So where did you start? Once you'd decided, "I want to look at this history," what were the first things you did?*

SF: First, I wanted to understand how those two previous films that I mentioned were made. It turned out they're both based on books. I thought, "Okay, let me find the trans book on this history." But there was nothing! Well, there was one book written by John Phillips called *Transgender on Screen* (2006). You're familiar with it?

LH: *Yes, I know it . . .*

SF: That one was not helpful. So, I quickly realized I had to make the primary document to base this film on. I did not want to do this in a vacuum, alone in the archive picking out what was important. So, I got on the road and spent the next eight months doing on-camera research interviews with trans people who worked in front of or behind the camera. From those interviews, I started the database and built it up from there.

LH: *Your own film career has been forged in the world of queer and trans independent filmmaking. Why did you decide to focus* Disclosure *on Hollywood rather than independent film?*

SF: When I was embarking on *Disclosure*, I naively thought that I could make an all-inclusive trans media doc. And since most of the people I knew are indie filmmakers, I thought the interviews would reveal a more inclusive history. I assumed that people were as uninterested in Hollywood as I was. When I was in my early twenties, I intentionally looked away from the dominant media because it offended all of the social issues I cared about and my aesthetic senses. But everyone I interviewed referred back to Hollywood. Especially when I'd ask, "What images do you remember seeing that you've carried around which have influenced your identity and the way you understand yourself in the world?" It was naive of me to be shocked, but I was. I came to see that Hollywood is where the collective shared memory is.

I'm more familiar with indie trans film history and how it reflects conversations in the queer and trans communities. My first film, *Boy I Am*, was released in 2006. It was about the rise of visibility of trans guys and the backlash that trans guys were experiencing in dyke space, particularly in New York. While I was screening *Boy I Am*, Kate Huh, an illustrious New York queer, stood up and said, "I'm sick of all these films about trans guys, where's the film about trans women?" But when I started making *Disclosure*, I was hearing trans guys say, "Filmmakers only care about trans women!" I was surprised that people who were invested in trans male representation had no knowledge of that history in indie trans films. In talking to Susan Stryker about it, she told me how she would see headlines from centuries back about what we would understand as trans men that would dominate for years and years, and then it would only be trans women for years and years. There was a constant flip-flop.

Anyway, the research interviews kept going back to Hollywood. And honestly it wasn't the story I wanted to tell. I dragged my feet for a while, but eventually I realized that this is what people want to talk about. This is where the data is. After those eight months, I had a database of six hundred television titles and four hundred film titles from nearly one hundred research interviews.

LH: *So even when you were talking to people in the independent film world, the things that they had in common were Hollywood and mainstream television.*

SF: Yeah, the majority of my research interviews were with indie filmmakers, and it was all Hollywood references.

LH: *It's funny, because there has been a film festival circuit for trans films for the last several decades. It's interesting that there are no independent trans-made films that made the same kind of impact on people across regional differences. Like* By Hook or By Crook *(dir. Harry Dodge and Silas Howard, 2001), for example.*

SF: *By Hook or By Crook* is one of my touchstones, but most people didn't know it. I'm trying to think—*Tranny Fags* (dir. Morty Diamond, 2003), that was also something I saw early on. *Southern Comfort* (dir. Kate Davis, 2001), *A Boy Named Sue* (dir. Julie Wyman, 2000). A few older trans men were familiar with them. Certainly, trans women didn't know about movies about trans guys. And mostly trans guys dominated in trans work in queer festivals. There was so much, but unless you were a programmer or really into the topic, people didn't know these trans-made films.

LH: *I think that says something about this lack of continuity in trans independent filmmaking. Things get made and are huge, and everyone sees them, and then they get forgotten, and it just keeps happening. One of the remarkable things about this film is how many trans people there were behind the camera. Can you talk about why that was important to you and the pragmatics of how you implemented that?*

SF: Right, so everyone you see in front of the camera is trans, and we prioritized having trans people behind the camera. It was very important that the messages of the film were reflected in the filmmaking process, that the film itself be an embodiment of the change we want to see in storytelling. We prioritized hiring trans people, and when we couldn't hire a trans person, we mentored a trans person. It was not easy. It took a long time. We did a national search. And so often press and nontrans filmmakers say, "That seems really hard if not impossible. There isn't enough talent, blah, blah, blah." But my response is always the same—making a film is *really hard* and you get to choose what's important to you. Ava DuVernay speaks beautifully about the "intention of your attention"

(Van Valkenburg 2015). My intention was to bring as many trans voices into this project as possible because it was not only essential for this story, but also because I know how hard it is to get your foot in the door. And when you do you might be on edge and distracted by the overt or subtle transphobia. I wanted to create an environment that centered trans people and valued trans voices where trans people could be focused on their work and not constantly looking over their shoulders.

It was dreamy—I would look in one direction and see someone drawing diagrams on the ground to teach a trans fellow how to light a scene. Somewhere else, a trans person would be talking about questions that we should ask in our next interview. Some of the best questions came from those conversations. At our first shoot in January 2018, our gaffer, a white cis queer woman, was so impacted by the set. She realized that her union, IATSE (International Alliance of Theatrical Stage Employees, Moving Picture Technicians, Artists and Allied Crafts), which is the largest tech union in the world, would not be the most welcoming place for trans people. So she helped to institute the first trans sensitivity training at IATSE. Within a couple of months four other states had implemented the same training, and now, I've been told, it's being done across the country. That's the invisible work that I think is just as important and maybe even more important than the film.

LH: *That's great. I think that's exactly what people need to be learning how to do, how to walk the walk when it comes to diversifying who's making films at every level. How did you and the project get connected with Laverne Cox? And how did that affect the direction that it went in?*

SF: That was, as Laverne says, *bashert* (destiny)! After two years of doing research, I was invited to give a presentation at the Outfest Trans Summit. I had a twenty-minute clip reel and I gave a ten-minute talk. At one point, I looked up into the audience to where my producer was sitting, Amy Scholder. And sitting right in front of her was this beautiful blonde with huge sunglasses on and a hoodie over her hair, trying to be incognito. Immediately I knew it was Laverne Cox. And she was totally engaged, nodding along, and listening really intently. Afterward, she ended up coming right up to us and said, "I have been thinking about making a movie about this for so long. The timing couldn't be better. I just happened to come to this talk today, because I was missing my community. How can I help you make this movie?" We had lunch a week later and she came on as our executive producer.

In terms of how the project changed, it only got better. She and I are so aligned regarding process, ethics, and values, in how to tell stories. We love nerding out on the history. The film would have had a lot more early history if we had our druthers, but Amy is a lot cooler than us and pushed us to bring in more pop culture because that would open it up to a wider audience. Laverne and I are both deeply committed to nuance, and that there's no single answer to any question. There are many ways of seeing the same thing. Often people don't know what they don't know, so we paid a lot of attention to holding everything within complex conversations. One example is in the scene about *The Crying Game* (dir. Neil Jordan, 1992). Most people talked about the trauma of seeing Fergus vomit when he saw Dil's body. And all the copycats of that scene. But then we have Zachary Drucker, who shared, "When I saw *The Crying Game*, I just saw a beautiful woman who had a penis, and that opened up a world of possibility to me." How beautiful that people have such different experiences of the same thing. This film was about ways of looking. There are moments that seem to be so particular to a trans way of seeing, but it's also about nuanced media literacy. Media is the most powerful institution that the majority of people in our society have access to. We need to be more media literate and more critical of the media. We have to be active consumers of media. That's at the heart of *Disclosure*.

Not least of all, Laverne is an encyclopedia with a photographic memory of history. And with that she brings so much nuance and life experience that beautifully complicates it all. We spent weeks doing research together. Collaborating with her made everything I wanted to do all the more possible.

LH: *Laverne was such a wonderful guide for the audience in this film. I know you collected hundreds of hours of archival footage and also hundreds of hours of interviews. How did you decide which things to keep and which to leave out?*

SF: The narrative was a puzzle based on personal anecdotes and historical touchstones. We always went back to the question, "Where's the personal story? How does it connect to history?" Finding those moments guided us through the edit. It was based on how memories unfold and how we share that with another when we want to be known by them. And how the past and present folds in on itself and divergent views on the same material.

LH: *I was fascinated by the structure of the film. You start with silent cinema and you end with contemporary film and television, but in the middle, it doesn't go chronologically at all. Tell me more about the logic you used to go from one part of the film to another.*

SF: I did not want it to be chronological—that felt too easy and boring. When people haven't seen the film yet, they refer to it as a survey film, which it is not. I love that genre, but that's not going to reach a mass audience. Also, I saw in the history that these tropes and images repeat themselves so much that showing it chronologically would be a little bit like *Groundhog Day* (dir. Harold Ramis, 1993). I had to figure out a way to hold the tropes and the storytelling in their own universes, so we could also talk about race and movements in time. The only way to make those stick was to base the narrative on personal anecdotes. So, that was always where we returned to.

Initially it felt too predictable to put silent cinema at the beginning. I wanted the viewer to earn that, because it's amazing to see how far back this history goes. It concretizes how trans people have always been a site of fascination in film, how transgressing gender expectations has always been a storytelling tool. I wanted the viewer to have that same experience of spending some time with the material and then realizing how far back it goes, as I had when I was doing the research. But after a couple of cuts, the feedback was that the history needed to come sooner because we need to have that foundation. But I knew the film was not going to take a chronological path. That's not how our memories work. When we're thinking about our experiences in the world, it doesn't start from the beginning of our lives and come into the present. It's always turning around itself and constantly informing our present. And the way we're living in the present informs how we understand our past. I wanted the viewer to experience that, too.

LH: *It's so interesting to hear about these other versions of the film and how many possible permutations there could be, because the way it makes connections sideways is really effective. This film seems to be made for both trans and cis viewers. How do you handle that kind of multiple address?*

SF: You know, first and foremost, I had trans audiences in mind, as I always do. In terms of having it be accessible to nontrans viewers, I think that comes with the content, because the material is so universal. But the interviews are so specific. Zachary Drucker talks about how the more specific a story is, the more universal it becomes. I sat with that a lot. I didn't want to spoon-feed a nontrans audience, and I didn't want to alienate a trans audience. I think when you stick to the specificity of the message you're trying to get across, somehow that opens the doors up. Even if someone doesn't understand all the references, they feel like they're getting an inside view—which they are, and there's a lot of joy in that. I also think that the nostalgia in seeing these clips that we're so familiar with—and understanding our part in laughing at them before we understood what was problematic—makes it accessible, because we're all complicit in this history.

LH: *I've heard from a few trans viewers that it was extremely hard to watch a lot of these clips, especially right in a row (e.g., Greenberg 2020). So sometimes they would take a break from the film and come back to it. I'm wondering how you thought about the issue of re-presenting sometimes extremely difficult material.*

SF: I constantly wrestled with that. There are two scenes that I could barely watch during the edit—the *Ace Ventura* (dir. Tom Shadyac, 1994) scene and the *Boys*

Don't Cry (dir. Kimberly Peirce, 1999) scene. But I knew they needed to be there. And something my friend Nat said helped to understand why. Nat Ruiz Tofano, a nonbinary trans person who was facilitating a Q&A I did for the "Getting Real 2020" conference, said that they felt that watching *Disclosure* was like therapy. It was painful at times, but then healing. And I hoped it would be a cathartic experience for trans people. Seeing all these images that you've experienced, often in isolation, over your lifetime—whether it's literal, physical isolation, or you're with people who don't understand you—seeing them it in a context that's held by trans people who might mirror your feelings can lead to a healing and cathartic experience where you can now move past it and contextualize it in a way that you haven't been able to before. So now when a parody of *Crying Game* shows up in *Family Guy* you may feel less alone in your reaction.

LH: *As you say, I've heard from trans folks about being the only person in a public cinema audience who isn't laughing—or who is laughing—and how alienating that can be. And by having this large group of trans people talking about their experiences, even if you might not be in the room with another trans person watching it, you still feel like you're part of this community of viewers who are going to laugh at the same time as you, and not laugh at the same time as you.*

SF: That's one of the most heartbreaking parts of releasing *Disclosure* during the pandemic. The film was meant to be seen in community, in theaters with your people. Our only public screening was the premiere at Sundance. There were thirty of us from the film there. All they heard were each other's reactions, thirty trans people watching the film together. And that was beautiful. That's how it is supposed to be. I don't know how the experience would have been different for people who are finding it difficult to watch if they could watch in community. I understand finding it difficult to watch alone. One person asked me and Laverne at a Q&A, "I'm scared to watch, is it going to be hard?" And I thought about when Yance Ford says in the film that there are some really painful and violent parts of our history, but we have to know them—we have to learn them.

LH: *Have you seen any impact already on the way Hollywood is making films?*

SF: Yes. And that's been incredible. I didn't think it'd be that fast. From the release in June, we saw people on social media who are in positions of power saying how they're seeing everything differently now. The COO at Netflix—yes, Netflix bought the film, but there's no reason that he would have watched it, but somehow he watched it—he was like, "This changes everything. I want everyone in Netflix to watch it." So that's exciting. Maybe they won't develop and buy films that follow these horrendous storylines anymore. And then actors like Ryan

Reynolds, who sent Laverne and Jen Richards private messages saying how this completely changed the way he's looking at films and how he's going to make films. And then he started a fellowship program (Kit 2020). When the news went out that Halle Berry was going to play a trans man in a film and she was referring to the character as a woman, within twenty-four hours, someone sent her *Disclosure*, and she was like, "Oh, okay, I'm not going to do this project." So that was wonderful.

Honestly, the impact outside Hollywood is even more interesting to me. We're looking to have an impact in judicial systems and the educational system, in DEI (diversity, equity, and inclusion), and trans wellness groups. I've worked with lawyers and judges—some who have come to me, which shocked me—who want to use clips from *Disclosure* to educate each other on the biases that they may have toward trans people in the courtroom. That kind of thing is what I'm most excited about—those are life-and-death situations, right? When a lawyer or a judge is looking at a trans person, now they're going to understand some of the bias they might have because they love this film they saw as a kid. If you read the transcripts of the Aimee Stephens trans antidiscrimination case that went to the Supreme Court, they were referencing Hollywood films. They were referencing Pat on *Saturday Night Live*. Those are the reminders that this is an important story to tell.

LH: *It is exciting to see* Disclosure *travel in these other circles in ways you couldn't predict.*

SF: Yeah. That's the utility of using Hollywood, right?

LH: *Yeah—lots of eyeballs.*

SF: If this had been what I originally wanted it to be, an indie trans story, I don't know if it would have caught the attention of these people. Which is sad, which sucks, which is offensive. But now, they're bringing me in to tell them how to hire trans people.

LH: *In 2016 you and AIDS activist media scholar Alex Juhasz published a fantastic conversation in* Jump Cut *called "Does Visibility Equal Progress?" (Feder and Juhasz 2016). In this interview you ask some hard questions about the implications of media representation of trans people. Now that you've made* Disclosure *and talked to so many trans creatives, I was wondering what your thinking is today about these questions. Here is one thing you say in that interview:*

> *To what point are we tipping? Visibility of whom to whom? Social justice for whom? Assimilation of whom? A shift in public discourse by whom and about whom? Does*

visibility actually mean serving as a profitable commodity? Trans people are not yet authorized to set the terms of our own visibility. To be visible, we must conform to the demands placed on us by a public that wants to buy a story that affirms their sense of themselves as ethical.

What would you say about these issues today?

SF: Since *Disclosure* was released, I've been getting pitched various projects. I'm actually in the middle of a reading a book that was optioned—the script hasn't been written yet. But they wanted me to read the book because they've hired the screenwriter, and they want to bring in a director to work with the screenwriter. The people who optioned it are not trans, but they know enough to have hired a screenwriter who is trans and looking for a director who is trans. The scope is that this trans kid switches schools because he was bullied at his previous school. At the new school no one knows he's trans. He tries out for and gets on the soccer team and no one knows he's trans. So again the narrative device is relying on transness as a secret that needs to be hidden, and the reader is constantly wondering how his coach, teammates, or love interest will react when and if they find out.

LH: *It sounds like some kind of trans remake of* Just One of the Guys *(dir. Lisa Gottlieb, 1985) or* She's the Man *(dir. Andy Fickman, 2006)!*

SF: Right? Same issue! But here we have a trans guy (not a cis woman disguised as a boy), and they want trans people to make the movie. But the people in decision-making positions (producers) still don't see what's a stake. When I meet with them, I'll share my views and we'll see if they let me make some big changes. As a culture it seems we understand that we should have empathy. But empathy isn't enough if we don't understand the roots of the problem. There's still a long way to go. We're still in this place where nontrans people are setting the terms so the questions you shared above from 2016 are still top of mind. I never had aspirations of working in Hollywood. Even when *Disclosure* finished and we were at Sundance, I did not think I'd work in Hollywood. And with the Netflix sale, we did not make a profit. So I figured I'd go back to New York and continue making films in the same ways I always have.

People are more and more interested in trans stories, they understand there's an audience, they understand it's interesting. But trans people are still not in decision-making positions. I think about these questions all the time. Who's benefiting from this? What is the utility of visibility? Can we be visible in this culture without becoming a commodity? Where is that space? Do we want to exist in this culture without being visible? On some level we all need to be visible, we need to be seen, we need to be mirrored, we need to be reflected. But when that comes hand in hand with being more vulnerable. . . . How do you live in this world sticking to your values while the rest of the world is profiting off your identity? I don't have the answers. I do know that visibility is deeply problematic. There's a deep paradox when it comes to visibility. This was the impetus of the film. It's bookended by that question. The whole reason I made the film was to address that question. And we needed this shiny Hollywood conversation in order to even address the paradox to a mass audience because paradox makes people uncomfortable. People want to think, "Yes, visibility is good, everything's great. We have Laverne Cox, everything is great." People are comfortable with that. And they're deeply uncomfortable with the fact that visibility is actually really dangerous. The questions I asked in that article in *Jump Cut* are still relevant. Very few trans people benefit from the rise of visibility, financially or in terms of any security. Trans people are still disproportionately underemployed, three times the national average, or four times if you're a trans person of color. I certainly tried to have an intervention in that fact while making *Disclosure* by hiring trans people, training trans people when we couldn't hire a trans person, and paying everyone on both sides of the camera. But those questions remain. And I don't know if I'll have answers in my lifetime.

LH: *Given that Hollywood is always going to prioritize profits over social justice and will probably always center young, slender, traditionally attractive people—even if a few marginalized people can sneak into that group—is it worthwhile for trans creators to put up with Hollywood's bullshit enough to have a mainstream career?*

SF: As a director who's motivated by social justice, I wonder about that. But then I think about someone like Ava DuVernay. You see her activist work in everything she does. It's not all perfect: you can see some places that she's had to compromise, but she's still doing the work. The bullshit that directors have to put up with behind the scenes is often invisible. When I was telling nontrans people that I was hiring a trans crew, they often said, "You just have to hire the best people if you want to make the best movie." We knew that trans people *were* the best people to make the movie. And since we were not beholden to anyone, we didn't budge. But it took five years to make the movie. I can't afford to do that again, literally. Then, in distribution, buyers said, "Oh, we already have a trans film." Or, when *Disclosure* finally got sold to Netflix, knowing that David Francis's documentary (*The Death and Life of Marsha P. Johnson* [2017]) was sold for seven digits and our film was sold for half of what it cost us to make it. What does that tell you? Was it worth it for me to put up with all that to now have more of a platform? We'll see.

LH: *I think it comes back to something you said earlier, which is that even amongst trans indie filmmakers, the films and TV shows they shared in common were ones made by Hollywood. And so even though Hollywood demands constant compromises,* *it does seem like that's one place that touches people, even if you can never make exactly the film you want.*

SF: It's true. But also, who gets those opportunities? If I were not white, would my critique of Hollywood have been accepted the way it is? There are a few people that have said they're not going to promote *Disclosure* because they don't like how I talked about their film in it. That's fine. But had I not been white, I think powerful people in Hollywood would have been a lot nastier to me. Who gets to be contrary, who gets to push back, to be a squeaky wheel?

LH: *You said in a recent discussion that you were initially not sure you agreed with Jen Richards when she said that "we just need more" trans representation (Chair in Transgender Studies 2021). Why were you ambivalent? And what's your thinking on that now?*

SF: I was ambivalent, because—more of what, more crap? For the most part we have either sanitized images that are kind of boring or violent, dehumanizing images. I was ambivalent because I didn't understand what the utility of the "more" would be. In *Disclosure* we edited that comment of Jen's to be left open to interpretation, but the film doesn't go into what I feel is conflicting about it. So yes, if there's more media, more people are going to have access to seeing themselves. But I felt conflicted because I hadn't seen anything that I thought was good or interesting—until I saw *Veneno* (2020). You're familiar with that series?

LH: *I've been hearing great things, but I haven't seen it yet. It's not commercially available in Canada.*

SF: You have to see it. This is the "more" we need to see. It has plenty of stereotypes and tropes and it's messy. But it's complicated and nuanced. These are people that I know. They are sex workers, there is violence, there is prison. It's messy, it's dirty, there is addiction. And it's in community—there is love, it's intergenerational, it's just beautiful. There's romance you can identify with that is empowering. *Veneno* is where I finally see possibility in mainstream media. That's the kind of show that gives me hope.

Laura Horak is associate professor of film studies at Carleton University on unceded, unsurrendered Algonquin territory and director of the Transgender Media Lab and Transgender Media Portal. She is the author of *Girls Will Be Boys: Cross-Dressed Women, Lesbians, and American Cinema, 1908–1934* (2016) and coeditor of *Silent Cinema and the Politics of Space* (2014), *Unwatchable* (2019), and a special issue of *Somatechnics* on trans/cinematic/bodies. Horak is a white cis queer settler who is here to leverage her privilege and institutional resources for the revolution.

References

Chair in Transgender Studies. 2021. *"Disclosure" Panel*. YouTube video, 1:00:34. www.youtube.com/watch?v=C-5DeoHpS2o.

Feder, Sam, and Alexandra Juhasz. 2016. "Does Visibility Equal Progress? A Conversation on Trans Activist Media." *Jump Cut*, no. 57. www.ejumpcut.org/archive/jc57.2016/-Feder-JuhaszTransActivism/text.html.

Greenberg, Slava. 2020. "Disclosure: Toward Communal Trans Spectatorship." *Docalogue*, September.docalogue.com/disclosure/.

Kit, Borys. 2020. "Ryan Reynolds Launches Diversity Program 'The Group Effort Initiative' (Exclusive)." *Hollywood Reporter*, July 31. www.hollywoodreporter.com/news/ryan-reynolds-launches-diversity-program-group-effort-initiative-1305234.

Phillips, John. 2006. *Transgender on Screen*. New York: Palgrave Macmillan.

Steinmetz, Katy. 2014. "The Transgender Tipping Point." *Time*, May 29. time.com/135480/transgender-tipping-point/.

Van Valkenburg, Julia. 2015. "Ava DuVernay on the Intention of Your Attention." *Catch-All* (blog), March 19. thecatchallblog.com/2015/03/19/ava-duvernay-on-the-intention-of-your-attention/.

"Naming Their History"

EMILY SKIDMORE

Female Husbands: A Trans History
Jen Manion
Cambridge: Cambridge University Press, 2020. 342 pp.

Jen Manion's *Female Husbands: A Trans History* is the most recent addition in a series of important books on trans history published in the last decade. Throughout the text, Manion serves up powerful and persuasive analysis that will push the field for years to come—forcing scholars to reconsider the ways in which we have categorized our gender-transgressive historical subjects.

Female Husbands focuses on the figure known by the same name, "a term that persistently circulated throughout Anglo-American culture for nearly 200 years to describe people who defied categorization" (1). The term first emerged in England in 1682 and was used frequently by journalists on both sides of the Atlantic to refer to individuals who were assigned female at birth and who assumed the role of husband to a woman. While this may at first seem like a narrow topic, Manion convincingly illustrates how a close examination of this single figure can provide a window into the historic construction of gender. Indeed, as Manion writes, "Female husbands invite us to grapple with what exactly gender is" (6). Manion builds on the work of Clare Sears (2014), who introduced the notion of trans-ing analysis in their *Arresting Dress*. As Manion writes, "To say someone 'transed' or was 'transing' gender signifies a process or practice without claiming to understand what it meant to that person or asserting any kind of fixed identity on them" (11). To that end, Manion uses the gender-neutral pronouns *they*/*them*/*their* and in so doing hopes to "offer a model for people reading, writing, and thinking about the past and present in a more expansive manner, freeing stories and experiences from a telling that has been for far too long reduced and contained by the gender

TSQ: Transgender Studies Quarterly ∗ Volume 8, Number 4 ∗ November 2021   **572**
DOI 10.1215/23289252-9336238   © 2021 Duke University Press

binary" (14). I believe Manion does this, as what follows in *Female Husbands* is rich and compelling and will no doubt inspire scholars for many years to come.

Unlike previous recent work on gender-transgressive individuals assigned female at birth pre-1900, *Female Husbands* is not bound geographically by a single city (like Sears's *Arresting Dress*) or within the United Sates (like my own *True Sex* [2017]) but, rather, examines Anglo-American culture more broadly. Manion examines stories about female husbands from the United Kingdom as well as North America, across a fairly wide chronological timeframe (1746 to the 1910s). This broad scope offers readers a chance to watch the ways in which narratives about female husbands changed over time and across space, inflected by concerns about woman suffrage, patriarchy, and sexual desire at different intervals. Manion includes some figures that are somewhat familiar to scholars and students of trans history, including Robert Shurtliff, born Deborah Sampson, who fought in the American Revolution, and Alan Hart, who in 1917 pursued gender-affirming surgery. These two illustrate the breadth of Manion's book chronologically and topically. Indeed, Shurtliff returned to presenting as a woman after the Revolutionary War, married a man, and had several children. Hart, on the other hand, fought hard to pursue a medical transition and lived as a man for several decades. Despite the divergences in their stories, Manion refers to both figures using *they/them*, a choice that some readers might question. However, it is in such cases where Manion's commitment to highlighting the ways in which the subjects of the book transed gender comes through clearest, and where Manion's call for us to eschew tellings of the past that are reduced to the gender binary are most powerful.

Another aspect that I appreciate about *Female Husbands* is that Manion includes the stories of the wives of the female husbands in the narrative. In previous works, the partners of female husbands are often ignored, in part because they often claimed ignorance of their partners' bodies when questioned. In such framing, not only are female husband's marriages presumed to be asexual, but their wives are presumed to be not queer. Manion recovers the queer potential in these wives, asking in one case, "What if Abigail pursued James, persuading James that she could see them and would love them for who they were? What if their life and love together was her idea?" (119). In addition, Manion considers the power the female wives had in such relationships—the power of knowledge about their partners that they could use to defame them at any time. "This fact made female wives of female husbands unlike any other wives in the UK or US in the nineteenth century," Manion writes (123). As such, including female wives in the narrative does more than simply add new queer figures to the past; it pushes us to consider what their marriages were like with greater complexity. Overall, *Female Husbands* is provocative and insightful, while also written in a way that is accessible to wide audiences.

It is worth lingering for a beat longer on Manion's choice to use *they/them* and consider the significance of this move in pushing the field forward. Since its inception in the 1970s, queer history has been rife with border wars, as authors challenge one another on their classification of the subjects. Part of this, of course, was animated by queer and trans folks wanting to claim antecedents; as Leslie Feinberg (1996: 11) writes in *Transgender Warriors*, "I couldn't find *myself* in history. No one like me seemed to have ever existed." And now, thanks to the scholarship of Feinberg and many others (Susan Stryker and Joanne Meyerowitz foremost among them), we now know that our past is full of individuals who have moved away from the gender they were assigned at birth. And yet the debate over who can "claim" whom has raged on, with the rise of trans studies creating anxiety among some lesbian writers who worry that labeling historical trans masc figures as trans men is tantamount to the erasure of historical butch subjectivities. And of course, layered on top of these "border wars" as Jack Halberstam famously called them in 1998, is the potential violence of applying modern terminology, like *transgender*, to subjects who lived prior to the emergence of such terms. Manion's *Female Husbands* seeks to push the field beyond such debates and encourages readers to be comfortable with the idea that we cannot know with certainty how historical subjects understood their gender. Of course, there are some who may disagree with Manion that assigning the pronouns *they/them* is any less fixed than labeling them as butch women or trans men because it is still ultimately assigning a label. However, *Female Husbands* productively reminds us that fighting over labels is far less interesting than examining the ways in which gender is made and remade, and far less powerful than focusing on the ways in which female husbands resisted gender norms and forged lives for themselves.

Emily Skidmore is associate professor of history at Texas Tech University. She is the author of *True Sex: The Lives of Trans Men at the Turn of the Twentieth Century* (2017). Her work has also appeared in *GLQ* and *Feminist Studies*.

References

Feinberg, Leslie. 1996. *Transgender Warriors: Making History from Joan of Arc to Dennis Rodman.* Boston: Beacon.

Halberstam, Jack. 1998. "Transgender Butch: Butch/FTM Border Wars and the Masculine Continuum." *GLQ* 4, no. 2: 287–310.

Sears, Clare. 2014. *Arresting Dress: Cross-Dressing, Law, and Fascination in Nineteenth-Century San Francisco.* Durham, NC: Duke University Press.

Skidmore, Emily. 2017. *True Sex: The Lives of Trans Men at the Turn of the Twentieth Century.* New York: New York University Press.

Breaking All the Rules

BILLY HUFF

Unbound: Transgender Men and the Remaking of Identity
Arlene Stein
New York: Pantheon, 2018. 352 pp.

Whenever I read work about trans people published by a cis scholar, I return to Jacob Hale's (1997) "Suggested Rules for Non-transsexuals Writing about Transsexuals, Transsexuality, Transsexualism, or Trans _____." Although Hale's suggestions were first published in 1997, they remain salient even within the rapidly changing field of trans studies. Among the suggestions are for non-trans authors to interrogate their own subject positions and privileges in relation to trans subjects, to avoid speaking of trans as a monolithic trope, and perhaps most important, to be aware of the multiple conversations in which trans people participate, including their places within communities and power structures. Hale's "suggested rules" form the criteria with which I evaluate sociologist Arlene Stein's *Unbound: Transgender Men and the Remaking of Identity*.

 Unbound follows three trans masculine subjects and one cis woman through the journey that brought them to and through "top surgery." Much of the book focuses on one of Stein's participants, Ben, and his parents, Gail and Bob. Gail and Bob allow the reader into their struggles with Ben's decision to transition, including bouts of deadnaming, misgendering, and negotiating questions faced by many parents of trans children, such as what to do with family photographs from the past. Ultimately, it is parents of trans masculine people who will perhaps benefit most from the book. Stein initially met Ben in person at Dr. Charles Garramone's plastic surgery office in South Florida the day before his surgery. According to Stein, Garramone is one of the few plastic surgeons who devotes his practice to the surgery, and he has performed more top surgeries

TSQ: Transgender Studies Quarterly * Volume 8, Number 4 * November 2021   **575**
DOI 10.1215/23289252-9336253   © 2021 Duke University Press

annually "than anyone else in the world" (113). The remainder of Stein's three participants happened to share a surgery date with Ben.

Although the book focuses primarily on Ben, a self-identified trans man, and his parents, the brief encounters with Stein's other participants allow her to somewhat resist essentializing moves that reduce all trans subjects to a single story. For example, while Parker identifies (at least in the beginning) as a rather traditional binary man, Lucas identifies as genderqueer, and Nadia identifies as a lesbian who desires to modify her body while still being recognized as a woman. Stein's overall stated goal is to better understand what brings trans masculine people to Garramone's office for gender-affirmative surgeries, as well as to understand how "collectively, transmasculine people are challenging popular understandings of gender" (9).

Stein names her intended audience for *Unbound* as "general readers who may have limited acquaintance with the transgender world and wish to learn more about it" (20). Perhaps owing to her focus on a more general audience, Stein does not name any particular theoretical framework that guides her analysis or describe her methodological approach in-depth. She does, however, mention that she incorporates interviews with her participants' family members, friends, and coworkers, as well as medical and psychological experts, and trans activists. Although Stein's lack of engagement with scholarship in trans studies and her discussion of methodology might seem overly simplistic to scholars, it is likely appropriately critical for her intended general popular nonacademic audience.

Stein attempts to practice self-reflexivity throughout the text. She engages with her own identities as a middle-aged, cisgender, lesbian feminist woman and the ways that she is variously positioned in relation to her participants. For example, Stein recounts, "For me, identifying as a feminist and a lesbian enables me to express my femaleness in ways that seem true enough. But over the years I learned that there are others who feel that they were assigned a gender at birth that seems inauthentic and wrong—so much so that many seek out body modifications to bring their bodies into alignment with their selves" (9). Stein's participants related varied stories of what being trans means to them, and she even states that "few of the transgender men [she] interviewed spoke about being trapped in the 'wrong body'" (71). Yet there are numerous moments when Stein repeats the common "born in the wrong body" trope that many trans people experience as limiting and problematic. At other points, however, Stein privileges the ways that "a younger generation of transgender men are prying open many of our assumptions about what it means to be men and women" (20), a move that is equally as troubling to some trans men who identify strongly within the gender binary.

There are admittedly several cringe-worthy moments in the book. For example, in chapter 7, "Last Butch Standing," Stein seems to mourn the loss of butch lesbians to gender transition and even states that "it is difficult, if not impossible, to prove the existence of 'real' differences between trans men and butch lesbians" (182). This statement communicates that Stein does not understand trans men as "real" men. There are obviously very real differences between men and lesbian women. Stein mentions trans exclusionary radical feminists (TERFs) once in the text, but she explains that their position results from a backlash against the gains of feminism; in her view, TERFs feel a sense of loss rooted in nostalgia and demographic decline (195). She does not mention that TERFs most often target trans women, and her explanation does not point out the violence TERFs inflict on trans populations. Finally, as a self-identified gay trans masculine person who is not attracted sexually to women, I cannot overstate the offensiveness of statements that view my identity as identical to that of a butch lesbian, especially given that my existence depends on my distance from that category.

Unbound overall lacks a thorough intersectional analysis that acknowledges that gender identity and expression cannot be separated from race, class, ability, national identity, settler colonialism, and other social and institutional characteristics. The reader is led to believe that the participants are all white, although it is never stated in the text. There are scant mentions of the ways that poor people and trans women of color are the most at risk for violence, poverty, lack of medical access, and other effects of marginalized status, but the analysis mostly illuminates gender and sexuality and brackets other categories of difference. To cite one example, Stein admits that her set of four participants "are hardly an exhaustive portrait of individuals who seek out top surgery" (40), but she continues to point out only their relative affluent class status as a difference that matters to the exclusion of race and other significant characteristics. Later Stein discusses that trans people are more likely to live in poverty and be rejected by their families, and she includes that trans women of color "are particularly vulnerable to economic exclusion and experience higher rates of violence" (41). She never expands on why that is the case, nor does she explain the privileges that whiteness affords her participants. Instead, she concludes, "Even relatively privileged transgender people, such as the ones I profile here, face considerable challenges, too" (41).

Returning to Hale's "Suggested Rules for Non-transsexuals," Stein's *Unbound* partially misses the mark. It does, at times, exoticize trans masculine subjects (e.g., claiming that "transgender is the hot new thing" [196]). It also lacks an intersectional lens, and there are moments when Stein's own political positions seem to uncritically influence the analysis. She does mostly give primacy to the voices of her participants, and she takes care to share various stories of trans experience that avoid overly essentializing trans subjectivities.

I do not recommend *Unbound* for an audience of trans studies scholars and/or gender scholars. However, I would like to conclude by adding an important consideration to Hale's "Suggested Rules." Through its frank attention to the struggles and support of Stein's participants' partners, friends, and family (like Gail and Bob), *Unbound* is a book that has the potential to improve the lives of some trans people. That is to say that *Unbound* can accomplish the labor of educating families, friends, and partners of trans masculine people about gender, sexuality, and transition in accessible ways that might lead to better understanding. Outside critical theory and substantial contributions to academic conversations in trans studies, Stein gives us a book that provides an insufficiently critical but accessible explanation of gender and sexuality for parents of trans masculine people who have likely not thought much about gender. Stein paints a portrait of parents struggling with their child's decision, even as they attempt to demonstrate unconditional love. She allows the reader to witness their failures, changes, and eventual growth. In the end, I argue that Stein's missteps are not so egregious as to render them dangerous. As a trans scholar, I did not find *Unbound* particularly useful. I was even offended by some of the claims of the book discussed above. That did not prevent me, however, from sending my own parents a copy. *Unbound* was always intended for them anyway.

Billy Huff (PhD, 2010, Georgia State University) is a lecturer of communication at the University of Illinois Urbana-Champaign and a research associate with the Unit for Institutional Change and Social Justice at the University of the Free State in Bloemfontein, South Africa.

Reference

Hale, Jacob. 1997. "Suggested Rules for Non-transsexuals Writing about Transsexuals, Transsexuality, Transsexualism, or Trans _____." SandyStone.com, last modified November 18, 2009. sandystone.com/hale.rules.html.

Parenting Trans Kids in a Cisgender World

ALITHIA ZAMANTAKIS

Trans Kids: Being Gendered in the Twenty-First Century
Tey Meadow
Oakland: University of California Press, 2018. 320 pp.

What does it mean to do gender in a world in which the system of gender, from a white, cisgender perspective, is seemingly changing? Tey Meadow's *Trans Kids: Being Gendered in the Twenty-First Century* aims to answer this question by utilizing ethnographic analyses that provide thick description, complex answers, and even more questions for future research. The book makes valuable contributions to the sociology of gender and families, but its lack of engagement with critical trans epistemologies and use of outdated language limit its contributions to trans studies. In *Trans Kids*, Meadow argues that parents' and adults' perceptions of trans kids are shifting within the family, medicine, and activist spaces. The majority of the parents in the study utilized essentialist logic to understand their child's transness. Such logic ranged from gene mutations to psychological and neurological divergences to spiritual ideas of transness being "a status that's entrusted to souls" (204). While parents accepted their children, Meadow details how their acceptance hinged on an essentialist discourse that has historically been used to invalidate trans people's gender identities. Parents also assessed the differential levels of risk and access to resources to decide whether to move their children to a new area and school. Parental decisions ranged from facilitating a "stealth" identity by having their children keep their transness a secret to "monitoring" children by deciding when and where a child could engage in "atypical" gendered behavior. Meadow explicates how such parental decisions and discourse reified and perpetuated the gender binary rather than deconstructing it. As such, Meadow

TSQ: Transgender Studies Quarterly ∗ Volume 8, Number 4 ∗ November 2021
DOI 10.1215/23289252-9336267   © 2021 Duke University Press

contributes to literature in the sociology of gender by analyzing how trans boy-hood and girlhood do not automatically rupture cisnormative notions of a gender binary. This literature has historically utilized trans individuals and trans expe-riences to highlight that the binary is a social construction; however, Meadow details how the parents of trans kids actively aid in the cementing of the binary.

One of the strongest and richest, ethnographic conceptualizations Mea-dow offers is that of "gender fragments," or the moments, interactions, behaviors, and words that "cohered into something [parents] understood" as the core gender of their child. Parents questioned whether their child was gay, a "tomboy" vis-à-vis kids assigned female at birth (AFAB), going through "a phase" of exploration, and then, eventually, transgender. Parents' questioning of whether their child is transgender was ultimately a final step in the process and was brought into the conversation after multiple "gender fragments" cohered into an image that seemed transgender, genderqueer, or something other than cisgender. These fragments could include a moment an AFAB child refers to himself as a boy, a moment when a child assigned male at birth (AMAB) says they want a dress for their birthday, or a moment when a child plays with a toy that is deemed too "masculine" or too "feminine" for their sex assigned at birth. A single fragment alone did not result in parents questioning if their child was trans. However, at a certain point, these "gender fragments" coalesced into something parents felt they could no longer ignore.

While titled *Trans Kids*, Meadow's analysis focuses on the decision mak-ing, discourse, and advocacy of parents, adults, and clinicians. Trans kids, themselves, are not at the center of the analysis. Meadow notes in the appendix that this was an intentional decision, as observing and analyzing the behavior of children felt uncomfortable. Meadow did not want to reproduce the "othering psychiatric gaze" (237). As such, Meadow instead details how trans kids were viewed, treated, and raised by cisgender adults. Meadow's work builds on soci-ology of family scholarship that analyzes how cisgender parents respond to, treat, and raise trans children.

While Meadow provides a nuanced and complex analysis of cisgender adults, they do this less so with trans adults. In the introduction and conclusion, Meadow describes the raising of a "new generation" of trans kids as distinct from contemporary trans adults. Trans kids are said to be raised within organizations that center a cisgender, heterosexual perspective. As such, Meadow predicts that this "new generation" of trans kids will align much more with their cisgender parents than with current trans adults compared to "previous generations of gender outlaws" (96). In the process, future generations of trans adults may find greater comfort in the heteronormative, nuclear family, conservative politics, and the gender binary. Trans children are conceptualized as a novelty to be compared to contemporary trans adults. Trans adults, in comparison, supposedly distance themselves from notions of gender normativity, binary gender identities, and medical models of transness. This analysis constructs trans adults as a monolith and lacks an awareness of hyperconservative, heterosexual, white trans men and women of days past and present (for example, Caitlyn Jenner and Blaire White).

One of the most difficult things to get through in the book is Meadow's language. The book is filled with repeated use of the term *transgenderism*, reference to kids assigned male at birth as being "born little boys," reference to sex assigned at birth as "natal gender," and other such cisnormative language. This includes Meadow noting, "Their children became not atypical, but gender nonconforming; not boys or girls, but transboys and transgirls" (26). Meadow notes that language shifts, and it even shifted during their fieldwork. It is difficult to understand, though, how scholarship on transness published in 2018 could justify including the phrase "the transgender" or the description of a trans girl as having a "boy history." Throughout, it felt as though Meadow were attempting not to say *trans*, instead leaning on these various, cissexist descriptors. In the process, the very clinical gaze Meadow wished to steer away from by not interviewing trans kids presented itself in the clinical, othering, and cisnormative language used to speak of trans people. *Trans Kids* ends up reifying cisnormativity at the same time as Meadow is analyzing it.

Alithia Zamantakis is a PhD candidate in sociology at Georgia State University. She is also the director of LGBTQ+ Programs and Services at Shippensburg University. Zamantakis is a scholar of racialized cissexism, trans/nonbinary dating and hook-up culture, and critical cisness studies.

A Gender Journey
Without Gender Studies

LAZARUS NANCE LETCHER

Passing to América: Antonio (Née Maria) Yta's Transgressive, Transatlantic Life in the Twilight of the Spanish Empire
Thomas A. Abercrombie
University Park: Pennsylvania State University Press, 2018. 272 pp.

Thomas A. Abercrombie's historiography is an impressive tome tracing gender roles, expression, and fluidity from the metropole through the Spanish colonies in the eighteenth century. Abercrombie spent the better part of a decade piecing together the story of the book's protagonist, Yta, to explain the layers of fashion and fashioning that would make a transatlantic gender journey possible. Abercrombie draws largely from primary documents, namely, the court transcriptions of Yta's divorce filings, which priests and lawyers later label a confession of Yta's sex assigned at birth. The author handedly paints a picture of what life would be like for someone of Yta's station and gender expression existing in places ranging from convents to mines, occasionally weaving in a discussion about the development and deployment of race in the colonies.

Abercrombie makes clear that he is not here to label Yta with "the terms represented in the acronym LGBTQIA" (8), arguing that it would be anachronistic to use words that did not exist in Yta's time. Yet a few pages later he muses, "Was Don Antonio transgendered? A butch lesbian? Queer? Or, perhaps, intersexed?" (11), setting the stage for two hundred pages of genitalia obsession and surface-level queer questions. In the book's first chapter, he analyzes the confession Yta gave after his wife left him and accused him of deception. Abercrombie seeks to understand the confession through other popular genres at the time, taking care to note that the confession was mediated through scribes and not directly from

Yta's hand. Throughout the text he wrestles with pronouns—in the confession Yta's attorneys, mother, and wife use different pronouns, and adding the level of translation creates additional problems. Abercrombie chooses to use *she/her* for Yta when describing Yta's life in Spain and switches to *he/him* once Yta arrives in the colonies.

In the chapters that follow, Abercrombie creates a compelling analytic, *hábitos* (a nod to Yta's garb in the convents), to unpack Yta's shift in expression and presentation in the larger scope of Spain and its empires. The author excels in describing the worlds of Yta—carefully depicting the fashions of the time, the economic climate, and the changing tide as the Spanish empire falls. While Abercrombie credits Yta's birth in the metropole as one of the key factors in helping him pass—essentially the creation of whiteness in the colonies—the author does not expand on the violence of colonization on the Indigenous peoples Yta oversaw or the African "servants" that were symbols of status.

Abercrombie branches out from the original documents describing Yta's life and ventures to touch on some dramatic retellings of Yta's life and loves, noting that Yta has become a bit of a queer icon in the last few decades. Thus begins his turn to queer and trans studies. While Abercrombie claims in the introduction to not perpetuate the judges' of Yta's obsession with genitalia, the entire book focuses on what was in Yta's pants. The final chapter aims to tell the history of sex and its move from the ecclesiastic to the medical realm. Abercrombie closes his text with an analysis of the role of deception in narrative, briefly noting that linking the term *deception* to gender nonconformity is life threatening for some. The author draws from (white) performance studies, queer theory, and gender studies from the 1980s and 1990s, namely, Jack Halberstam, Esther Newton, Judith Butler, and Jay Prosser, to seemingly argue that queer identity stands in opposition to trans folks that "pass," contending that doing so upholds the heteropatriarchy. I am still unsure what this has to do with Yta, but it seemed to be just a half-baked and outdated literature review from the fields of (white) performance studies and queer theory.

The book's dedication gestures toward an emancipatory reimagining of historical trans lives: "For Don Antonio Yta and all those who have paid a high price for confounding or transgressing cisgender heteronormativity." Yet this gesture falls flat in the author's persistent attempts to pin down "what" or "who" Yta was, and especially in his obsession with Yta's genitals. While Abercrombie attempts to engage with transgender and queer studies in the final chapter of the text, his use of language reserved for the tabloids and daytime TV confessionals reveals that his dive into transgender studies was surface level at best. The dedication is the only time the term *cisgender* is used—Abercrombie opts for other terms like *real* or *true sex, biological man,* or *normal,* even calling Yta a "sex-ambiguous freak of nature" (179). Similarly, he frequently uses *transgender* as a noun and opts for using the term *hermaphrodite* while also acknowledging that the appropriate term is *intersex*. I was disappointed and angered by his final argument, a played-out contestation that being trans means reifying gender norms and undoing queer efforts to unsettle them. He leaves no room for non-binary identities or the possibility that trans people can be queer as well. While Abercrombie includes some voices from trans studies, I would not consider this text a part of the field. Abercrombie does an adequate job explaining gender roles and expression within the context of eighteenth- and nineteenth-century Spain and its colonies but falls short in his engagement with queer and trans studies from this century.

Lazarus Nance Letcher is a graduate student at the University of New Mexico on Tiwa Pueblo land. Laz studies Black and Indigenous solidarities, the roots of transphobia in white supremacy and settler colonialism, and pop culture.

Transgressing Criminology and Victimology

SERGIO DOMÍNGUEZ Jr.

Transgressed: Intimate Partner Violence in Transgender Lives
Xavier L. Guadalupe-Diaz
New York: New York University Press, 2019. 224 pp.

Even though the lifetime prevalence of intimate partner violence (IPV) in trans populations is around 50 percent (Messinger and Guadalupe-Diaz 2020), there is an alarming absence of trans-specific and trans-inclusive research and interventions to address IPV. For sociologist Xavier L. Guadalupe-Diaz, this absence raises two important questions: 1) Under what conditions are trans people's experiences of IPV erased? and 2) To what extent does intimate partner violence produce "genderist" systems? Answering these questions first requires a historical tracing of social scientific understandings of IPV, which stem from 1970s feminist activism and scholarship that understood gender in binary-essentialist terms. This work resulted in legal and institutional adoption of cis- and heteronormative approaches to domestic violence work (as it was called at the time) that continue to center white cisgender women in discourses on the gendered nature of violence in romantic relationships. *Transgressed: Intimate Partner Violence in Transgender Lives* invites us to examine the ways that systems of power foster IPV while also examining the ways that IPV replicates and reinforces systems of power, namely, genderism.

Transgressed is a sociological study that uses a modified grounded theory framework to expand our knowledge of the relationship between interpersonal violence and structural, institutional, interpersonal, and intrapersonal genderism. The text begins from the assumption that little scholarship in trans studies has focused on IPV and little criminological scholarship has focused on trans

TSQ: Transgender Studies Quarterly ★ Volume 8, Number 4 ★ November 2021 **585**
DOI 10.1215/23289252-9364141   © 2021 Duke University Press

survivors. *Transgressed* is based on data from thirteen personal interviews and five online free-write questionnaires with eighteen trans survivors of IPV. This study contributes to our knowledge about trans survivors of IPV by providing empirical evidence for existing claims made by activists and scholars, most notably that genderist social and legal structures erase trans people from social institutions meant to reduce the incidence of IPV. Contemporary interventions within health care, in schools, on college campuses, and in the workplace thus often only account for cis people, leaving behind fertile grounds for intimate abusers to disproportionately harm trans people.

Throughout the book, *Transgressed* includes vivid descriptions of abuse by contextualizing survivors' experiences in terms of genderist systems that assume that only cisgender men are perpetrators of abuse and only cisgender women are victims of abuse. Guadalupe-Diaz frames individual stories within broader genderist systems to paint a picture of the ways that understandings of trans IPV both converge with and diverge from patterns of violence represented in mainstream victimology. Abuser attacks reflect genderist systems in that they "regulate the boundaries of appropriateness as defined by a genderist culture and the abuser" (77), while "positive attacks" reinforce "a limited conception of the victim's gender expression" through positive reactions to gender conformity (77). Transphobic attacks, on the other hand, are aimed at trans survivors' trans identities by "belittling bodies, making victims feel that the abuser was doing *them* a favor in staying, stereotyping and misunderstanding their transition processes, or threatening to 'out' them" (79). In effect, these attacks work only in societies and cultures where trans identities are institutionally antagonized, including through cultural scripts, lack of legal protections, and unequal access to health care.

In his richest chapter, Guadalupe-Diaz moves beyond documenting abuse and toward participants' understandings of their experiences. Most participants "saw many of their experiences with abuse as attempts by abusers to control [gender] transition and define them on the abusers' own terms" (87). That is, abusers manipulate and limit survivors' ongoing gender embodiments and imaginaries, fostering a dynamic and mutually constitutive disempowerment loop. This inter- and intrapersonal entrapment leads us to ask not only when this loop is maintained, but also how it is broken. When describing victim identities in the help-seeking process, participants appropriated the notion that victims were "submissive, traditionally feminine, and . . . did not fight back" (121). Paired with their abusers' genderist and transphobic attacks, as well as awareness that resources such as police and shelters often benefit only cis people, participants struggled to see themselves as victims able to access formal resources. While some did access formal resources, queer kinship structures, informal resources, and fighting back more often fostered avenues for trans IPV victims to move toward survivorship.

Although topics like immigration are alluded to in the text, intersectional factors (e.g., ableism, classism, racism) do not receive the attention I crave. Guadalupe-Diaz correctly avers that failure to adopt intersectional frameworks results in goals that remedy individual problems but "merge with the neoliberal state" (49). *Transgressed* at times centers some narratives of multiply marginalized participants, yet the extent to which gendered understandings of IPV otherize multiply marginalized people goes unremarked. For instance, how are gendered understandings of IPV artifacts of class privilege that collude with structures of class domination? Limitations notwithstanding, Guadalupe-Diaz has crafted an engaging and valuable study that synthesizes, contextualizes, and elevates the voices of privileged trans populations who have sustained violence from intimate partners. This study would fare well for courses in criminology and victimology, gender studies, and social science approaches to trans studies. *Transgressed* invites us all to examine and challenge genderist systems that facilitate IPV.

Sergio Domínguez Jr. is a doctoral student in counseling psychology at the University of Wisconsin–Madison. Their research and clinical interests lie in trans well-being, relationship-centered methods, and ethical and legal issues for mental health practitioners.

Reference

Messinger, Adam M., and Xavier L. Guadalupe-Diaz, eds. 2020. *Transgender Intimate Partner Violence: A Comprehensive Introduction.* New York: New York University Press.

New Books from Duke University Press

Philosophy for Spiders
On the Low Theory of Kathy Acker
MCKENZIE WARK

"In this brilliant reading of one of the late twentieth century's most interesting writers, language 'messes with flesh' while 'logic messes with language,' transmuting Kathy Acker's sign-worlds into philosophy. I love the fearless way in which McKenzie Wark thinks. I also love the calm voice with which she walks herself (and us) through difficult spaces in theory and memory. Exploring how gender structures writing in ways related to, but ultimately different from, the norms that structure heterosexuality, Philosophy for Spiders radically expands the field of trans girl lit." — Sianne Ngai

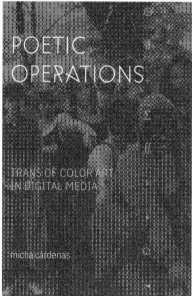

Poetic Operations
Trans of Color Art in Digital Media
micha cárdenas
ASTERISK

"In this beautifully written book, micha cárdenas directs us to look at how the algorithm, as analytic and praxis, holds the possibility of trans of color survival. Deftly moving across numerous geographies, texts, and fields of inquiry, Poetic Operations is a bold contribution to trans of color studies."
— C. Riley Snorton

DUKE UNIVERSITY PRESS

   dukepress.edu